That His Spirit May Be Saved

That His Spirit May Be Saved

Church Discipline as a Means to Repentance and Perseverance

Jeremy M. Kimble

WIPF & STOCK · Eugene, Oregon

THAT HIS SPIRIT MAY BE SAVED
Church Discipline as a Means to Repentance and Perseverance

Copyright © 2013 Jeremy M. Kimble. All rights reserved. Except for brief quotations in critical publications or reviews, no part of this book may be reproduced in any manner without prior written permission from the publisher. Write: Permissions, Wipf and Stock Publishers, 199 W. 8th Ave., Suite 3, Eugene, OR 97401.

Wipf & Stock
An Imprint of Wipf and Stock Publishers
199 W. 8th Ave., Suite 3
Eugene, OR 97401

www.wipfandstock.com

ISBN 13: 978-1-62564-210-3

Scripture quotations are from The Holy Bible, English Standard Version® (ESV®), copyright © 2001 by Crossway, a publishing ministry of Good News Publishers. Used by permission. All rights reserved.

This work is dedicated to my loving wife, Rachel, whose love for God and others is so readily demonstrable.

"Many women have done excellently, but you surpass them all."

Proverbs 31:29

Contents

Preface by | ix
Acknowledgments | xi
Abbreviations | xiii
Introduction | xv

1 *The Need for Discipline in the Church* | 1
2 *A Biblical Analysis of Church Discipline* | 16
3 *A Historical Analysis of Church Discipline* | 63
4 *A Theological Analysis of Church Discipline* | 112
5 *Implications of This Study and Conclusion* | 146

Bibliography | 175

Preface

AFTER A LONG AND somewhat awkward period of silence, discussions concerning church discipline are beginning to be heard again, as some are recognizing the role of church discipline in church health. Though still few in number, they raise a biblically based, clearly mandated, and critically important church practice. A valuable and distinctive contribution to that discussion is given in this book by Jeremy Kimble. I had the pleasure of supervising Jeremy's work on this topic as a doctoral student at Southeastern Baptist Theological Seminary, and the additional pleasure now of providing this foreword.

Several distinctive features call for attention in this work. First is the helpful inclusion of Old Testament teaching that forms the background for church discipline. While scholars differ on to what degree the New Testament people of God (the church) has continuity with the Old Testament people of God (Israel), there is no question but that Paul based his commands concerning church discipline to the Corinthians on Old Testament teaching (1 Cor. 5:13, citing an Old Testament formula repeated numerous times in the book of Deuteronomy). Kimble analyzes the material Paul draws upon, and sees it as part of an Old Testament trajectory that leads to the more explicit New Testament teaching, which he also ably expounds.

The second important feature is the demonstration that the practice of church discipline, and especially the understanding of church discipline given by Kimble, is not a historical novelty, but firmly rooted in the teaching of luminaries such as Luther and Jonathan Edwards and the entire Anabaptist movement, as exemplified in the works of Balthasar Hubmaier. Edwards's example is especially instructive, showing that church discipline and evangelistic revival are not antithetical, as Edwards was a key figure in the First Great Awakening.

But the most important and distinctive contribution of this work is his exposition of the purpose of church discipline. It is fairly common (and accurate) to say that church discipline should be redemptive for the one disciplined and protective for the church; Kimble explains how church discipline serves its redemptive and protective functions. God authorizes the church to issue a warning of potential eschatological judgment, thus giving the offender the strongest possible inducement to repent. It is the church speaking its strongest and most fervent and loving word of warning, and therefore must be undertaken with the utmost of seriousness, as a responsibility laid on the church, and especially the church's leaders. Discipline serves its protective function, not merely by removing the unrepentant member, but by calling all its members to persevere in the faith. As Galatians 6:1 says, those called to the task of restoring the one caught in sin must also watch themselves, lest they be tempted themselves.

This is a fuller, more comprehensive explanation of church discipline than commonly given, and is the most distinctive contribution of the book. But Kimble places us further in his debt by showing the significance of this understanding of church discipline for practical issues in the life of the church such as maintaining regenerate membership, pastoral leadership and shepherding, and faithful observance of the ordinances.

I am pleased to commend this book to what I hope will be a wide readership, and pray that it will contribute to the upbuilding of many local churches toward the goal of being the radiant bride of Christ, "without stain or wrinkle or any other blemish, but holy and blameless" (Eph 5:27 NIV).

John S. Hammett
Professor of Theology
Southeastern Baptist Theological Seminary

Acknowledgments

THIS WORK ORIGINATED AS a doctoral dissertation for my PhD in theological studies from Southeastern Baptist Theological Seminary in Wake Forest, North Carolina. It was fulfilled with the local church in mind, and as such it is my hope that, along with scholars, pastors and church members would truly benefit from its contents. There are many people I would like to thank in making this project a reality. First, I want to thank the many students at Southeastern who sharpened and encouraged me throughout my studies. Critique in various seminars was always coupled with grace and a desire to better the other person, and this was absolutely vital in developing a more robust theological acumen. In particular, I would like to thank Jake Pratt, Mark Catlin, and Grant Taylor. Your friendship, encouragement, and constancy in sharpening one another's thinking has been of great benefit.

I also want to sincerely thank several professors who have been shaping in my life and ministry. Dr. Gregg Allison served as the initial inspiration and encouragement of this topic. I am grateful for his insights and probing questions regarding the details surrounding this proposal. Dr. Danny Akin has been an inspiration as a professor and president, exuding an unforgettable passion for God and all the peoples of the earth. Dr. Nathan Finn, who taught an outstanding seminar on the history of revivals, demonstrated that theology, history, and Christian living can and should be wedded together. Dr. Bruce Ashford has offered helpful wisdom and insights at various junctures of this process, for which I am truly grateful. And most especially, to my mentor, Dr. John Hammett, I owe a debt of gratitude. Dr. Hammett has patiently read multiple drafts of this work, and has always offered keen insights in a patient and gracious manner. He is a tremendous example in the realm of Christian scholarship of theological rigor, genuine humility, and a love for students.

Thanks must be extended also to my family, beginning with my parents. Your diligence, perseverance, and dedication to the Christian faith has had a profound influence on my own life. You have loved me faithfully and sacrificed much in allowing me to take part in higher education. I love you both deeply. To my children, Hannah and Jonathan. You have endured many hours where daddy is reading, studying, and feverishly typing on the computer. Thank you for your support, patience, and love throughout this process. To my wife Rachel, this book is dedicated to you. Words cannot express the gratefulness that wells up in my heart at the thought of our journey together. You have shown more grace and patience than I could ever deserve, and through the good times and the bad you have been my partner, confidant, and true love. I love you.

Finally, my greatest thanks go to the God who has called me out of darkness into the kingdom of his beloved son, Jesus Christ. I am grateful that he has opened my eyes to the truth that his glory and my joy are not at odds, they are the same path. Christ loves his church exceedingly and desires she be pure and blameless before him. This dissertation is devoted to pursuing that end with greater vigor and resoluteness.

Abbreviations

ABR	*Australian Biblical Review*
BCOB	Baker Commentary on the Bible
BDAG	Bauer, Danker, Arndt, and Gingrich. *A Greek-English Lexicon of the New Testament and Other Early Christian Literature.* 3rd ed. Chicago, 2000.
BECNT	Baker Exegetical Commentary on the New Testament
BHH	*Baptist History and Heritage*
BibSac	*Bibliotheca Sacra*
BNTC	Black's New Testament Commentary
BZNW	Beihefte zur Zeitschrift für die neutestamentliche Wissenschaft
CBQ	*Catholic Biblical Quarterly*
CH	*Church History*
CNTUOT	Commentary on the New Testament Use of the Old Testament
CQ	*The Covenant Quarterly*
CTR	*Criswell Theological Review*
DTIB	Dictionary of Theological Interpretation of the Bible
EBC	Expositor's Bible Commentary
EDT	Evangelical Dictionary of Theology
EQ	*Evangelical Quarterly*
EvJ	*Evangelical Journal*
ExpTim	*Expository Times*
FM	*Faith and Mission*
ICC	International Critical Commentary
IVPNTC	IVP New Testament Commentary
JBL	*Journal of Biblical Literature*
JETS	*Journal of the Evangelical Theological Society*

JIH	*The Journal of International History*
JSNTSup	*Journal for the Study of the New Testament: Supplement Series*
LCC	*Library of Christian Classics*
LQHR	*London Quarterly and Holborn Review*
LW	*Luther's Works*
MAJT	*Mid-America Journal of Theology*
MSJ	*The Master's Seminary Journal*
NAC	*New American Commentary*
NDBT	*New Dictionary of Biblical Theology*
NICNT	*New International Commentary on the New Testament*
NICOT	*New International Commentary on the Old Testament*
NIDNTT	*New International Dictionary of New Testament Theology*
NIGTC	*New International Greek Testament Commentary*
NIVAC	*NIV Application Commentary*
NTS	*New Testament Studies*
PNTC	*Pillar New Testament Commentary*
RE	*Review and Expositor*
ResQ	*Restoration Quarterly*
RJ	*Reformed Journal*
RR	*Review of Religion*
SBJT	*Southern Baptist Journal of Theology*
SCJ	*Sixteenth-Century Journal*
SJT	*Scottish Journal of Theology*
StudBib	*Studia Biblica*
TDNT	*Theological Dictionary of the New Testament*
TJ	*Trinity Journal*
TNTC	*Tyndale New Testament Commentary*
TOTC	*Tyndale Old Testament Commentary*
TynBul	*Tyndale Bulletin*
VT	*Vetus Testamentum*
WBC	*Word Biblical Commentary*
WJE	*Works of Jonathan Edwards*
WUNT	*Wissenschaftliche Untersuchungen zum Neuen Testament*
ZECNT	*Zondervan Exegetical Commentary on the New Testament*

Introduction

I LOVE THE CHURCH, and this study is dedicated to its success. Having grown up in church and serving in vocational ministry for a decade of my life, I have been exposed to the good and bad of church life. At times one can note the beauty of the body of Christ working together in unity, dedicated to the task of making disciples. At other moments, one can sense that sin is being ignored, disunity is entrenched, and the church is not thriving as it ought to. While not the only answer to building a flourishing church, one key component to seeing God's people grow into Christian maturity is the practice of church discipline.

This work is by no means some detached study focusing on esoteric matters that hardly relate to the church. The proper understanding and implementation of church discipline is crucial for the health of God's people. It is not an inconsequential matter; rather, it is of utmost importance for any church as they seek to proclaim the gospel. To protect our witness and purity, church discipline must be upheld. And as I continued to read and study this matter in greater detail, I found that this practice holds more significance than I previously realized.

The thesis of this work is that one purpose of church discipline is to serve as a declaration of potential eschatological judgment both to warn offenders of their need to repent, and, by implication, to exhort the church members to persevere in their faith. It argues from biblical, historical, and theological grounds that, while only God can make ultimate pronouncements concerning the salvific status of individuals, it must be acknowledged that Christ has given his church authority and, though not ultimate, it is to be used as a warning to unrepentant sinners and a means to restore them. One can observe this convergence of discipline, final judgment, and the call to perseverance and note the heightened importance of ecclesial discipline. If this is a proper understanding of discipline—and I argue throughout that it is—then it will be difficult to dismiss the practice of church discipline out of hand in the local church. This becomes a crucial means by which the people of God are built up, and as such, calls for churches to rightly implement the kind of discipline called for by Jesus and the apostle Paul.

It must be acknowledged that there could be some reading this book that have seen or experienced church discipline exacted in an unbiblical manner. Unfortunately there are many cases of such abuses, and God is certainly not pleased with them. However, this does not give us permission to rid ourselves of discipline, but rather to take up the Scriptures once again and align ourselves with its teachings on the subject. This work is an attempt at such a synthesis. It is my sincere hope that scholars will benefit, but my eager expectation is that pastors and churches would not only learn, but also be exhorted to exercise proper church discipline for the glory of God and the upbuilding of the church.

1

The Need for Discipline in the Church

THE PRACTICE OF CHURCH discipline, though not always implemented consistently in contemporary Protestant circles, has deep biblical moorings that must be clearly understood and practiced in order for the church to function properly.¹ Due to misapplications and misunderstandings, discipline has been ignored by many congregations, resulting in communities of faith that neglect many of the moral absolutes laid out in Scripture.² When one understands, however, that there is a "holiness without which no one will see the Lord" (Heb 12:14), the church is compelled to use various means to pursue that goal in a corporate manner.³ As such,

---

1. For a specific portrayal of the decline of discipline among Southern Baptist churches see Haines, "Southern Baptist Church Discipline," 14–27; Wills, *Democratic Religion*, 11–140. For a more current assessment of the application of discipline in local churches see Hammett, *Biblical Foundations for Baptist Churches*, 110–16; Mohler, "Church Discipline," 16–27. It should also be noted that there has been a resurgence in teaching and practicing church discipline, and one crucial figure leading the way is Mark Dever through his ministry with Capitol Hill Baptist Church and 9Marks Ministries. See especially Dever, *9 Marks of a Healthy Church*, 167–94.

2. Albert Mohler elaborates on this point, saying, "As a matter of fact, most Christians introduced to the biblical teaching concerning church discipline confront the issue of church discipline as an idea they have never before encountered. At first hearing, the issue seems as antiquarian and foreign as the Spanish Inquisition and the Salem witch trials. Their only acquaintance with the disciplinary ministry of the church is often a literary invention such as *The Scarlet Letter*." See Mohler, "Discipline," 43. Brown similarly asserts, "If discipline is a mark of the true church, as several Reformers insisted, then hardly any modern congregations possess that mark." Brown, "Role of Discipline," 51–52.

3. Unless otherwise noted, this work will be citing from the English Standard

church discipline is an essential ingredient to the church's health. Therefore, it is vital that the church come to a coherent, robust understanding of ecclesial discipline, knowing that God desires a people who are holy, as he is holy (1 Pet 1:15–16).

STATEMENT OF THESIS

The thesis of this dissertation is that one purpose[4] of church discipline is to serve as a declaration of potential eschatological judgment both to warn offenders of their need to repent, and, by implication, to exhort the church members to persevere in their faith.[5] As such, church discipline is a means God uses to save and preserve his people to the end.[6] It should be noted that only God can make ultimate pronouncements concerning the salvific status of individuals; the church is simply a messenger and steward of the message he has given. While this is the case, it must also be acknowledged that Christ has given his church authority and, though not ultimate, this authority is to be used as a warning to unrepentant sinners and as a means to restore them.

This work, therefore, will address the issue of church discipline in such a way as to offer robust theological support for its implementation, and also

---

Version of the Bible.

4. It must be acknowledged that there are a variety of purposes for church discipline. Dever helpfully summarizes, "Finally, church discipline should be practiced in order to bring sinners to repentance, a warning to other church members, health to the whole congregation, a distinct corporate witness to the world, and, ultimately, glory to God, as his people display his character of holy love (see Matt 5:16; 1 Pet 2:12)." Dever, "Doctrine of the Church," 809.

5. It must be acknowledged that the origin of this thesis was brought to fruition through dialogue with Dr. Gregg Allison during my time as a student at Southern Baptist Theological Seminary. Since that time Allison has written a chapter on church discipline that is largely in agreement with this work in Allison, *Sojourners and Strangers*, 179–204. Regarding the specific nuancing of this thesis, a helpful paragraph was found on the idea of church discipline being a "sign of eschatological judgment." He elaborates on this idea, saying, "Just as God's future 'intrudes' on the present through Word and sacrament (the inauguration, sign, and seal of the new creation and the wedding feast), excommunication is an eschatological sign of the last judgment in the present. As a sign, however, it is declarative and not definitive: absolution is always held out as the end goal." Horton, *Covenant and Eschatology*, 272.

6. A similar argument is made in Schreiner and Caneday, *Race Set Before Us*, 38–45, wherein the authors argue that biblical warnings and admonitions serve as the means used by God in calling the saints to persevere in their faith. While this work is quite thorough in the exegesis of various texts on perseverance, particularly in the NT, there is relatively little data regarding church discipline, though there seems to be a very close connection between the warning passages in Scripture and the warning that comes through ecclesial discipline.

concurrently seek to assuage the fear many churches and leaders harbor regarding this topic. It is hoped that this effort will elevate the place of church discipline in ecclesiastical life in such a way as to strengthen both the faith of individual believers, as well as the corporate health of the Christian community. If purity is to be sought, sin is to be dealt with, and restoration is to occur, this practice must be understood and applied. When biblical discipline is consistently undertaken, blessing and benefit will be the ultimate result.

CHAPTER SUMMARIES

The opening chapter contains the introduction to the dissertation, beginning with a brief summary of pertinent background regarding church discipline. Following the articulation of the thesis of this work will be an attempt to define terms such as "church discipline," "eschatological judgment," and "perseverance of the saints." Due to the fact that these specific terms will be repeatedly referenced, a proper understanding of their respective definitions is crucial to understanding the overall argument of the dissertation. Each of these concepts will be elaborated upon textually and theologically as the work progresses. Finally, we will note the contribution made by this dissertation in relation to other works dealing with this specific topic, as well as the particular methodology that will be employed throughout.

Chapter 2 focuses on the biblical teaching regarding church discipline and its relationship to divine judgment and the perseverance of the saints. Since OT texts will be considered, this chapter will begin with a brief reflection of how one should understand continuity and discontinuity between the OT and NT, specifically in reference to the people of God.[7] Based on this brief study, one can see that while there is a degree of discontinuity that one must take into consideration when approaching this topic, there are also OT trajectories that point toward the practice of ecclesial discipline in the NT church.

Three such trajectories will be analyzed: First, this study will investigate Adam and Eve's exile from Eden for their disobedience to God's command. Second, expulsion from the camp of Israel for various infractions of the Mosaic law will be considered. Finally, this chapter will take note of Israel's continual disobedience and eventual exile to Babylon. In rightly understanding God's discipline in the OT as evidenced through these three examples, one can see that God operates in a manner that displays his holiness

---

7. For an excellent study on this topic that offers multiple perspectives, see Feinberg, *Continuity and Discontinuity*, 37–86, 221–59.

and deals with sin in a fitting manner. However, it should also be noted that this discipline is always done with the goal that his people would repent, be restored, and endure in their obedience to him.

This OT foundation leads to a more comprehensive understanding of NT discipline. While there are a number of texts one could consider, this work will focus primarily on five: Matthew 16:13–19, 18:15–20, 1 Corinthians 5:1–13, Galatians 6:1, and 2 Thessalonians 3:6–15. Each of these texts will be examined thoroughly in order to rightly understand the data concerning church discipline, while also noting the various implications for eschatological judgment and perseverance.[8] Other relevant texts regarding ecclesial discipline will be cited throughout this work, but they must be treated briefly since these five passages comprise the main focus of this study. Taking these various texts on discipline from the OT and NT will allow for an opportunity to bring the seemingly disparate ideas of the different passages together into a cohesive and fruitful arrangement. Ultimately, one will be able to observe that discipline is a warning of potential eschatological judgment, as well as a means of perseverance for the people of God.

Chapter 3 contains a historical analysis of church discipline, demonstrating that specific figures from church history conceived of discipline in eschatological and soteriological terms, similar to the way in which it is described in this dissertation. This chapter is important to our study in that it offers sufficient historical evidence for categorizing church discipline within a soteriological and eschatological framework. The chapter will begin with a brief history of church discipline leading up to the Reformation. This section will demonstrate that while disciplinary action within the church had its controversial and contentious moments, it appears that for the first several centuries the church consistently sought to apply disciplinary measures according to the biblical witness.[9] According to Greg Wills, however, the practice of church discipline eventually declined and an emphasis on penance transformed church discipline largely into a private affair between the priest and layperson.[10] As such, the communal role of church discipline

---

8. While one could elaborate a great deal on these passages and the data they possess regarding church discipline, space constraints demand that the focus of our investigation will be directed toward the issues delineated within the thesis. As such, there are exegetical and theological details that may not be thoroughly considered, and thus the reader is encouraged to consult other works listed in the bibliography that deal specifically with the topic of church discipline.

9. For accounts of the discipline of the early church, see Ferguson, *Christian Life*; Haslehurst, *Some Account of the Penitential Discipline*; Lea, *Studies in Church History*.

10. Wills, "Historical Analysis of Church Discipline," 140–41.

dissipated, and private confession and works of merit were common fare in the days leading up to the Reformation.[11]

After this brief survey three figures will receive attention: Martin Luther, Balthasar Hubmaier, and Jonathan Edwards. These figures were chosen for specific reasons. Luther is a critical figure in that he serves in a transitional time from the medieval period to the Reformation era, asserting that church discipline, not penance, is a scriptural practice. Hubmaier is an influential Anabaptist, a movement that was well known for its strict application of discipline, making him worthy of study for this particular work. Finally, Edwards, while not often noted for his ecclesiology or disciplinary measures, is an extremely influential theologian in America and dealt with a number of significant disciplinary cases. Thus, each person was involved both in articulating the theology of church discipline, as well as in practicing discipline within differing congregational contexts. This section will examine the historical setting of each figure and will look predominantly at primary sources to ascertain their particular understanding of discipline. Where applicable, this work will consider specific cases of ecclesial discipline in which each individual was involved. One will thus be able to ascertain that historical warrant does exist for the thesis of this work, even if these figures did not elaborate on the topic as systematically as does this work.

Chapter 4 will present a theological synthesis based on the conclusions of the previous two chapters. While the connection between discipline, eschatological judgment, and the perseverance of the saints will be alluded to in previous sections, here is where the connections will be made explicit. This chapter will also take into account how this conception of church discipline highlights the missional nature of the church. As a warning of potential eschatological judgment and a means by which members of the church are called to persevere, ecclesial discipline calls for a church made up of believers in Jesus Christ who are dedicated to God's mission and held accountable to specific standards by fellow members. Emphasis will again rest on the fact that while church discipline is a warning of potential eschatological judgment, the main goal of discipline is to call sinners to repentance and to serve as a means of perseverance for the people of God. After this synthesis the chapter will conclude by answering potential objections and questions related to the overall argument of the dissertation.

The final chapter of this dissertation will conclude with the practical implications this study yields for local churches. First, the connection

---

11. For greater understanding of the development of medieval penitential practices, see McNeill and Gamer, *Medieval Handbooks of Penance*; Hamilton, *Practice of Penance*; Firey, *New History of Penance*.

between church membership and discipline will be demonstrated. The exercise of faithful discipline demands that a particular culture is set up within the church, wherein regenerate church membership is taken seriously, members care for one another deeply, and rightly understand their responsibility to hold one another accountable. Second, pastors of local congregations must understand that they are stewards of the gospel and shepherds of their people. As stewards, churches must be dedicated not only to corrective church discipline, but also formative discipline. This includes faithful preaching and teaching, leadership, as well as the proper administration of regenerate church membership. Personal attention should also be directed toward all members within the church in order to assess their spiritual vitality and provide them with proper oversight. Finally, attention will be given to the proper observance of the ordinances and their significance in relation to the view of discipline espoused in this dissertation. It is hoped, therefore, that this study will inspire such measures so that scholars, as well as pastors and church members, may see the connection between church discipline, the warning of final judgment, and the call to persevere in the faith.

DEFINITION OF TERMS

Several terms will be emphasized throughout this study, including "church discipline," "eschatological judgment," and "perseverance." Since these terms can take on different meanings depending on one's theological presuppositions it is imperative that definitions are sufficiently delineated so as to provide continuity and clarity throughout.

Church Discipline

Since there are a number of factors involved in the process of discipline, definitions of this practice can vary, but they are typically situated around several common themes. These themes include accountability, exhortation, dealing with sin, authority of the church, excommunication, repentance, and reconciliation. Throughout this study the concept of church discipline will be understood as divine authority delegated to the church by Jesus Christ to maintain order through the correction of persistently sinning church members for the good of those caught in sin, the purity of the church, and the glory of God.[12] Thus, when gross, habitual, unrepentant sin occurs within

12. This definition is derived from a number of sources dealing with the topic of church discipline. Notable contributions to this doctrine include Adams, *Handbook of Church Discipline*; Blue and White, *Church Discipline That Heals*; Dever, *Polity*; Jeschke,

the church, it must be dealt with accordingly, "but always with a view to bringing about repentance."[13]

The concept of church discipline can be understood as both "formative" and "corrective." Leeman notes, "In broad terms, church discipline is one part of the discipleship process, the part where we correct sin and point the disciple toward the better path.... And a Christian is disciplined through instruction and correction."[14] He continues and states that the idea of both instruction and correction is why "there's a centuries-old practice of referring to both formative discipline and corrective discipline."[15] As such, churches do well in not separating discipline a great distance from their pursuit of discipleship, recognizing that the former is a crucial aspect of the latter.[16]

Formative discipline means order is maintained in the church through measures such as regenerate church membership, the right preaching and teaching of Scripture, proper administration of the ordinances, and observing the many "one another" commands contained in the New Testament.[17] Formative church discipline, according to Don Cox, "is broader than corrective discipline and refers to the nurture of believers through instruction and their shared life in the body."[18] While many churches enact these kinds of practices, it is often not referred to as formative church discipline, though this may help to give a particular mindset to the life of the church. This type of discipline is exercised in the Christian community as the members express genuine concern for each other and become dynamically involved with one another in deep interpersonal relationships, recognizing that God holds all accountable for their stewardship of life.[19] Thus, the purpose of formative discipline is to enlighten, encourage, support, and sustain one another in the discipline under which they live and in the fulfillment of their divine mission.

Discipling the Brother; Knuteson, *Calling the Church to Discipline*; Laney, *Guide to Church Discipline*; Lauterbach, *Transforming Community*; Leeman, *Church Discipline*; Oden, *Corrective Love*; South, *Disciplinary Practices in Pauline Texts*; Wray, *Biblical Church Discipline*.

13. Kingdon, "Discipline," 450.
14. Leeman, *Church Discipline*, 27.
15. Ibid.
16. See Schreiner, "Biblical Basis for Church Discipline," 105.
17. For a more thorough study of this type of discipline, see Cox, "Forgotten Side of Church Discipline," 44–58.
18. Ibid., 44.
19. See ibid., 44–45.

While a crucial component of the disciplinary process, this work will focus on the corrective aspect of church discipline, which deals with the direct confrontation of sin. A forthright approach to the process of discipline is elucidated by Jesus, which helps to form a pattern for how one should approach these kinds of situations (Matt 18:15–20).[20] Jesus states that one should go directly to the person who sinned against them to see if they can restore the relationship. If reconciliation does not take place, one or two witnesses are to be brought along in order to restore fellowship. If there is no reconciliation at this point the matter is brought before the church so that the sinner can be confronted corporately. If this does not achieve the goal of reconciliation the person is to be removed from the membership of the church and treated as a "Gentile or tax collector."[21] In each of these steps, love and forgiveness are to be extended, since the goal of discipline is ultimately reconciliation.

This last step of the discipline, known as excommunication, is more rare in church settings, since issues typically are dealt with in the first or second step. Nevertheless, this area of discipline demands our attention. Piggin astutely defines this aspect of discipline:

> The most extreme disciplinary measure of the church, excommunication is the exclusion of an irrevocably rebellious sinner from the communion of the faithful. In most periods of the church's history, excommunication has been understood primarily as a medicinal measure, to recall to repentance and obedience. A secondary purpose is to safeguard the community's purity. When excommunication is rightly understood, punishment has never been the object.[22]

This step of discipline does not mean that a person cannot attend a church service; rather it involves a removal of that person from the membership rolls and the exclusion of the person from partaking of the Lord's Supper. Church members must also know that they are to treat the excommunicant

---

20. It should be noted that this pattern may not necessarily apply in all cases. One can see this as evidenced in 1 Cor 5 where Paul calls for the immediate excommunication of the sinning member without going through the other steps as seen in Matt 18.

21. More detail will be given later regarding this phrase from Matt 18. At this point it is sufficient to say that Jesus appears to be saying that a congregation should treat one who is excommunicated as if they were an unbeliever. As such, it is crucial to note Marlin Jeschke's exhortation and note that church discipline is nothing less than a "renewed presentation of the gospel message to the impenitent persons in that it confronts them with the truth." Jeschke, *Discipling in the Church*, 88. As such, church discipline has both ecclesiological and soteriological concerns.

22. Piggin, "Excommunication," 256.

as if that person were an unbeliever, based on a lack of repentance.[23] This understanding of excommunication is needful in embracing both the love as well as the holiness of God, noting that both attributes are exercised in this practice.

Eschatological Judgment

While fiercely debated from a number of vantage points,[24] the concept of final judgment is thoroughly biblical and intrinsically connected to the concept of church discipline. Motyer depicts final judgment and states, "The Lord Jesus spoke plainly about the dreadful aspects of the last day (Matt 10:28; cf. 5:29; 23:33; Luke 12:5), and placed himself at the center of the eschatological events. His coming signals the ingathering (Mark 13:26–27) and 'out-gathering' (Matt 13:41–42)."[25] He continues, "All will stand before him, to receive either eternal life (Matt 25:34, 46) or eternal fire (Matt 25:41, 46)."[26] There are no exceptions; this truth applies to all people in the earth throughout the course of history (2 Cor 5:10). Eschatological judgment, therefore, denotes a reality that all of humanity will face, though not all will face the same eternal destiny.[27]

When surveying the passages detailing the final judgment, it should be noted that individuals are judged according to what they have done (e.g., Matt 25:31–46; 2 Cor 5:10; Rev 20:13). As such, to be completely accurate to Pauline language, we are justified by faith and judged according to works.[28]

---

23. Dever and Alexander, *Deliberate Church*, 71. Again, this statement does not infer that the church is the final authority regarding one's salvation; however one must take seriously removal from a local church, since this serves as a warning of potential final judgment and serves as a means by which the saints are called to persevere in their faith.

24. One need only recount the firestorm of controversy that erupted over Rob Bell's book *Love Wins*, which questioned the traditional doctrines of hell and God's final judgment. Two of the better known responses to this work are Chan and Sprinkle, *Erasing Hell*, and Galli, *God Wins*.

25. Motyer, "Judgment," 615.

26. Ibid.

27. For another helpful source dealing with the final judgment see Vos, *Pauline Eschatology*, 261–87.

28. See Ortlund, "Justified by Faith," 323–39. Ortlund provides a helpful taxonomy of views regarding this thorny matter, and ventures to understand this difficult tension via a robust understanding of our union with Christ. See also Thiselton, *Life after Death*, 178–79, who makes use of speech-act theory and asserts that while Christians are sinners "within the realm of law and history," God looks upon them as put right with God in the "framework of eschatology and Christology."

This reality, though it remains a difficult paradox to explicate exhaustively, is what connects church discipline to the perseverance of the saints. Believers are called to persevere in a faith that works itself out in love (Gal 5:6), for it is this kind of life that demonstrates true faith (Jas 2:14–26). Conversely, if a church member is not persevering in this kind of faith, and instead indulges in habitual, unrepentant sin, the disciplinary process should be applied.

Horton makes this point and contends that in this time where the kingdom of God has been inaugurated, "the business of the church is receiving and delivering the gift of salvation, not contributing to the gift, negotiating its terms, or determining its content."[29] Thus, the message proclaimed by the church is encapsulated in the gospel of Jesus Christ, and the keys granted by Christ to the church (Matt 16:18–19; 18:15–20) designate the church's authority to bind and loose, to receive in and to shut out. As such, Horton continues,

> Through preaching, baptism, and admission (or refusal of admission) to the Communion, the keys of the kingdom are exercised. After all, it may be said that the "binding and loosing" involved in church discipline is at issue in every liturgical absolution, sermon, baptism, and Communion. On all of these occasions, the age to come is breaking into this present age: both the last judgment and the final vindication of God's elect occur in a *semi*realized manner, ministerially rather than magisterially. The church's acts are not final—they do not coincide univocally with the eschatological realities, but they are signs and seals. Christ's performative speech is mediated through appointed officers.[30]

As the church, therefore, seeks to maintain its doctrinal fidelity and pursue holiness, it must be willing to remove a sinning, unrepentant member from fellowship, participation in the ordinances, and also "from the company of players if not from the play itself."[31] In other words, the practice of church discipline, specifically excommunication, warns of the eschatological reality of divine judgment, and thus while one is justified by faith alone, it is crucial to also note the importance of the obedience that comes from faith (Rom 1:5).

---

29. Horton, *People and Place*, 242.
30. Ibid., 243; italics in original.
31. See Vanhoozer, *Drama of Doctrine*, 425.

Perseverance of the Saints

One final category to define is the biblical concept of perseverance. Understood simply as enduring in one's faith until the end, there is disagreement over whether apostasy is a genuine possibility for believers. Schreiner observes, "The debate centers particularly on the severe warnings in the NT that threaten judgment for those who apostatize (e.g., Rom 11:22; Gal 5:2–6; 2 Tim 2:11–13; Heb 6:4–8; 10:26–31). . . . Preserving the tension between assurance and warnings is necessary to be faithful to the biblical witness."[32] This tension is key in not allowing believers to become lethargic in their faith, and also not living in constant fear and doubt.

Schreiner and Caneday survey four differing views on the topic of perseverance.[33] First, there are those who would assert that it is possible for believers to lose their salvation and apostatize from the faith. They maintain that the Bible's warnings and admonitions make it clear that heirs of God's promise can fail to persevere in faithfulness, and thus forfeit the inheritance of salvation. Current proponents of this view would include I. Howard Marshall[34] and Scot McKnight,[35] who would both be classified in the Wesleyan/Arminian camp. While it may appear that this reading may be the most straightforward as it relates to these warning passages, it seems to do away with the tension that must be held between warning and assurance, as stated previously.[36]

Schreiner and Caneday document three other views: the loss of rewards, test of genuineness, and hypothetical loss of salvation. The first and third, while advocated by a number of proponents,[37] do not seem to do justice to the tenor of the biblical texts. Neither seems to deal with the force of these texts in a satisfactory manner.[38] The test of genuineness view

---

32. Schreiner, "Assurance," 71.

33. These four views can be found in Schreiner and Caneday, *Race Set Before Us*, 21–38. See also Schreiner, "Perseverance and Assurance," 32–62.

34. Marshall, *Kept by the Power of God*.

35. McKnight, "Warning Passages of Hebrews," 21–59; McKnight, "Apostasy," 58–60.

36. For an excellent example of how one can refute the Arminian reading of Heb 6, arguably the most difficult warning passage for non-Arminians to explain, see Grudem, "Perseverance of the Saints," 133–82.

37. For the loss of rewards view, see Eaton, *No Condemnation*; Hodges, *Gospel Under Siege*; Kendall, *Once Saved, Always Saved*; Wilkin, *Confident in Christ*. Regarding the hypothetical loss of salvation view, see Kent, *Epistle to the Hebrews*; Westcott, *Epistle to the Hebrews*.

38. While outside the purview of our immediate discussion here, one can analyze the arguments more definitively in Schreiner and Caneday's work.

advocates that biblical warnings are addressed to people who profess faith in Jesus Christ, but who prove to be false in their confession. Supporters of this view, such as John MacArthur,[39] maintain that perseverance in holiness is essential for salvation, because perseverance is the necessary evidence that belief is genuine.

Schreiner and Caneday's own view is most similar to the position just mentioned, though unique in its own right. They assert that God's promises and warnings do not conflict; rather, "the warnings serve the promises, for the warnings urge belief and confidence in God's promises. Biblical warnings and admonitions are the means God uses to save and preserve his people to the end."[40] They also seek to hold the tension of an already / not yet salvation, wherein we are already saved and we still await eschatological salvation. As such, they seek as much as possible to do justice to the biblical texts with a view to understanding them within their textual and canonical context.

While a complex discussion and worthy of much inquiry, Schreiner observes that, regardless of one's interpretation, all would agree, "good works are *evidence* of genuine saving faith." He also understands good works as a fruit of faith, which are necessary for eschatological salvation (cf. Jas 2:14–26).[41] This dissertation will adopt the view of Schreiner and Caneday, understanding the warnings in Scripture to serve as means for believers to persevere in their faith. This understanding appears to best fit with the biblical data, and also helps to make sense of the tension one sees in church discipline and final judgment. Discipline serves a redemptive purpose, but, if not properly acknowledged by repentance (i.e., lack of perseverance), it can be a strong indicator that those under discipline will not inherit eschatological salvation at the final judgment.

UNIQUENESS AND CONTRIBUTION OF THE STUDY

Ecclesiology is often a category of theology that is overlooked due to its seeming "secondary" status. When broaching this topic, however, one can see how matters of ecclesiology can directly bear on matters related to the gospel and salvation. Thus, the importance of church discipline can be seen not only in an academic sense, but also on a practical and pastoral level. First, this topic will show the connection that should be made between this aspect of ecclesiology and specific areas of soteriology (e.g., perseverance) and

---

39. MacArthur, *Gospel according to Jesus*.
40. Schreiner and Caneday, *Race Set Before Us*, 40.
41. Schreiner, "Assurance," 71.

eschatology (e.g., judgment). This reality calls for greater care and attention in implementing the practice of church discipline in local congregations. As such, the significance of this study is evident, since right understanding of this crucial aspect of ecclesial discipline will in turn give greater determination in implementing and exercising discipline when necessary.

As a contribution to the fields of biblical and systematic theology, this study will endeavor to trace data from both the OT and NT in apprehending the nature and importance of church discipline. In seeking to investigate OT data, an example will be given of how one can best understand varying degrees of continuity and discontinuity between the Testaments. This understanding will be beneficial as one seeks to understand the relationship between Israel and the Church, and how God interacts with these groups within the framework of redemptive history.

This work will also demonstrate how various loci of theology can and should be thought of in relationship to one another. Often, distinctive aspects of theology are considered in isolation, thus allowing for greater depth of research. However, this does not necessarily foster the kind of rigorous interaction that could yield more fruitful results. While working primarily in the area of ecclesiology, this study will show that considerations from the fields of soteriology and eschatology enrich one's understanding of the church and its role and function in ecclesial discipline. Finally, pastors can benefit from this work, not primarily in better understanding how one practically implements church discipline within a local congregation,[42] but why they should do so theologically. It is hoped that this study will serve as a catalyst for loving discipline within churches for the good of God's people.

In the way of originality, a search of pertinent dissertations on the area of church discipline revealed that while a number of works have been written on related areas of discipline, none seem to address directly the fact that it is a warning of potential eschatological judgment and a means by which the people of God are called to persevere in their faith. Many of these dissertations focus on a historical era or figure in delineating the role church discipline played in that particular milieu.[43] Others center their attention on exegetical concerns, seeking to explicate the pertinent passages relating to the practice of discipline.[44] One dissertation focused its attention on the subject of excommunication in relation to the particular *Sitz im Leben* of

---

42. For more on this topic, see esp. Leeman, *Church Discipline*, 67–124.

43. See, e.g., Bezzant, "Orderly but Not Ordinary"; Burnett, *Yoke of Christ*; Goncharenko, "Importance of Church Discipline"; McMullan, "Church Discipline"; Oberholzer, *Delinquent Saints*.

44. See Kitchens, "Church Discipline"; Pascuzzi, *Ethics*; Smith, *Hand This Man Over*; South, *Disciplinary Practices in Pauline Texts*.

each community.⁴⁵ Two more recent works have shown both the role of over-realized eschatology in church discipline,⁴⁶ as well as how discipline manifests God's fatherly love.⁴⁷ While these works all make contributions in their own distinctive way, it appears there is ample room for a study that incorporates the ideas of eschatological judgment and perseverance in the faith in relation to ecclesial discipline.

RESEARCH METHODOLOGY

This dissertation will seek to build on the evidence in a logical and progressive fashion, beginning with Scripture. The issue of discipline and exclusion from the covenant community is a rather broad biblical topic. Often, however, when the issue of church discipline is discussed from a biblical perspective, relatively few texts are considered.⁴⁸ This is an unfortunate practice and can often cause a shortsighted understanding of all that is actually involved in church discipline. The intention of this dissertation is to avoid such a limited approach. This study will consider the subject by taking into account the broader canonical context of the Scriptures and its contribution to the topic, though admittedly not in an exhaustive manner. When one takes this broader context of Scripture into account, it can be seen that discipline plays a fundamental role in the storyline of the biblical narrative.

Unlike many studies regarding church discipline, this study will begin with the OT, noting several trajectories that point forward to NT discipline: exile from Eden, expulsion from the camp of Israel, and ejection from the land of Israel. These three examples provide a helpful foundation in understanding NT discipline, as they model how God deals with those who persist in their sin within the covenant community. The focus of this work will then shift to the NT, looking at pertinent texts in the Gospels as well as Pauline literature. This will allow for an opportunity to bring the seemingly disparate ideas of the various texts together into a cohesive understanding.

After this study of the various biblical passages, three historical figures will be analyzed, demonstrating that this perspective on church discipline

---

45. Storm, "Excommunication."
46. Canham, "Not Home Yet."
47. Bargerhuff, *Love That Rescues*.

48. Although other passages of Scripture certainly are cited, the texts that are typically appealed to are Matt 18:15–20 and 1 Cor 5. One example of this is found in the overall structure of Adams, *Handbook of Church Discipline*. Here Matt 18:15–20 is given precedence as the guiding framework of how to approach church discipline, which is certainly appropriate, though not exhaustive.

also contains sufficient historical warrant. The data culled from the previous chapters will then be brought together for a coherent theological synthesis, noting the relationship between ecclesial discipline, eschatological judgment, and the perseverance of the saints. This synthesis will inevitably demonstrate the ways in which discipline should directly affect the practices of the church today. Church discipline must be understood theologically, but always with a view to proper application within the local church so that the church may be presented to Christ "without spot or wrinkle or any other blemish" (Eph 5:27). Thus, the research methodology will begin with exegetical study, then compare the findings to historical precedents, leading to a theological formulation, which in turn serves as the basis for practical application.

2

A Biblical Analysis of Church Discipline

THIS CHAPTER WILL FOCUS on the biblical teaching regarding church discipline and its relationship to divine eschatological judgment and the perseverance of the saints. The purpose here is to provide biblical evidence supporting the thesis that church discipline serves as a declaration of potential eschatological judgment. Thus, this chapter will serve as a foundation for the remainder of this work, as the historical, theological, and practical formulations are rooted in the conclusions derived from the biblical data.

Unlike many studies regarding church discipline, this study will begin with the OT, noting several trajectories that point to NT discipline: exile[1] from Eden, expulsion from the camp of Israel, and ejection from the land of Israel. These trajectories provide a helpful foundation and understanding for NT discipline. The focus of this work will then shift to the NT, looking at pertinent texts in the Gospels as well as Pauline literature. This will allow for an opportunity to bring the seemingly disparate ideas of the various texts together into a cohesive arrangement. Before this study of the pertinent biblical texts is undertaken, however, one must first consider the relationship that exists between the OT and NT to ascertain if it is legitimate to draw from OT texts in order to illuminate NT practices.

---

1. Duguid defines the concept of exile in the following manner: "Exile, in theological terms, is the experience of pain and suffering that results from the knowledge that there is a home where one belongs, yet for the present one is unable to return there." Duguid, "Exile," 475.

CONTINUITY AND DISCONTINUITY BETWEEN THE TESTAMENTS

The relationship between the OT and NT is filled with complexity.[2] While apparent similarities and parallels between the Testaments occur on a number of themes, a degree of discontinuity also exists.[3] Thus, for our purposes, both continuity and discontinuity must be acknowledged when speaking of Israel, the church, and the subject of discipline.

Mark Dever helpfully distinguishes between Israel and the church, saying, "Though some Christians use the phrase 'New Testament church,' the shape of the visible church today bears a clear continuity—though not identity—with the visible people of God in the Old Testament."[4] Millar summarizes this reality when he asserts, "The entire Bible speaks of God's plan to create his people, in his place, under his rule. He commits himself to working with one people, and follows this commitment through to the end, though he extends the scope of his people infinitely through the work of Christ."[5] Thus, a pattern is seen beginning in the OT where God is interested in blessing a group of people, beginning with the saving of a few families from the flood (Gen 6–8), and coming into greater focus in the covenant made with Abraham (Gen 12). God promises a land and blessing for Abraham's descendants, and this reality comes to fruition in the nation of Israel, whom God leads out of Egypt and calls his own people (Exod 1–20). God shows great interest in calling a particular people to be his own.

In noting further continuity between Israel and the church, one can observe that the two primary terms used to refer to God's people in the OT are קהל (*qhl*) and עדה (*ēdâh*). In the NT the word translated "church"

---

2. In seeking to understand this relationship, a divide has typically been driven between covenant and dispensational theology. For the covenant position, see Horton, *God of Promise*; Robertson, *Israel of God*; Reymond, *New Systematic Theology*, 503–44. A traditional dispensational view would be represented by Ryrie, *Dispensationalism*. For the progressive dispensationalist position, see Blaising and Bock, *Progressive Dispensationalism*; Saucy, *Case for Progressive Dispensationalism*. For a mediating position between covenant and dispensational theology, see Gentry and Wellum, *Kingdom through Covenant*.

3. For an excellent study on this topic see Feinberg, *Continuity and Discontinuity*.

4. Dever, "Church," 768. Tidball, agreeing with this assertion, states, "The church traces its roots back to the OT people of God. The new covenant community, although in some ways radically different from the community of the old covenant (Jer 31:31–34), nonetheless has much in common with it." He goes on to demonstrate that continuity regarding the people of God is found in that the OT and NT contain a people who are the elect of God, are called to worship God as a royal priesthood, and function as an organized assembly who are called to obey God in holiness. Tidball, "Church," 407–8.

5. Millar, "People of God," 687. See also Martens, "People of God," 225–53.

is ἐκκλησία (*ekklēsia*), which has three primary usages, all connoting an assembly of people.⁶ Hammett notes, "The translators of the Septuagint used *ekklēsia* to translate *qāhāl* nearly one hundred times, but never to translate *ēdâh*. For *ēdâh* they usually used the Greek term *synagōgē*, which is used only once in the New Testament to refer to the church (James 2:2)."⁷ Taking this data into consideration, Dever asserts that there is a rich association between the assembly of God in the OT (*qāhāl*) and the NT church by virtue of the etymological connection that exists as evidenced by the LXX.⁸

Another evidence for continuity includes the way in which the NT associates Israel and the church. In Galatians 6:16, Paul referred to "all who follow this rule" in the Galatian church as "the Israel of God." While some suggest this title refers to ethnic Jews in the congregation,⁹ others believe that earlier Paul referred to all Christians, Jew and Gentile, as "Abraham's seed," and thus the link between Israel and the church is deliberate.¹⁰ Peter also uses OT language specified for Israel to refer to the church as "a chosen race, a royal priesthood, a holy nation, a people for his own possession" (1 Pet 2:9; cf. Deut 10:15; Exod 19:5–6; Deut 7:6). Acts 15 is also a significant passage dealing with this issue. At the Jerusalem Council, James quotes Amos 9:11–12, a prophecy promising that David's fallen tent would be restored and that Israel would come to possess the nations. Dever asserts, "James affirmed that this prophecy points toward the church's present circumstances and the recent influx of Gentile believers."¹¹ Thus, according to the affirmation of the apostles, a prophecy made to Israel in the OT includes in its fulfillment, at least in part, Gentile believers coming into the church.

---

6. BDAG, s.v. "ἐκκλησία."

7. Hammett, *Biblical Foundations for Baptist Churches*, 27. Hammett derives this data from Coenen, "Church," 1:292–96. Coenen further maintains that *qāhāl* "embraces only those who have heard the call and are following it. *Ēdâh*, on the other hand, is the permanent community into which one was born." See Coenen, "Church," 295.

8. Dever, "Church," 769.

9. See, e.g., Johnson, "Paul and 'The Israel of God,'" 41–55; Walvoord and Zuck, *Bible Knowledge Commentary*, 611.

10. See Köstenberger, "Identity of the Ἰσραὴλ τοῦ θεοῦ," 3–24; Ridderbos, *Epistle of Paul*, 227. Schreiner states the entirety of the letter to the Galatians is dealing with whether one must become a Jew to be saved. Paul has argued throughout that circumcision is unnecessary and that those who put their faith in Christ belong to the family of Abraham. Seemingly, it would be very confusing to argue for the equality of Jew and Gentile in Christ (3:28), assert that all believers are Abraham's children, and then conclude that only ethnic Jews who believe in Jesus belong to the Israel of God. See Schreiner, *Galatians*, 381–83.

11. Dever, "Church," 770.

While one should note that these continuities are present, it is crucial also to consider the differences that exist between Israel and the church.[12] For example, God's people in the OT are ethnically distinct, while the NT church includes both Jew and Gentile. Israel in the OT lived as a separate nation with its own laws; the church in the NT lives among the rulers of the nations, called to obey God's commands, but also subject to the governing authorities (Rom 13:1–7). A covenant sign for Israel was physical circumcision, while in the NT baptism and the circumcision of the heart mark out the church. Discontinuity also exists because of the coming of Christ and all that he accomplished, as well as the inauguration of the new covenant and the indwelling of the Holy Spirit.[13] Thus, discontinuity must be maintained, even while one can rightly see the relationship between Israel and the church. As such, Dever avers, "Though Israel and the church are not identical, they are closely related, and they are related through Jesus Christ (Eph 2:12–13). . . . Christ is the fulfillment of all that Israel points toward (2 Cor 1:20), and the church is Christ's body."[14] Seemingly one can agree that God has consistently planned to glorify his name through groups of people whom he chooses.[15]

As it relates to discipline—if one acknowledges this connection between the OT and NT people of God—the pattern of OT discipline is foundational for understanding the enactment of discipline within the NT church. God exists in holiness, and he requires his people to be holy if he is to dwell in their midst (Lev 11:44–45; 19:1–2; cf. 1 Pet 1:14–16). This expectation of holiness grounds God's actions as it relates to his covenant with Israel. God, who is certainly loving and merciful, will not allow his people to dwell in sin for long without enacting dire consequences (Deut 28:15–68). Holiness means that God will discipline those in unrepentant sin, though he does so with an end to love and forgive the one in sin (Deut 30:1–10).

---

12. For further thoughts on the discontinuity between Israel and the church beyond what is mentioned here, see Saucy, "Israel and the Church," 239–59.

13. For an excellent study on the indwelling of the Spirit as a new reality in the NT, see Hamilton, *God's Indwelling Presence*.

14. Dever, "Church," 770. Robert Saucy, a progressive dispensationalist, while seeking to highlight the discontinuity between Israel and the church, argues, similarly to Dever, that although the church does not now assume the position of Israel exclusively in some replacement fashion, the use of OT terminology to refer to the church "does clearly indicate that the 'people of God' has been enlarged to include those from nations other than Israel." Saucy, "Israel and the Church," 241. For more thoughts on this topic from an author advocating "moderate discontinuity," see Allison, *Sojourners and Strangers*, 39–43.

15. On this point, see Ladd, *Gospel of the Kingdom*, 120.

As holiness was held as a standard for Israel, so it is also required of the NT church (Heb 12:14). Richard Haslehurst, noting the OT roots of church discipline, maintains, "The apostles when they administered discipline as leaders of the Christian Church were only carrying on a principle with which they had been familiar from childhood."[16] One example of this can be seen in Paul's use of Deuteronomy when telling the church in Corinth to "purge the evil person from among you" (1 Cor 5:13). More will be stated on this passage below, but it is sufficient at this point to note that Paul's admonition to the Corinthian church to discipline is rooted in an OT practice. Thus, while admitting distinctions between the OT and NT people of God and how discipline was actually administered, it is beneficial to see the OT background that gave grounding to NT practices. As such, one must seek to rightly understand the trajectories that the OT offers in order to attain a more thorough comprehension of the practice of church discipline.

OLD TESTAMENT TRAJECTORIES

With this comprehension of the continuity and discontinuity between the Testaments one can now observe the patterns offered in the OT that help to make sense of the NT practice of church discipline. One can begin with the story of God's creation, the fall of humanity, and the resulting consequences.

Exile from Eden

The biblical narrative begins with God's creation of the universe, climaxing in the creation of humanity (Gen 1).[17] Man and woman are created in God's image to reflect his glory and exercise dominion over the face of the earth (Gen 1:26–28). God blesses Adam and Eve, who are to function as his vice-regents,[18] and places them in a garden where they will experience blessing and God's presence, provided they obey God's command to not eat from one particular tree in the garden (Gen 2:15–17). They, however, succumb to temptation, rebel, and eat from the tree of the knowledge of good and evil (Gen 3:1–7). While the prospect of death—along with other negative results of the fall—is made clear as a consequence (Gen 3:8–19), what the reader sees happening presently is the exile of Adam and Eve from

---

16. Haslehurst, *Some Account of the Penitential Discipline*, 1.

17. This summary draws heavily from Ciampa, "History of Redemption," 257–58.

18. For a more detailed understanding of man acting as God's vice-regent in the Garden, see Dempster, *Dominion and Dynasty*, 59–62.

their garden paradise (Gen 3:23–24). The rest of the biblical story revolves around the question of eventual restoration of the relationship between God and humanity.

While the preceding paragraph serves as an adequate summary of the narrative concerning creation and the fall, it is imperative to look more closely at the results of Adam and Eve's sin, especially their exile from Eden. God proclaims, due to the choice to rebel against his command, that humans are now in a sinful state, and, seemingly, if they take of the tree of life they will live forever in this state (Gen 3:22). Therefore, he drives Adam and Eve from the garden of Eden and places an angel at the entrance of the Garden to keep people from partaking of the tree of life (Gen 3:23–24). This latter passage evidences increasingly intensive language being used. First, God says he will "send" the man out, and then he actually "drove" them out.[19] Thus, God removes humanity from his blessing, immediate presence, and protection.[20]

If the story ended there it would be a rather morbid conclusion; however, there is hope to be seen in this passage, as well as God's gracious character. House affirms this fact and asserts,

> With the consequences of sin clearly stated and with a long-term promise of the serpent's defeat in place, God acts in mercy to sustain the fallen couple. God clothes them (3:21). The Lord also removes them from the garden to protect them from eating of the tree of life, which had not been forbidden previously, so that they will not live forever in a sinful condition (3:22–24). Not even their sin can separate them from God's concern for and commitment to the well-being of the people he has created.[21]

---

19. Of this latter term, Wenham states, "It is often used in the Pentateuch of the expulsion of the inhabitants of Canaan (e.g., Exod 23:28–31). It is coupled with 'send out' in Exod 6:1; 11:1, and in each case it adds emphasis." Wenham, *Genesis 1–15*, 85. Hamilton concurs with this assessment and elaborates: "The juxtaposition of these two verbs reinforces the idea that man does not leave the garden of his own will. Nor is he gently escorted to the garden's edge. In fact, he is thrown out! Sin separates from God. Intimacy with God is replaced with alienation from God." Hamilton, *Book of Genesis*, 210.

20. Detailing this particular point from Gen 3:22–24, Sailhamer asserts, "The sentence of death now leveled against the man and the woman consists of being cast out of the garden and being barred from the tree of life. The penalty is later taken up as being part of the Mosaic law: to 'be put to death' (*môt yûmat*, lit., 'he shall surely die') is to be 'cut off from [one's] people' (Ex 31:14). The transgression of Adam and Eve means they will be cast off from the protection of the garden (cf. Gen 4:14)." See Sailhamer, *Genesis*, 94.

21. House, *Old Testament Theology*, 66.

Beyond what is mentioned here, God also pronounces the *protoevangelion* in Genesis 3:15, promising a seed of the woman—namely, Jesus Christ (Gal 3:16)—who would one day crush the head of the serpent, Satan. Thus, Calvin also asserts that, for Adam, a "solemn excommunication" was administered not so the Lord would cut him off from all hope of salvation, but rather would cause individuals to seek new assistance elsewhere. He continues, "From the moment in which he became alienated from God, it was necessary that he should recover life by the death of Christ, by whose life he then lived."[22] God, therefore, demonstrates his justice and grace, showing that sin is a grotesque affront to his holiness, while also providing for humanity in a temporal and eternal fashion.[23]

This act of discipline on God's part is profound in that it serves as a model of the way in which sin will merit serious consequences. Duguid asserts that the expulsion of Adam and Eve from the garden of Eden is the archetype of all subsequent exile (Gen 3:24), stating, "Throughout the rest of the Bible, the state of God's people is one of profound exile, of living in a world to which they do not belong and looking for a world that is yet to come."[24] Anderson elaborates on this point, specifically regarding the connection between the exile of Adam from Eden, and the exile of Israel from the land, which is a topic that will be taken up in greater detail at a later point. He declares,

> Biblical writers believed that the human condition was best described through what happened to Israel. On the face of it then, we should expect some similarity between what happened to Adam and Eve and what happened to Israel. And this expectation bears fruit. Just as Adam and Eve receive a commandment prior to their entrance into Eden, so Israel is given a set of commandments prior to her entrance into the Promised Land. Just as in the Garden Adam and Eve's well being is predicated on their obedience, so for Israel. And, most important, just as the tree of life remains a tantalizing reward for Adam and Eve

---

22. Calvin, *Commentaries on the First Book of Moses*, 1:184.

23. Knuteson, *Calling the Church to Discipline*, 21–22, states, "Discipline is God's business. How graphically this is seen in the beginning years of human history. Adam and his wife Eve were driven from the Paradise of God and cherubim with a flaming sword guarded the way to the tree of life (Gen 3:24). A loving Creator thus excluded the first couple by disciplinary action. We must realize that if He had allowed them access to the Tree of Life, after spiritual death had begun its awful toll, our first parents would have lived endlessly in aging and weakening bodies. This discipline of exclusion was for their own good. . . . Divine discipline has always been exercised as a means of grace; it is the evidence of love and a tangible sign that God really cares."

24. Duguid, "Exile," 475–76. See also Alter, *Genesis*, 18.

should they be found virtuous, so life itself is offered as a reward to Israel should they be faithful to the covenant.[25]

Ciampa agrees and suggests that Adam and Eve face not only exile, but also specific curses. Thus, the suggestion that the Genesis narrative reflects what he would describe as a "covenant, sin, exile, restoration structure," which applies to all of creation, obviously entails "reading the early Genesis narratives in the light of the covenantal background of their Pentateuchal context, where blessings or curses in the land and the covenantal curse of exile from the land are well-established explicit elements of the narrative."[26] Therefore, the act of expelling Adam and Eve from the garden of Eden serves as a kind of prototype for how God will deal with sin throughout the rest of redemptive history.

It is important to note again at this point that exile from Eden—along with expulsion from the camp and ejection from the land—serves as a trajectory. It is not a perfect parallel to NT church discipline. The OT pattern often denotes God as the initiator of the discipline, whereas in the NT God has given authority to the church to exercise discipline. Most often, OT discipline had a decisive and definitive end in death, and in NT discipline the process is often drawn out for the purpose of repentance and reconciliation. NT discipline is also exacted in an ecclesial context, not within a socio-political milieu, as was the case with Israel. While the trajectory is important to trace, one must also keep in mind the progressive shifts that occur within salvation history.

As such, while this narrative is quite removed from the NT context of local church discipline, a distinct link can be seen between Adam and Israel and the discipline they received from God. This link serves to solidify the

---

25. Anderson, *Genesis of Perfection*, 120. Subsequently he summarizes the relationship between Eden and Sinai in the following way:

Eden	Sinai
God creates man	God elects Israel
Command is given	Torah is revealed
Violation	[Should] Israel violate the law
Expulsion from Eden	Expulsion from the promised land

26. Ciampa, "History of Redemption," 259. Ciampa believes this to be a right reading contra Wright, *Resurrection of the Son of God*, 122, who "wonders whether the story in Genesis 3, of Adam and Eve being expelled from the garden, was read in this period as a paradigm of Israel's expulsion from the promised land," concluding that "direct evidence for this connection is lacking." Ciampa believes that "in view of the clear parallel to the Deuteronomic pattern so essential to so much other Old Testament material, I think it unlikely that readers sensitive to the logic of the narrative development would not read the opening of Genesis in the light of the clear SER [sin, exile, restoration] patterns found elsewhere." See Ciampa, "History of Redemption," 259; Duguid, "Exile," 475; cf. Waltke, *Old Testament Theology*, 150–51.

connection between the first man and God's chosen people, and, as was seen earlier, there is an association to be made between Israel and the church of God under the new covenant.[27] This narrative also demonstrates God's abhorrence toward sin and disobedience, his determination to execute justice for that sin, and the fact that God desires good to be done to his people through the administration of discipline.

Expulsion from the Camp

After the exile of Adam and Eve, as well as a global flood (Gen 6–8) and the scattering of the peoples of the earth (Gen 11), God made a covenant with a man named Abram, to give him a land, bless him, and make a great nation by his descendants (Gen 12:1–3). That nation is Israel, who is later brought out of captivity from Egypt in the exodus and brought into covenant relationship with God (Exod 1–20). The Lord makes his law known through the Mosaic covenant, covering a variety of subjects, including disciplinary measures that must be exacted upon certain offending sinners within the nation of Israel. One such measure was expulsion from the camp of Israel, which was their temporary abode prior to their entry into the promised land.

Physical Removal from the Camp

Being taken outside of the camp was a way in which Israel sought to maintain its holiness and purity before the Lord.[28] As such, corpses were taken outside the camp (Lev 10:4–5), along with lepers and those who were unclean (Lev 13:46; 14:3–9; Num 5:1–4; 12:15; Deut 23:10–11). The sacrifice that bears the sin of the nation on the Day of Atonement was also taken outside the camp (Lev 16:20–22), along with those who were to be punished for blasphemy or breaking the Sabbath (Lev 24:14, 23; Num 15:32–36), and those who were foreigners (Josh 6:23).

These kinds of commands were to be taken seriously since God called his people to be holy, for he was holy (Lev 11:44–45). As seen in Leviticus 13:46, the diseased person had to live alone outside the camp. A solitary

---

27. For further information regarding the connection between Israel and the church beyond what was cited above, see Clowney, *Church*, 30–47.

28. Ortlund elaborates on this point: "In contrast to the moral chaos widely accepted in the nation which God is expelling from the promised land, Israel is to observe the distinctions entailed in God's moral order. To transgress his boundaries is to deny one's consecration to Yahweh, making one indistinguishable from those not covenanted to him, as if he had not bound Israel to himself at all." Ortlund, *God's Unfaithful Wife*, 35.

existence was viewed as a calamity in itself in ancient times (cf. Lam 1:1). It was not that everywhere outside the camp was unclean; there were clean places outside the camp (e.g., Lev 4:12). However, as Wenham notes, "It was the place farthest removed from God, the place to which the sinner and the impure were banished (Lev 10:4–5; Num 5:1–4; 12:14–15; 31:19–24). It was the place where wrongdoers were executed (Num 15:35–36)."[29] Being taken outside the camp signified a way in which God sought to keep the people of Israel pure.

Capital Punishment as Removal from the Camp

Beyond mere temporal expulsion from the camp, Verbrugge also notes two different strands of discipline detected in the OT, the second of which we will discuss at a later point in this chapter. This first type of discipline still involves expulsion from the camp, but the intensity of that expulsion picks up in these specific instances. Here discipline is undertaken, most often, as capital punishment. Verbrugge elaborates,

> There are five major areas of serious deviation from the laws of God, and in each case the punishment to be meted out was death. Those who worshiped false gods, engaged in serious ritual offenses, practiced certain sexual impurities, committed social crimes (murder, disrespect of parents, kidnapping), or scorned Yahweh through blasphemy, forfeited the right to live. The classic example of this type of Old Testament "excommunication" is preserved for us in the story of Achan in Joshua 7. Obviously, when discipline in the Old Testament took this severe form—death for the offender—there was no opportunity for repentance and restoration. Not only was the individual cast out of the visible nation of Israel; he was also cut off from the covenant of God with all its privileges. Physical death was but a sign of his spiritual death, his removal from the book of life (cf. Deut 29:18–21). The primary purpose of this type of discipline is the purity of the community, not necessarily the salvation of the sinner.[30]

Thus, it is important to note that in this instance, while the salvation of the sinner may not be in view explicitly, one reason these kinds of laws were designed seems to be for the people to persist in their faith and covenant obedience.

29. Wenham, *Book of Leviticus*, 200–201.
30. Verbrugge, "Roots of Church Discipline," 18.

One should be aware of the crucial link to be made between this type of serious correction and NT discipline. Paul, for example, cites a repeated phrase from Deuteronomy connecting this kind of discipline to what is seen in 1 Corinthians 5. In verse 13 of this passage, one can discern this connection to NT church discipline with the phrase, "purge the evil person from among you." This phrase is paradigmatic for Paul, a point that will be addressed in more detail when we look at discipline in Pauline literature. At this point the phrase as seen in the near context of Deuteronomy will be taken into consideration.

Deuteronomy, the final book in the Pentateuch, is set directly prior to the people of Israel entering the land of Canaan. It is a crucial juncture in Israel's history and appears to be significant theologically to NT authors, as they cite from the book numerous times.[31] Deuteronomy begins with a recounting of Israel's history (1:1—3:29), followed by the stipulations of the law (4:1—26:19), the specific blessings and curses that will accompany obedience to this law or lack thereof (27:1—30:20), and the arrangement of succession in leadership from Moses to Joshua (31:1—34:12). Fundamentally, these stipulations found in Deuteronomy appear to flow from the command to Israel to love the Lord with their entire being (6:1—9).[32] In essence, this is a book about a holy God who has elected a people for himself and made a covenant with them to bless and multiply them, if they put their faith in the Lord and obey his commands. The persevering obedience of his people is a serious matter to the God of Israel.[33]

With this background in mind, one can now observe more closely the various texts dealing with discipline as capital punishment. The first use of this phrase ("purge the evil person from among you") is found in Deuteronomy 13:1–5, which is contained in a passage that speaks of how Israel should respond to false prophets in their midst. Here, and in most other instances of this phrase in Deuteronomy, the people of God are told to put the sinner, in this case the false prophet, to death. Thompson avers, "The threat of execution for such an offender was designed to prevent the spread of infection and purge out the evil from the midst of Israel (cf. 17:12; 19:11–13; 21:18–21; 22:21–24; 24:7). The question was: how could the corporate life of

---

31. For a helpful monograph on this subject, see Maarten and Moyise, *Deuteronomy in the New Testament*.

32. See Waltke, *Old Testament Theology*, 483–86. Waltke asserts partially that this is so based on other ancient Near Eastern documents that use the same language of their kings and expect obedience from their subjects based on their love for the king.

33. Information for this section was derived from LaSor et al., *Old Testament Survey*, 111–27; Longman and Dillard, *Introduction to the Old Testament*, 102–19.

Israel be kept true to Yahweh?"[34] The corporate obedience of God's people was of utmost importance.

A second use of this phrase is found in Deuteronomy 17:2–7 where the text speaks explicitly about the way in which Israel should deal with those who worship other gods. The law required at least two valid witnesses against the accused person in order for a case to be established and the death penalty to be put into effect (17:5–7).[35] Having given true testimony to the idolatry of the accused, the witnesses cast the first stones, but shared the responsibility with the whole community. The capital punishment of the offender removed the evil, which had, by the nature of the crime, endangered the continuation of the covenant community of God (see especially 17:2 and the fact that this sin had violated the covenant of God).[36]

After saying that a person can undergo capital punishment at the testimony of two or three witnesses in Deuteronomy 17, the next use of this saying is found in connection with false witnesses (19:15–21). If a malicious witness rises up against another person and the witness is found to be speaking lies about the other individual, then *lex talionis* is to be put into effect, which could certainly include death for that individual, depending on the specific crime (19:19–21; cf. Exod 21:23–25; Lev 24:17–20). Israel is called to "do to him as he had meant to do to his brother," which could include, "life for life, eye for eye, tooth for tooth, hand for hand, foot for foot" (Deut 19:19, 21). In this way evil is removed from the community. Thus, one of the purposes for this practice is to deter a further breach of the covenant in the community, and instead encourage people to fear God and obey his commands (Deut 19:20).[37]

In Deuteronomy 21:18–21, this phrase is again used in reference to a rebellious son who refuses to submit to the authority of his mother and father (cf. Exod 21:15; Lev 20:9). The parents, after seeking to discipline the son themselves but making no progress, are to bring him before the elders of the city. At this point the parents make known the situation to the

---

34. Thompson, *Deuteronomy*, 174. So also Driver, *Critical and Exegetical Commentary*, 152, who states that this formula of purging the evil from the midst of the nation of Israel is "always at the close of instructions for the punishment of a wrong-doer, and always, except [possibly] 19:19, with reference to capital punishment. A formula peculiar to Deuteronomy, whereby the duty is laid upon the community for clearing itself from complicity in a crime committed in its midst, and of preventing, as far as possible, an evil example from spreading."

35. One can see Matt 18:16, 2 Cor 13:1, and 1 Tim 5:19 for evidence of the principle of establishing a testimony on the basis of two or three witnesses carrying over into the NT.

36. Craigie, *Book of Deuteronomy*, 250–51.

37. Ciampa and Rosner, "1 Corinthians," 709.

leadership of their community and disclose their efforts to bring the son into submission. The men of the city, therefore, are to stone the son to death, and thus purge evil from the midst of Israel.[38] This is done so that others will hear of it, and, as a result, turn from their sin and avoid such practices.[39]

This particular expression is seen again in Deuteronomy 22 where it is cited for a number of offenses, all of which deal with the sin of sexual immorality (22:13–21). If a young woman is found to not be a virgin by a man who has taken her as his wife, she is to come to the door of her father's house where the men of the city will stone her to death (22:21). A second instance pertains to a man and a woman who commit adultery (22:22). As in the previous example, both of these individuals are to be put to death by the community. A final case dealt with in this chapter is an instance where a man commits sexual sin with a "betrothed virgin"[40] in the city (22:23–24). Both of these individuals are to be put to death: the woman because she did not cry out for help, indicating the sexual act was consensual, the man because he sinned by violating his neighbor's wife. This command, in these three instances, is to be followed so that the evil is purged from Israel.

---

38. Craigie helpfully comments on why this individual was stoned by the men of the city: "Here, the allocation of responsibility within the community is made clear. The parents had a responsibility to prosecute their son for the offense in question; they could not take the law into their own hands, however. Judgment would then be carried out by the men of the city. The reason for the men [of the city] carrying out the judgment lies in the nature of the crime; although it took place initially within the sphere of the family, the crime was one affecting the whole community of God. Therefore it was to be punished by representatives of that larger community." See Craigie, *Deuteronomy*, 284–85.

39. Sailhamer agrees with this assertion, saying, "The stated purpose of the law was to eliminate the evil influence of such a child from among the people (Dt 21:21). Moreover, it was also to provide a warning to parents and children alike of the consequences of disobedience and rebellion." Sailhamer, *Pentateuch as Narrative*, 460. This is important to keep in mind, as one of the primary motivations for Paul in addressing the Corinthian church and commanding them to expel the evildoer was to prevent the sin from spreading any further in the community so that the Christians would effectively persevere in their faith.

40. It is beneficial to consider what is meant in this particular text by the phrase "betrothed virgin." Currid offers the following explanation: "Betrothal status in Israel reflected a stronger tie and commitment than engagement in modern times. A contract has been made and a marriage price has been paid. The woman is still living in her father's house, yet she is treated as if she were already married." See Currid, *Study Commentary on Deuteronomy*, 370. So also Walton et al., *IVP Bible Background Commentary*, 195, who states, "Once a [marriage] agreement is in place, it is expected that other persons will respect the betrothed status of the woman as technically already married (see Gen 20:3). Thus the laws of adultery are in full force even before the actual ceremony and consummation of the marriage."

The final use of this phrase in Deuteronomy can be found in dealing with one who seeks to steal a fellow citizen for the purpose of selling him into slavery (Deut 24:7; cf. Exod 21:16).[41] It appears that this offense may have been common in the ancient Near East, since other law codes from various nations legislate against such practices.[42] This offender must also die, as did the other sinners previously noted in the Deuteronomic context. This is done in order that the evil might be taken out of Israel and their purity restored.

Thus, whether speaking of temporal expulsion or extirpation, discipline for sin was an explicit practice within the nation of Israel. Rosner conceives of these texts forming three distinct themes that are noteworthy for rightly understanding the pattern set forth in Deuteronomy. He asserts that in the OT "offenders are expelled because Israel is the sanctified (holiness motif) covenant (covenant motif) community (corporate responsibility motif) of the Lord, the holy God."[43] Israel is called to be holy as God is holy (Lev 19:2). They are in covenant with God, whereby he states that he will expel wickedness from the nation. Finally, God sees them as being corporately responsible for the sin of an individual, since Israel functions as a community (Deut 19:13; 21:9). Once again, God's hatred of sin and his exacting of justice are evident. One should also note God's motivation to expel and discipline for the sake of warning the community and exhorting them to continue in holiness before him.

Ejection from the Land

One final OT trajectory that points toward NT church discipline is the Babylonian conquest and Israel's exile from the land. As God's people were about to enter the promised land, they were told by God that if they were obedient to his commands they would enjoy his blessing, but if they were disobedient they would undergo his curse and would be cast out of the land (Deuteronomy 28–30). Leviticus 26 is a passage that details this type of punishment for disobedience.[44] Wenham, commenting on this text, asserts that the curses

41. Sailhamer interestingly notes, "The specific wording of the law is reminiscent of the story of Joseph, who was kidnapped and sold into slavery by his brothers (Ge 37:26–27; 40:15)." See Sailhamer, *Pentateuch as Narrative*, 466.

42. So Thompson, *Deuteronomy*, 246.

43. Ciampa and Rosner, "1 Corinthians," 706. See also Rosner, *Paul, Scripture and Ethics*, 61–93; Rosner, "Drive Out the Wicked Person," 25–36.

44. Kingdon helpfully delineates the meaning of discipline as it relates to God's character: "In Deuteronomy 8:5 the nature of God's covenant discipline is made clear. It

are a denial of all the hopes enshrined in the covenant with Abraham, that his descendants would become a great nation, inherit the land of Canaan, and so on (cf. Gen 15, 17). They represent a reversal of the blessing in vv. 11–13 that God would be present with his people.... Yet the judgments are still described as "discipline" (v. 28, cf. v. 18 above). They are not God's last word to his erring people. Rather he punishes them because they are his own (Amos 3:2). So if they confess their sin and humble their hearts God will remember his covenant with the patriarchs (vv. 42–45). What this remembering will mean in practice is not spelled out here, but Deuteronomy 30, a similar passage in a similar context, explains that it will mean restoration to the land of promise and prosperity there. This would seem to be implicit in this Leviticus passage too.[45]

Thus, God promised that Israel would undergo his discipline, but the discipline was aimed at bringing them to the point of repentance and sustained obedience.[46]

In the book of Deuteronomy the story of the Lord's relationship with Israel reaches an important landmark. As Israel stands poised to take possession of the land of Canaan, Moses sets before a new generation of adult Israelites the obligations which they must fulfill in order to enjoy God's blessing there (Deut 4–28). At the heart of these obligations is the requirement to love the Lord wholeheartedly (Deut 6:4–5). Significantly, Israel's

---

is not so much the discipline of a suzerain towards a vassal, as the discipline of a father towards his child. It is therefore prompted by a tender love and deep concern for the child's development as a person.... However, the covenant curses of chapters 27 and 28 warn us against sentimentalizing God's love so as to preclude the exercising of severe discipline, of which the destruction of Jerusalem and the Babylonian exile constitute the paradigm." See Kingdon, "Discipline," 448

45. Wenham, *Book of Leviticus*, 332. Hartley similarly states, "Whenever Israel failed to keep the covenant, Yahweh committed himself to chastise them. These curses, though, were not self-operating. They would begin only when Yahweh activated them, and he would direct their course. Yahweh's use of these curses was based on a definitive program. He would employ them in sets of increasing severity sevenfold in order to discipline his people and motivate them to repent and seek his favor. Should the people persist in their rebellion against him, Yahweh, like a master teacher, would increase their discipline by unleashing on them harsher and harsher curses, ever hopeful that they might recognize their sinful ways and return to him." Hartley, *Leviticus*, 472.

46. Waltke confirms this interpretation and elaborates on the point of restoration: "In Deuteronomy 29:2–30:20, Moses exhorts the people to covenant fidelity. Moses looks to the future of Israel's existence and, knowing the depravity of Israel, Moses foresees national apostasy and exile. However, Moses also knows the faithfulness of God to his covenants, and thus he also anticipates repentance and restoration. The blessings of God, and not his curses, will have the last word." Waltke, *Old Testament Theology*, 495.

future in the promised land is tied directly to their willingness and ability to fulfill their covenantal duties.[47] Deuteronomy 30, another passage that proclaims future blessing or cursing, describes the choice between obedience and disobedience, not only as a choice between blessing and curse but also as a choice between life and death (Deut 30:15, 19).

That same chapter (Deut 30:1–6) predicts that Israel will repeat the history of humanity and find itself choosing disobedience and unfaithfulness, resulting in death and exile (cf. Lev 26:1–13, 14–39, 40–45). It also hints at the nature of the problem that would lead to such exile and the solution God would provide in the time of restoration. The problem was a hardness of heart that led to constant rebellion and disobedience. The solution would come in an eschatological circumcision of the heart at the time of Israel's restoration (Deut 10:12–16; 30:1–6; cf. Ezek 36:25–27).[48] "While Deuteronomy holds out the prospect of divine blessing in the Promised Land . . . it also envisages a future in which Israel, through failure to fulfill the covenant obligations, will come under God's curse."[49]

Thus, even before God's people entered the land he had promised them under the leadership of Joshua, the prospect of their exile from that land as a punishment for disobedience was in view. The land, which had been given to Israel as a gift, would be removed from their care if they were disobedient. Duguid states, "If the people failed to keep the terms of the covenant they would be scattered among the nations (Lev 26:33; Deut 28:64; 30:3–4). . . . However, for Israel exile is not simply loss of the land. More importantly, it is the loss of the Lord's presence with them."[50] This reality of exile is a major part of the discipline God would exact upon Israel should they choose to disobey, which points to the seriousness of their sin and the tenacity with which God held to his covenant stipulations.

As one continues to read through the history of the OT, it becomes apparent that Israel, while experiencing times of blessing and obedience, eventually comes to a place of continual disobedience to God. As observed by Waltke, "God sent prophets to turn a sinful nation back to the Mosaic standards. Some kings repented at the prophetic rebuke and found blessings

---

47. See Currid, *Study Commentary on Deuteronomy*, 421.
48. See Ciampa, "History of Redemption," 269.
49. Alexander, *From Paradise to the Promised Land*, 171–72.
50. Duguid, "Exile," 476. He continues, "For that reason, even though the land had not been lost, the loss of the ark to the Philistines in 1 Samuel 4 can be described as the glory of the Lord 'going into exile' (1 Sam 4:22). This prefigured the visionary departure of the glory of the Lord from the Jerusalem temple in Ezekiel 10, which itself preceded the historical exile in 586 B.C. After the Lord had abandoned the land, it was only a matter of time before the people would go into exile." Ibid.

(1 Chr 17:1–15; 2 Chr 11:1–23; 19:1–11), but those who did not repent suffered (2 Chr 16:7–10; 18:1–34)."[51] Eventually, despite these preventative measures sent by God, the northern tribes were taken into captivity by Assyria in 722 BC, and the Babylonians systematically overtook Judah beginning in 606 BC. Under Zedekiah, the nation revolted against the ways of God, succumbed to idolatry, and repudiated God's prophets to the point of bringing the wrath of God upon themselves in the form of exile from the land (2 Chr 36:15–16).

The latter prophets speak a great deal regarding the exile and understand this event not as mere coincidence, but as brought about directly by God as a result of Israel's ongoing sin. Waltke concurs and states, "The prophets interpret the invasions by Assyria (ca. 750–626 B.C.) and Babylon (605–586) as the fulfillment of the covenant curses to purge the land: Israel is losing the Land because she is abusing her usufruct just as the covenant curses had warned (Lev 26:34; Deut 28:64–68)."[52] One can certainly note that a pattern of God's justice and holiness is exercised in the context of covenant.

One also sees a pattern of grace and forgiveness exuding from God and his covenants. While God is faithful to discipline his children, he is also faithful to his promises to restore his people to the land as they come to a point of repentance. As such, seventy years after Israel was taken forcibly from their land, they return to rebuild and start afresh. However, while physical restoration begins on the wall and the temple of Jerusalem, there is still a spiritual need that must be addressed for Israel.[53] In essence, the history of the OT ends by demonstrating that, due to sin and stubborn rebellion, God's people failed to find righteousness and blessing through keeping the

---

51. Waltke, *Old Testament Theology*, 763. These blessing and judgments took different forms, such as military victories and defeats (2 Chr 14:8–14; 20:1–30), the increase and decline of progeny (1 Chr 14:3–7; 10:4), prosperity and poverty (1 Chr 18:7–8; 2 Chr 12:9; 36:3, 7, 10), and either healing and long life or sickness, death, and exile (2 Chr 32:24–26; 15:13; 23:7). Thus, these OT forms of blessing and judgment point forward to the call for the church to persevere in their faith (Heb 3; 6; 10:35–39) and explain the reason why God implements disciplinary measures in the church both directly (1 Cor 11:30; Heb 1:3–11) and indirectly by means of church discipline (Matt 18:15–20; 1 Cor 5). See ibid.

52. Ibid., 831.

53. Several authors actually maintain that at a deeper level, the prophets, such as Isaiah and Ezekiel, were prophesying not only a physical return to the land along with its inherent blessings, but also the end of exile from Eden as narrated in Gen 3. Dempster, *Dominion and Dynasty*, 67; Hamilton, *God's Glory in Salvation*, 357; N. T. Wright, *New Testament and the People of God*, 268–72.

law. Israel experiences the exile and then God's restoration, and all the while they look for the anticipated promises given by God through the prophets.[54]

Hamilton summarizes the point of ejection from the land effectively, noting its essence in a way that gives theological grounding for rightly understanding discipline in the NT era. He asserts,

> It is God's holiness that has been defiled, his name that has been profaned, and it is his faithfulness to his word that is displayed when Israel is finally cast out of his presence. The long history of disobedience only highlights the loving-kindness of the Lord, which clothes justice with faithfulness, patience, and mercy, without which trust and hope are impossible. The story does not end with judgment. Judgment serves as the backdrop, and through it salvation comes as mercy shines against it.[55]

God disciplines his children as a Father in order that they might share in his holiness (Deut 8:5–6; Prov 3:11–12; Heb 12:4–11; Rev 3:19). That is, as a parent God afflicts disobedient children in order to keep them from ever leaving his family and falling under the ultimate curse of the covenant. Jealously he disciplines them, seeking to produce in them "the peaceful fruit of righteousness" (Heb 12:11).

When Israel came to live in the land of their captors, if they acknowledged that they had walked contrary to him and repented of their sins, God promised to hear their cries and forgive their sins (this would also prove true in the time of the church).[56] As noted previously, one must rightly observe the degree of discontinuity that exists between OT and NT discipline. However, these trajectories highlight key principles that carry over into NT practice. In rightly understanding God's discipline in the OT, therefore, one can see that he operates in a manner that displays his holiness and deals with sin in a fitting manner, but with the goal that his people would repent, be restored, and endure in their obedience to him.

---

54. Thus, Israel's history "points to the need for a king who is greater than David. It also suggests the need for a new covenant, one in which the promises of the Abrahamic and Davidic covenants can find ultimate fulfillment and thus lead to ultimate restoration and blessing." These promises would eventually be inaugurated at the coming of Jesus Christ. Pate et al., *Story of Israel*, 67. See also Hamilton, who maintains God brought the exiles back to the land as he promised in 539 BC, but other new exodus promises were yet to be fulfilled (e.g., Isa 11:9; Hab 2:14). Israel was back in the land, but the desert was yet to bloom, the enemies of God were yet to be defeated once and for all, the Spirit was yet to be poured out on all flesh, the new and greater David was yet to sit on the throne. See Hamilton, *God's Glory in Salvation*, 355–59.

55. Hamilton, *God's Glory in Salvation*, 350–51.

56. See Hartley, *Leviticus*, 472–73.

THE SHIFT IN DISCIPLINE

Observing the transition from later writings in the OT to the NT, one can see a shift in practice as it relates to discipline.[57] Earlier in this chapter reference was made to the first of Verbrugge's two strands of OT discipline, namely, capital punishment. The second strand is connected largely with the point in redemptive history immediately leading up to the NT era. After the exile a new development in discipline arose: separation from the community of Israel without the accompanying death motif. In Ezra 10:7–8 the same Hebrew word is used as in Deuteronomy 29:21 for separating a person from the covenant community (בָּדַל), but with quite a different connotation: the opportunity was given for repentance and restoration of the sinner.[58]

Here in Ezra there is the only clear OT example of formal exclusion, in which the offender is neither put to death nor solely given over to the punishment of God.[59] In other words, seemingly at this stage in God's progressive revelation in the OT, the task of expelling rebellious Israelites from the community was no longer necessarily connected with their physical and spiritual death. The reason for this change is not apparent.[60] Perhaps

---

57. This section is largely dependent on Verbrugge, "Roots of Church Discipline," 18–19.

58. See Kitchens, "Church Discipline," 26–28.

59. As one moves into Second Temple literature, it becomes apparent that while capital punishment is present as outlined in Deuteronomy, excommunication seems to also become a dominant form of discipline. In citing this shift in understanding, Rosner notes, "In the history of its transmission and interpretation, regularly in Targum Onkelos, Targum Pseudo-Jonathan and Sifre and usually in the LXX, a curse of exclusion is substituted for the death penalty in these formulae. Similarly in 1 Corinthians 5:13b we find 'the evil man' instead of the 'the evil' is to be 'put away.'" See Rosner, "Drive Out the Wicked," 27. Horbury, who works through the details of documents from Qumran, such as the Damascus Document and the Rule of the Community, along with several others (e.g., Josephus, 3 Maccabees), demonstrates that Paul's understanding of excommunication in 1 Cor corresponds with the practice of Second Temple Judaism, which regularly understood exclusion as a surrogate or preparation for execution. Horbury, "Extirpation and Excommunication," 27–30. See also Kitchens, "Church Discipline," 29–37.

60. The reason for this shift in discipline could be as simple as Israel no longer possessing authority to exact discipline as a nation under Rome. Roetzel goes further and, showing connections between the NT and literature from the Second Temple period, provides what may prove to be significant assistance in answering that question. He states, "It is not necessary, for example, to explain the shift of capital punishment to God as resulting from Roman restrictions placed on the Jews. Given the tendency in Jewish apocalyptic to shift judgment more and more into a realm beyond history, shifting the administration of the death penalty to God might be expected. . . . The new element in Paul, however, is his belief that the *final* vindication has already begun. Paul's concern for the purity of the church resembles not only the emphasis of the priestly writers,

it came as a result of the revelation of God in the exile itself. In Judah's case for example, God's punishment, his casting his people out of the promised land, was followed up with the possibility of repentance and restoration. At this point in the history of revelation, God revealed a "new side" to his nature—not that he was not a forgiving God (for many passages in the Pentateuch testify to this), but that those whom he had excommunicated he did not necessarily cut off completely; rather, he extended the possibility of repentance and restoration. This strand is the one taken up in the NT regarding ecclesial discipline.[61]

NEW TESTAMENT

Taking into account God's discipline of his people as evidenced in the exile from Eden, expulsion from the camp of Israel, and ejection from the land, we will now turn our attention to the NT. With the coming of Jesus Christ a new era dawns as it relates to salvation-history, the people of God, and the practice of discipline.[62] As one notes the shift from the OT to the NT

---

but also the preoccupation of the Qumran community with purging the community of unclean members. Since membership in the Qumran sect was considered proleptic membership in the new covenant community of the future, strict discipline was imposed to keep life in the present congregation consistent with membership in the future family. Various degrees of punishment were imposed on offenders from a small fine to total exclusion in order to maintain a state of readiness for the coming Kingdom of God." Roetzel, *Judgement in the Community*, 117.

61. See Verbrugge, who asserts that this trajectory is important to note if one is to understand the shape that discipline takes in the NT: "That strand of the Old Testament which became the established policy in the New Testament church was the [latter] one which removed an individual from the visible community but contained no 'death warrant.' The decision regarding the invisible church, the kingdom of Christ, the book of life, was left completely in the hands of the Lord." See Verbrugge, "Delivered Over to Satan," 19.

62. This shift occurs in relation to the fact that the church is living in the era of the new covenant. As such the sinning individual is now being confronted after the life, death, resurrection, and ascension of Jesus Christ has taken place. In the OT those who committed certain blatant sins were put to death, as is evidenced by the Deuteronomic formula to put the evil one out of the community's midst. Schreiner notes, "Paul does not require, however, that the man committing incest be put to death (1 Cor 5:13). Still, the OT requirement finds a new fulfillment in Christ. The unrepentant member of the church is to be excommunicated for his sin and failure to repent." See Schreiner, *New Testament Theology*, 654. Schreiner goes on to demonstrate that Paul has already shown this type of pattern of OT reality and NT fulfillment in 1 Cor 5. "Observing the Passover is no longer binding for Christians, but such a conclusion does not cancel out the significance of the Passover, for Christ fulfills the Passover sacrifice by his death on the cross (1 Cor 5:7). Similarly, the command to remove leaven from houses is not mandatory for believers (1 Cor 5:6–8). It does not follow from this that the command

regarding the discipline of the people of God, it is important to observe, with Kingdon, "In the OT discipline is understood mostly in corporate terms (e.g., Deut 8:5), though the individual dimension is not lacking (e.g., Prov 3:11–12). While in the NT the corporate aspect is certainly present (1 Cor 11:27–32), the individual dimension assumes greater prominence (Heb 12:3–11)."[63] Neither aspect is minimized in either Testament, but one should note the shift in emphasis. One can also see a shift from physical consequences in the OT, with more emphasis on the spiritual in NT discipline. Kingdon summarizes the practice of discipline within the NT, saying,

> The community of faith exercises discipline over its members. They are members one of another, fellow members of the body of Christ (Eph 4:25). This body is to be marked by unity (Eph 4:3), "orthodoxy" ("one faith," v. 5) and purity. When believers refuse to be reconciled they deny the unity of the church and thus become subject to discipline by the assembly (Matt 18:17). When the truth of the gospel is denied church discipline is to be exercised (2 John 7–11; cf. 1 Tim 1:20). When there is open and scandalous sin it cannot be tolerated; severe action must be taken (1 Cor 5:1–5) but always with a view to bringing about repentance. Excommunication is the end of the disciplinary process, not its beginning, and is to be imposed only reluctantly.[64]

With these realities in mind this section will seek to understand the teaching of the NT regarding church discipline, beginning with the witness of the Gospels.

Gospels

Jesus did not speak in abundant detail about the issue of church discipline, but there are two key texts to be considered, namely, Matthew 16:13–19 and 18:15–20.[65] These passages have a close linguistic connection, particularly

---

about leaven is irrelevant for believers, for it symbolizes the need to expunge evil from their midst and to live with sincerity and truth." Ibid., 653. Therefore, since the law has reached its end and goal in Christ (cf. Rom 10:4), a law like this takes on a new and heightened reality. See ibid.

63. Kingdon, "Discipline," 448.

64. Ibid., 450.

65. One could also look at other passages that speak to this issue more indirectly: Matt 5:23–24; 7:1–5; Luke 6:37–42; 17:1–4; John 20:23. While beneficial to ascertaining a more holistic view of discipline, these texts lie beyond the purview of this particular study.

in their use of the term *ekklēsia*[66] as well as the concepts of "binding" and "loosing." They also offer direct instructions from Jesus as to how authority and discipline ought to be administered within the church. These two passages will be considered in detail alongside other ancillary texts that further clarify this issue.

Matthew 16:13–19

Matthew 16 begins with a conversation between Jesus, the Pharisees, and the Sadducees, as these religious leaders ask Jesus to show them a sign from heaven in order to confirm his messiahship (16:1–4). Jesus does not give them what they ask for and later tells his disciples to beware the leaven, or teaching, of the Pharisees and the Sadducees (16:5–12). The disciples and Jesus then arrive in the region of Caesarea Philippi, where Jesus asks his followers the crucial question, "Who do people say that the Son of Man is?" (16:13). The disciples report that many are identifying him with John the Baptist, Elijah, Jeremiah, or one of the prophets (16:14). Jesus then becomes more specific in his questioning and asks his disciples (the "you" in this verse is plural) who they believe he is, to which Peter replies with the famous confession, "You are the Christ, the Son of the living God" (16:15–16).

Here the text turns in a direction that is important to our discussion on church discipline, particularly as it relates to Matthew 18:15–20. Jesus answers Peter and calls him blessed, acknowledging that this information has not come from men but from God (16:17). He further declares that the man who made this confession is to be called *Petros*, and that on this *petra*, or rock, the Church would be built, which the gates of hell would not prevail against (16:18).[67] Though Peter is in view specifically in this text, progres-

---

66. See Ware et al., "Perspectives on Church Discipline," 87. Hammett also takes note of the fact that this word is used sparingly in the Gospels, observing, "Noteworthy is the surprising lack of references to *ekklēsia* in the Gospels. The only three references are found in two passages in Matthew (Mt 16:18; 18:17)." Hammett, *Biblical Foundations for Baptist Churches*, 28. Due to the rare usage of the term, some have doubted the veracity of its usage in the Gospel of Matthew. Two works that argue for the authenticity and the contextual and cultural fittingness of this term include, Clowney, "Biblical Theology of the Church," 16–27; Merkle, "Meaning of Ekklēsia in Matthew 16:18 and 18:17," 281–91.

67. There has been great debate concerning this verse. Roman Catholics have taken this text to refer to Peter as the first pope, as well as the doctrine of apostolic succession. Some have argued that Jesus was speaking of himself as the "rock" in this passage. See Lenski, *Interpretation of St. Matthew's Gospel*, 626; Walvoord, *Matthew*, 123. Other have argued that the "rock" refers to Peter's confession. For a thorough treatment of this viewpoint see Caragounis, *Peter and the Rock*. Jesus, however, seems to be referring to Peter as the rock upon which the church is built, since he will be a predominant

sive revelation points us to the apostles and prophets in general as being the foundation of the church, with Jesus being the chief cornerstone (Eph 2:20).

The climax of this section culminates with Jesus declaring, "I will give you the keys to the kingdom of heaven, and whatever you bind on earth shall be bound in heaven, and whatever you loose on earth shall be loosed in heaven" (16:19).[68] One must come to terms with what exactly Jesus means when he refers to the "keys of the kingdom of heaven," the issue of "binding and loosing," and how these concepts relate to church discipline.[69] First of all, regarding the keys, Blomberg claims, "'The keys to the kingdom' (16:19) almost certainly is based on the identical metaphor in Isaiah 22:22."[70] The prophet Isaiah is rebuking an unworthy steward of God's household and saying that authority will be transferred to Eliakim, who will, as a result, possess the key of David, with which he will "open and shut" (Isa 22:20–22). Motyer notes that contextually and culturally, a key denotes "the power to make and enforce binding decisions."[71] Beale elaborates on this point and gives further commentary concerning these texts:

> Like Eliakim, Christ establishes himself as having an authoritative position in the new temple in Matthew 16:18, and then extends his priestly authority to his disciples, who also have priestly authority. Matthew 16:19, in the light of 18:15–18 and John 20:23, says they express what would appear to be their

---

leader of the apostles (as evidenced in Acts 1–12). This best fits the Matthean context, and it also coheres with other NT texts that speak of an apostolic foundation for the church (Eph 2:20; Rev 21:14). See BDAG, s.v. "πετρα" and "πετρος" for support of this interpretation, along with D. A. Carson, *Matthew*, 368; France, *Gospel of Matthew*, 925; Turner, *Matthew*, 406–7.

68. Pennington notes, regarding the use of "heaven and earth" terminology in the Gospel of Matthew, that another clear function of Matthew's heaven and earth contrast theme is to provide a clear identity for the followers of Jesus. Matthew wants his hearers to understand that those who follow Christ are the true people of God and to encourage them with this reality. Jesus defines this new or true people not by ethnic pedigree, including having Abraham as one's father (3:9–10; 8:11–12; 23:9), nor by positions of honor (23:2–11), but as those who do the will of the Father who is in heaven (7:21; 12:50), as those whose lives bear the fruit of following God's commands from the heart (3:7–10; 7:15–23; 12:33–38). This theme creates a heaven-oriented identity for the disciples in the midst of a hostile earthly world. The world is depicted as bipartite—heaven and earth—and Jesus' disciples are the true people of God aligned with heaven, as opposed to the rulers (Roman and Jewish) on earth. In this way, Matthew's heaven and earth theme is an important part of his ecclesiology (see esp. 16:17–19; 18:14–20). See Pennington, *Heaven and Earth*, 348.

69. For a helpful article on the relationship between the gates of hell, the keys of the kingdom, and binding and loosing, see Marcus, "Gates of Hades," 443–55.

70. Blomberg, *Matthew*, 55. See also Carson, *Matthew*, 370.

71. Motyer, *Isaiah*, 157.

priestly task by declaring who is forgiven and who is not.... In both Isaiah 22 and 2 *Baruch* the keys are being taken away from unworthy keepers in Israel and transferred elsewhere, which appears to be the case here in Matthew 16: could the idea be that the keys to the true temple are being taken from old Israel and being transferred to true Israel, Jesus and his followers?[72]

Connecting Matthew 16:19 to Isaiah 22:22, taking into account the parallel concept of the keys, signifies that Jesus is extending authority to Peter in particular, and later on to the church as a whole (see Matt 18:18).[73] Peter and the other apostles carry out their foundational ecclesiastical role through handling the keys or exercising kingdom authority (Isa 22:15, 22; Rev 1:18; 3:7; 9:1-6; 20:1-3). This authority is exercised through binding and loosing.[74] The disciples are agents of the kingdom of God and, unlike the scribes and Pharisees, they are to use this authority to point others to God's kingdom (cf. Luke 11:52).

Closely tied to the idea of the keys is the statement about "binding and loosing." Certainly there is the idea of authority here, similar to the keys of the kingdom, but the meaning is once again disputed. Some scholars advocate this phrase to refer to authority in exorcism,[75] while others understand authority over entrance into the church to be in view.[76] Others compare Matthew 16:19 and 18:18 and conclude that binding and loosing refer to church discipline.[77] Turner avers, "Perhaps it is best ... to combine the ideas of entry into the kingdom (Matt 16:9a, the 'keys') and maintenance of acceptable life within the community (16:9b-c)." He continues and maintains that if this is so, the "doctrine" and "discipline" are really one, and through the preaching of the gospel, "the authorized agent opens the door to the

---

72. Beale, *Temple and the Church's Mission*, 188.

73. Allison comments further on Matt 16:19, specifically regarding the keys, stating, "Keys serve to open and close doors; as Jesus himself notes elsewhere (Rev 1:18; 3:7; 9:1-2; 20:1-3; cf. his denunciation of the Pharisees in Luke 11:52). Thus, the keys belonging to the church open up the kingdom or shut it off. The close association of Jesus' instructions about the keys with the prediction of his death and resurrection (Matt 16:21) help us interpret the keys as the preaching of the gospel of Jesus Christ, the good news of his cross work and resurrection on behalf of sinful people. According to their actions in the book of Acts, the apostles certainly understood the keys as a reference to the ministry of the Word of God." Allison, *Sojourners and Strangers*, 186.

74. Turner, *Matthew*, 407.

75. Hiers, "'Binding' and 'Loosing,'" 233-50.

76. See, e.g., Calvin, *Harmony of the Gospels*, 2.187-88.

77. Davies and Allison, *Commentary on Matthew*, 638-39; Overman, *Church and Community in Crisis*, 245-46.

Reign of God or shuts it off."[78] Thus, when considering this passage alongside of Matthew 18:15–20, which will be dealt with shortly, it appears that Jesus is giving authority to Peter and the other disciples to judge a person within the body of Christ based on the truths of Scripture and that person's adherence to the proclamation of the gospel, or lack thereof.[79]

An important parallel passage to consider alongside of Matthew 16 is John 20:23, where the disciples are told, "If you forgive the sins of anyone, they are forgiven; if you withhold forgiveness from anyone it is withheld." As we will note in our interaction with Matthew 18 more specifically, there is a similar use of phraseology and verb tenses being utilized here and in Matthew 16, namely, future perfect passive verbs.[80] While John 20 and Matthew 16 seem to be speaking more directly to the proclamation of the gospel, there appears to be a secondary sense—when understood in light of Matthew 18:15–20—in which these passages should be understood, namely how they serve to foreshadow more definitive teaching on the issue of church discipline.

---

78. Turner, *Matthew*, 408. Mohler also identifies the usage of this phrase with rabbinic language and maintains the terms "binding" and "loosing" used by rabbis in the first century to refer to the power of judging matters on the basis of Scripture. He claims, "The Jewish authorities would determine how (or whether) the Scriptures applied in a specific situation and would render judgment by either binding, which meant to restrict, or loosing, which meant to liberate." Mohler, "Church Discipline," 53.

79. See Carson, who states, "But exactly what is meant by this 'binding and loosing' of persons, and is it absolute? And how is it related to the power of the keys? Substantial help comes from comparing Jesus' denunciation of the teachers of the law in Luke 11:52. There they are told that they 'have taken away the key to knowledge' and have not only failed to enter [the kingdom] themselves but have 'hindered those who were entering.' Clearly, then, by their approach to the Scriptures, Jesus says, they are making it impossible for those who fall under the malign influences of their teaching to accept the new revelation in Jesus and enter the kingdom. They take away 'the key to knowledge.' In contrast, Peter, on confessing Jesus as Messiah, is told he has received this confession by the Father's revelation, and will be given the keys of the kingdom: i.e., by proclaiming 'the good news of the kingdom' (4:23), which, by revelation he is increasingly understanding, he will open the kingdom to many and shut it against many. . . . Peter accomplishes this binding and loosing by proclaiming a gospel that has already been given and by making personal application on that basis." Carson, *Matthew*, 373. See also Ladd, *Theology of the New Testament*, 115.

80. In Matt 16:19 and 18:18 one sees the words for "binding" and "loosing" as δεδεμένον and λελυμένον, respectively. These terms are perfect passive participles. In John 20:23 the terms ἀφέωνται and κεκράτηνται are present, each of which are perfect passive indicatives. Thus, while John 20:23 contains indicatives and not participles, a similar structure still exists in the kinds of terms used. More detail will be given in the section dealing with Matt 18:15–20 regarding the significance of the verb tenses in these passages.

One should also not ignore the parallel structure that exists linguistically between Matthew 16:19, 18:18, and John 20:23 in regards to the perfect passive verbs. Oden elaborates on this parallel when he says the following: "Three pairs of vivid metaphors describe this commission: lock/unlock (Mt 16:19), bind/loose (Mt 16:19; 18:18), remit/retain (John 20:23). The first two are symbolic ways of referring to the third. They authorize the offering of forgiveness and the withholding of forgiveness."[81] John 20:23 may primarily point out how people receive forgiveness through receiving and believing in the gospel of Jesus Christ, but as one takes this passage with Matthew 16 into account, along with the wider teaching of Scripture, forgiveness through the gospel is only truly possessed by those who persevere in their Christian faith (Heb 3:6; 6:1–2; 10:35–39). Jeschke explains this connection:

> Since the church is founded upon the gospel, entrance into the community and perseverance in it rest upon the same foundation. Hence the condition laid out in Matthew 18 upon which one remains in the community is nothing other than that spelled out in Matthew 16 and John 20 upon which one enters the community. To put it another way, the keys of the kingdom, or the authority to bind and loose, are not only a definition of the conditions for entrance into the kingdom; they also by their very nature define the ethical norms of life in the community.[82]

One must be careful not to extract from a text like Matthew 16 more than is actually there. However, one must also observe the linguistic parallels seemingly evident in Matthew 16, 18, and John 20. A connection seemingly exists, connoting a progression in understanding, revealing a crucial concept regarding ecclesial authority.

Thus, in its near context, Matthew 16:16–19 appears to refer to the apostles as the gatekeepers of the kingdom, guiding the authoritative proclamation of Matthew 16:16, permitting entrance to the kingdom through the church for those who confess Jesus.[83] Also, in an indirect way, this passage speaks to the authority of the church, an authority that is later shown as sufficient to take in members or expel them through church discipline, potentially demonstrating through lack of repentance that they may be recipients of God's condemnation rather than his forgiveness (see below on Matt 18:15–20). Thus, while the passages under present consideration offer helpful information relating to ecclesial discipline in a secondary manner,

---

81. Oden, *Corrective Love*, 35–36.
82. Jeschke, *Discipling in the Church*, 49.
83. Turner, *Matthew*, 408.

they only do so as they are connected with Matthew 18, a text that speaks more explicitly to the matter of discipline.

Matthew 18:15–20

Contextually Matthew 18 begins with Jesus telling his disciples that they must be humble in order to inherit the kingdom of heaven (18:1–4).[84] He then goes on to instruct his followers to avoid practices that would cause others to stumble into sin, even to the point of exercising extreme self-discipline, such as cutting off a sinning hand (18:5–9). Jesus then tells a parable in verses 10–14 describing the effort made by a shepherd and his rejoicing over the recovery of a lost sheep (a sinner who has turned aside from the teachings of God). After the text in view, Jesus also tells a parable dealing with the issue of forgiveness (18:21–35). Based on this discussion of sin and how a follower of Jesus is to respond to sin in their life and the lives of others, Jesus moves into one of the central texts regarding church discipline, Matthew 18:15–20.

Beginning in Matthew 18:15 Jesus states that if someone sins against another[85] there should be a private conversation aimed at addressing the sin issue.[86] Thus, church discipline begins in the private sphere, allowing the offender a chance to hear his sin and have an opportunity to repent and seek forgiveness of the one they sinned against. Chamblin points out the importance of such a first step: "In the church's intense fellowship, such

---

84. The near context of this passage will be considered presently. For an excellent article outlining the interpretation of this text based on the surrounding chapters as understood in a chiastic manner, see McClister, "Where Two or Three Are Gathered," 549–58.

85. One should take note of the textual variant in this verse, where the shorter reading simply says "sins," (ἁμαρτήσῃ) while the longer reading adds "against you" (ἁμαρτήσῃ εἰς σὲ). Turner observes that the shorter reading is supported by ℵ, B, and 579, while the longer reading garners support from D, L, Δ, θ, 078, *Byz*, and most Latin MSS. He continues, "A complicating factor is that the phrase in question, *eis se*, sounds much like the verb ending –*ēsē*, which could lead to accidental omission if the text was being dictated to the copyist by a reader." When one takes this into consideration, along with the context of the passage and Peter's use of the phrase "against you" in 18:21, it appears that the longer reading is plausibly authentic. Turner, *Matthew*, 444, 447; cf. Davies and Allison, *Commentary on Matthew VIII–XVIII*, 782. Ultimately, according to White and Blue, ". . . although the phrase is missing in some early manuscripts, the fact is unimportant. Other passages urge us to go whether the sin is directed against us or not." White and Blue, *Church Discipline That Heals*, 88.

86. Concerning this practice, Adams wisely states, "Anything that creates an unreconciled state between us and another must be brought up and dealt with." See Adams, *Handbook of Church Discipline*, 55.

sin [against one another] is perilous indeed, regardless of its exact nature (v. 18a). Whereas in [Matt] 5:23-24 Jesus instructed the offending brother, here he speaks of the offended party's responsibility."[87] One can see from this verse, therefore, that the overall goal of this kind of confrontation is not condemnation of sinners, but growth in sanctification through repentance of sin and the expressing of forgiveness by the one against whom they sinned.

Jesus continues his teaching in verse 16 because a person is not always won over in this first step, and thus one should go again and take one or two witnesses. The concept of two or three witnesses brings to mind Deuteronomy 19:15, which appears to be in a judicial context in relation to the nation of Israel. In Deuteronomy it would seem that the witnesses had seen the actual crime committed, whereas in Matthew 18:17, the witnesses bear testimony to the actual confrontation in the second step of church discipline. Norman agrees with this interpretation when he claims, "The witnesses are to assist in the attempted restoration of the errant church member, but if the attempt fails, they will serve as witnesses, not of the original transgression, but of the failure to repent."[88] However, it seems wise to involve one or two people who have at least some kind of knowledge of the sin that has been committed, and that at least one of these witnesses be a church leader (i.e. elder), though this is not dictated by the text itself.

Hopefully at this stage the offender has repented of his or her sin and reconciled with the person they offended, but if they still refuse, Jesus gives a final exhortation in verse seventeen to tell the offense to the church. If at this point the sinner still refuses to admit their wrongdoing and remain unrepentant, that person should be considered as a "Gentile or tax collector." In essence, if the person refuses to repent after being called out by the church, Jesus commands the congregation to view that individual as an

---

87. Chamblin, *Matthew*, 744. Carson concurs and states, "The proper thing is to confront the brother privately and 'show him his fault.' The verb *elenchō* probably suggests 'convict' the brother, not by passing judgment, but by convicting him of his sin. The aim is not to score points over him but to win him over (same verb as in 1 Cor 9:19-22; 1 Pet 3:1) because all discipline, even this private kind, must begin with redemptive purposes (cf. Luke 17:3-4; 2 Thess 3:14-15; Jas 5:19-20; cf. Ecclus 19:13-17)." Carson, *Matthew*, 402.

88. Norman, "Reestablishment of Proper Church Discipline," 214. See also Carson: "It is not at first clear whether the function of the witnesses is to support the one who confronts his erring brother by bringing additional testimony about the sin committed (which would require at least three people to have observed the offense) or to provide witnesses to the confrontation if the case were to go before the whole church. The latter is a bit more likely, because Deuteronomy 19:15 deals with judicial condemnation (a step taken only by the entire assembly), not with attempts to convince a brother of his fault." Carson, *Matthew*, 402-3. See also Blomberg, "Matthew," 56-58.

outsider of the new covenant community. Such an individual is to be cut off from church fellowship and suspended from typical social relations with other Christians.[89]

Carson affirms this understanding of the passage:

> The same three-step procedure is known elsewhere (1QS 5:25–6:1; cf. CD 9:2–3). Refusal to submit to the considered judgment of Messiah's people means that they are to treat the offender as "a pagan or a tax collector." It is poor exegesis to turn to [Matt] 8:1–11; 9:9–13; 15:21–28 and say that such people should be treated compassionately. The argument and the NT parallels (Rom 16:17; 2 Thess 3:14) show that Jesus has excommunication in mind.[90]

This last step may seem harsh,[91] but the intention in treating others as nonbelievers is not to injure them or punish them, but rather to help them see the seriousness of their sin and their need for repentance. If repentance does not occur, the person is potentially displaying evidence that he or she was never truly a part of the new covenant community and as such that person needs to confess their sin and place faith in Christ for salvation.[92]

---

89. Leeman gives pertinent advice on how members are to interact with those who are under excommunication: "The New Testament addresses this matter in a number of places (1 Cor 5:9, 11; 2 Thess 3:6, 14–15; 2 Tim 3:5; Titus 3:10; 2 John 10). The basic counsel the elders of my own church give is that the general tenor of one's relationships with the disciplined individual should markedly change. Interactions should not be characterized by casualness but by deliberate conversations about repentance. Certainly family members should continue to fulfill family obligations (see Eph 6:1–3; 1 Tim 5:8; 1 Pet 3:1–2)." Leeman, *Church Discipline*, 76. While various details could be cited regarding the application of discipline, the point is that our interactions are marked with pleas for repentance.

90. Carson, *Matthew*, 403.

91. Strauch points out just the opposite when he says, "A critical test of genuine love is whether we are willing to confront and discipline those we care for. Nothing is more difficult than disciplining a brother or sister in Christ who is trapped in sin. It is always agonizing work—messy, complicated, often unsuccessful, emotionally exhaustive, and potentially divisive. This is why most church leaders avoid discipline at all costs. But that is not love. It is a lack of courage and disobedience to the Lord Jesus Christ, who himself laid down instructions for the discipline of an unrepentant believer." See Strauch, *Christian Leader's Guide*, 152.

92. This understanding of the final step of church discipline, or excommunication, differs from the Roman Catholic view, according to Calvin, in the following way: "Excommunication differs from anathema in that the latter, taking away all pardon, condemns and consigns a man to eternal destruction; the former, rather, avenges and chastens his moral conduct. And although excommunication also punishes the man, it does so in such a way that, by forewarning him of his future condemnation, it may call him back to salvation." Calvin, *Institutes*, 4.2.10.

In Matthew 18:18 one can see linguistic connections that lead back to 16:19, as Jesus uses the exact same phraseology in regards to "binding and loosing."[93] The tenses are the same as in 16:19, as is the terminology; the only difference is in the fact that the text is addressed to the church and not just to Peter or the rest of the disciples. Daniel Wallace refers to these terms in Matthew 16:19, 18:18, as well as John 20:23, as proleptic perfect participles, and defines that concept in the following way: "The perfect can be used to refer to a state resulting from an antecedent action that is future from the time of speaking."[94] In other words, these perfect passive participles are communicating to the disciples that the heavenly decision to admit into or exclude from the kingdom preceded their declaration of it on earth.[95] Mohler further clarifies and supports this understanding of the verb tenses in Matthew 16:18–19, 18:18 when he asserts the following: "He is not stating that the church has the power to determine what shall later be decided in heaven. The verb tense indicates that as the church functions on the authority of Scripture, what it determines shall have already been determined in heaven."[96] Thus, the authority given to Peter as an apostle is applied in a particular way to the church as it relates to ecclesial discipline.[97]

Carson demonstrates the conceptual connection between Matthew 16:19 and 18:18 by saying,

> If the church, Messiah's eschatological people already gathered now, has to exercise the ministry of the keys, if it must bind and loose, then clearly one aspect of that will be the discipline of those who profess to constitute it. Thus the two passages are tightly joined: 18:18 is a special application of 16:19. Again, if we may judge from Paul's ministry, this discipline is a special function of apostles, but also of elders and even of the whole church (1 Cor 5:1–13; 2 Cor 13:10; Titus 2:15; 3:10–11)—an inescapable part of following Jesus during this age of the inaugurated kingdom and of the proleptic gathering of Messiah's people. The church of Jesus Christ is more than an audience. It is a group with confessional standards, one of which (viz., "Jesus is

---

93. As stated earlier, in Matt 16:19 and 18:18 the words used for "binding" and "loosing" are δεδεμένον and λελυμένον.

94. Wallace, *Greek Grammar*, 581.

95. See Carson, *Matthew*, 371–72, for detailed discussion on the tenses of "will have been bound," and "will have been loosed" being periphrastic future perfect passive participles. Also see Mantey, "Distorted Translations in John 20:23; Matthew 16:18–19 and 18:18," 409–16.

96. Mohler, "Discipline," 52.

97. See Hammett, *Biblical Foundations for Baptist Churches*, 147; France, *Gospel of Matthew*, 928; Keach, "Glory of a True Church and Its Discipline Display'd," 71.

the Christ") here precipitates Jesus' remarks regarding the keys. The continuity of the church depends as much on discipline as on truth. Indeed, faithful promulgation of the latter both entails and presupposes the former.[98]

This understanding corresponds with Jesus' words in 18:19–20, wherein the reader can note that if two or three agree about these types of matters on earth, their prayers will be heard by the Father. Practically, it should be affirmed that when the church deals with serious issues relating to church discipline, prayer should be offered constantly concerning the situation. This allows the ecclesial body to move forward with humble boldness, knowing that the matter has already been bound or loosed in heaven and they are acting in the authority of the Father and the Son.

This process of discipline must be enacted in a spirit that is ready to forgive, as evidenced by the parable Jesus tells immediately following his teaching (Matt 18:21–35). Contextually, it seems that Jesus is commanding the people of God to forgive a person who confesses and repents of his or her sin in matters of church discipline.[99] Thus, church discipline has specific regulations not only for the one who has committed a sin, but also for those within the church who are called to be forgiving.[100]

---

98. Carson, *Matthew*, 374 (cf. Calvin, *Institutes*, 4.11.2). Norman also makes a tight connection between Matt 16:19 and 18:15–20 in regards to binding and loosing, stating that the rabbinic practice of judging matters on the basis of the revelation of God is a pattern for what Jesus was calling the church to do. He asserts, "Christ has given the church the necessary authority to restrict a sinful person under a disciplinary process or to liberate a repentant believer from the process. The church exercises discipline with the authority of heaven, for the Lord is with them, providing assurance and guidance in the process." Norman, "Reestablishment of Proper Church Discipline," 200.

99. Chamblin asserts, "Failure to forgive fellow believers (none of whose debts to each other could compare with those incalculable debts that God has canceled) shows that one has never really understood God's forgiveness. The judgment threatening such a person is just as real and final (v. 34) as that which threatens the offender (cf. vv. 14–20)—strong incentive for offering genuine, not just apparent, forgiveness (v. 35b)." Chamblin, *Matthew*, 745.

100. This call to forgiveness brings to mind a passage such as Matt 6:14–15. There Jesus warns his followers, "For if you forgive others their trespasses your heavenly Father will also forgive you, but if you do not forgive others their trespasses, neither will your heavenly Father forgive your trespasses." It appears that these verses are citing forgiveness as a fruit by which we know that we belong to God. If we are an unforgiving people toward repentant sinners we are proving that we are not truly forgiven by God, and thus we ourselves could be subject to church discipline based on that particular sin. A person who has been forgiven by God through salvation must certainly confront and judge others who disobey the commands of God, but it is also very clear that we must forgive the repentant. For further thoughts on this particular subject, see Ferguson, *Church of Christ*, 372; Schreiner and Caneday, *Race Set Before Us*, 77.

In concluding this significant section on church discipline, it should be noted that God has given the church authority to render judgment concerning an individual if it comes to that point. This judgment is authoritative only insomuch as it abides by the standards given in the Scriptures, which are the words God has given to us for such matters. The goal for the offender is repentance, and the aim for the offended church is forgiveness. All of humanity has sinned, and through the practice of discipline church members are called to persevere in their faith to the end, and thus stand before God at the final judgment and receive mercy in Christ (2 Cor 5:10; Heb 10:32–39).

Pauline Literature

While Jesus addressed the issue of church discipline, the apostle Paul also spoke in vivid detail. Most of the references to discipline for Paul were rooted in congregational situations that needed to be addressed in order for the process of discipline to function properly.[101] While there are other minor texts regarding church discipline from the Pauline corpus (e.g., Rom 16:17)[102] the bulk of time will be spent dealing with Paul's instructions from 1 Corinthians 5:1–13, Galatians 6:1, and 2 Thessalonians 3:6–15.

1 Corinthians 5:1–13

Paul addresses a number of sinful issues with the church at Corinth,[103] one of which involves church discipline, as he rebukes the church for not dealing with a specific issue of sexual immorality in the proper way.[104] There is a kind of sexual immorality occurring within the church that is not even

---

101. Lane affirms that since Paul is the messenger of the new covenant (2 Cor 3:6), "In a situation of church discipline, the statement identifies the Apostle as the messenger of the covenant lawsuit God has brought against his rebellious vassals at Corinth." Lane, "Covenant," 18. This notion of covenant lawsuit involves the consequences meted out for rebellion against covenantal stipulations. See ibid., 1.

102. For commentary on this text dealing specifically with the context of church discipline see South, *Disciplinary Practices in Pauline Texts*, 114–15.

103. Thiselton contends that the topics addessed in 1 Corinthians do not represent a seemingly random set of pastoral and ethical problems that Paul is merely reacting to. Rather, there is a "systematic and coherent" dimension to the issues addressed due to the Corinthians' skewed triumphalistic eschatological viewpoint. See Thiselton, "Realized Eschatology at Corinth," 526.

104. For a helpful summary of the context of this epistle in general, and this chapter specifically, see Köstenberger et al., *Cradle, the Cross, and the Crown*, 482–92.

acceptable among the pagans,[105] namely, that a man "has his father's wife" (1 Cor 5:1). This is a somewhat ambiguous phrase, which makes it difficult to know for certain what has happened to the father, and if there has been a death or divorce. However, as Fee notes, "In either case what had been forbidden by all the ancients, both Jewish and pagans, is the cohabiting of father and son with the same woman,"[106] and as such the church should have immediately dealt with this issue.

Thus, this man was involved in a knowingly sinful relationship and committing an offense that should certainly be recognized and rebuked by a Christian church.[107] This action, however, had not taken place, as Paul indicted the Corinthians for being arrogant rather than mourning over this serious issue (1 Cor 5:2).[108] When Paul tells the Corinthians that they ought to mourn rather than be arrogant, some commentators take that to mean a mourning over the impending loss of the sinning brother.[109] However, the word is only used elsewhere in the NT in 2 Corinthians 12:21, where its sense closely parallels the concept of godly sorrow or repentance (cf. 2 Cor 7:8–11).[110] Paul, therefore, appears to be imploring the church to mourn

---

105. Hays notes, "The word *ethnē*, translated by NRSV and most English translations as 'pagans,' is Paul's normal word for 'Gentiles' (i.e., non-Jews). His use of this term here offers a fascinating hint that he thinks of the Gentile converts at Corinth as Gentiles no longer (cf. 12:2, 13; Gal. 3:28). Now that they are in Christ, they belong to the covenant people of God, and their behavior should reflect that new status." See Hays, *First Corinthians*, 81.

106. Fee warrants this claim in his commentary by citing both Jewish and Greco-Roman law regarding this type of sexual immorality. See Fee, *First Epistle to the Corinthians*, 200. See also Conzelmann, *1 Corinthians*, 96; Hays, *First Corinthians*, 80–81.

107. Many in the history of interpretation have linked this man to the one Paul calls the church to forgive in 2 Cor 2:5–11. It is, however, unclear as to whether this is the man Paul is discussing in his second letter to the Corinthians or not. Indeed, both of these passages reveal how Paul thinks the community should treat offenders, but the link is difficult to make. For a full discussion on the subject see Furnish, *II Corinthians*, 160–68.

108. Fee asserts, "Given their theological stance articulated in 6:12–13 and their sense of superiority to Paul, and therefore to Paul's ethical instructions given in his previous letter, it is just possible, nay probable it would seem, that this sin in their midst is something over which they have taken a certain amount of pride." Fee, *First Epistle to the Corinthians*, 201–2. Pascuzzi likewise maintains, "The Christian community cannot be a partner to moral relativism nor can it adopt a posture of non-interference. To do so would be to abdicate responsibility for the spiritual well-being of both the offender and the community. To prevent this, Paul intervened to rouse the community to assume its responsibility." Pascuzzi, *Ethics, Ecclesiology, and Church Discipline*, 196.

109. See Findlay, "St. Paul's First Epistle to the Corinthians," 808.

110. See Ciampa and Rosner, "1 Corinthians," 706; Hays, *1 Corinthians*, 82.

over this man's sin, as well as their own sin of arrogance,[111] because they are culpable and corporately responsible for the actions of individuals within their covenant community.[112] The Corinthian church must take action and exclude this person from the community of believers, and, in so doing, maintain their corporate holiness.[113]

Paul then exhorts the Corinthians to take care of this issue in a corporate fashion (5:3-5; cf. Lev 24:14; Num 15:35; Deut 19:16-20). Bargerhuff asserts, "For the discipline to be enacted properly and fully in accordance with Jesus' teaching, the formal assembly of the church, along with its communal power and authority to bind and loose, must be formally instigated."[114] Thus, when they assemble in the name of the Lord Jesus and the power of the Lord Jesus is with them (1 Cor 5:4), they are to deliver this man to Satan for the destruction of the flesh "so that his spirit may be saved in the day of the Lord" (1 Cor 5:5).

The content of 1 Corinthians 5:5 has been the subject of much debate as to its proper interpretation. While some commentators believe the "destruction of the flesh" refers to a curse that leads to physical death,[115] it seems more plausible to read this text as referring to the man's sinful nature being destroyed as he is excluded from the community of faith, an edifying and caring environment that contends for one another's sanctification,

---

111. Minear interestingly points out that "in chapter 5 one verse deals with the incestuous person and twelve verses deal with the culpability of the congregation." Minear, "Christ and the Congregation," 343.

112. The OT is replete with examples of this. In Exod 16:27-28, after some of the people had broken the Sabbath, God addresses the nation and asks how long they will refuse to keep his commandments and instructions. In Num 16:20-27 the people are warned to keep their distance from Korah, Dathan, and Abiram, lest they also be swept away because of all their sins (note especially Moses' prayer in 16:22). In Deut 19:13—a passage already considered—the nation of Israel is instructed to purge a sinning individual from their midst so that it may go well with them in the land. Other such examples can be found in Deut 29:19-21, Josh 7:1-26, Josh 22:16-18, 1 Sam 14:37-38, and Neh 13:18. See Ciampa and Rosner, "1 Corinthians," 706; Rosner, "*Ouchi mallon epenthēsate*," 470-71.

113. The findings of this study are in disagreement with Pfitzner, "Purified Community—Purified Sinner," 48, who states that in 1 Cor 5, "Paul shows, perhaps surprisingly, little or no interest in preserving the holiness of the church on a neo-levitical foundation."

114. Bargerhuff, *Love That Rescues*, 161-62. This assertion is in keeping with Matt 18:15-20, where heaven's sanction reinforces the assembled, gathered church who excommunicates the unrepentant sinner, pronouncing divine discipline and judgment on sin. See also Hays, *First Corinthians*, 84.

115. See, e.g., Conzelmann, *1 Corinthians*, 97-98; Kuck, *Judgment and Community Conflict*, 241; Smith, *Hand This Man Over*, 57-182.

and put back out into Satan's domain.[116] South contends for the latter interpretation and states, regarding the connection between 1 Corinthians 5:5 and 1 Timothy 1:20, "Here is the only true verbal parallel to 1 Cor 5.5 in the NT and it clearly excludes the idea of the offenders' deaths, since both Hymenaeus and Alexander are not expected to die but to learn something and correct their behavior."[117] Verbrugge concurs and cites important OT background for rightly understanding this phrase:

> Various suggestions have been made, but the most natural is an Old Testament text where the identical words are used. In the Greek version of Job 2:6, Satan is conversing with God, and God says, "I deliver him [Job] over to you; only spare his life." God permitted Satan to do as he wished with Job, to afflict him in any way he desired. He had free play over him, short of taking his life. Satan's goal was clear: to get Job to curse God to his face. In this he failed, for Job did not reject God. He cursed the day of his birth, but he did not curse the Lord. The final result of Job's having been delivered to Satan was a stronger, more deeply committed Job, not someone whom Satan was able to take to his realm of the abyss. This is probably why this phrase appealed to Paul, for the motivation behind his instruction in both passages under discussion is wholly positive.[118]

---

116. Lampe comments, "The 'destruction of the flesh' and 'his spirit may be saved' are to be understood according to Paul's usual contrast of flesh and spirit, according to which flesh refers to the sinful nature, the life lived according to human desires, and spirit refers to the spiritual nature, life lived according to the Spirit of God (cf. Gal 5:16–25)." Lampe, "Church Discipline," 350–51. See also Cambier, "La Chair et L'Esprit," 228; Garland, *1 Corinthians*, 169–77; MacArthur, "'Spirit' in Pauline Usage" 251–52; MacGorman, "Discipline of the Church," 77. For a more comprehensive understanding of this interpretation, see South, *Disciplinary Practices in Pauline Texts*, 38–68; South, "Critique of the 'Curse/Death' Interpretation," 539–61.

117. South, "Critique of the 'Curse/Death' Interpretation," 551. See also Fee, *1 Corinthians*, 209–13; Rosner, "Drive Out the Wicked," 32–33; Thielman, *Theology of the New Testament*, 293; Verbrugge, "Delivered Over to Satan," 17. Thiselton also rightly observes that if this verse is referring to an eschatological salvation, then the curse/death interpretation would seem to understand Paul as speaking of a post-mortem opportunity for salvation. This cannot be the case, and so it seems more likely that the verse is referring to the man's sinful nature that must be destroyed. Thus, according to Thiselton, "What Paul hopes will be destroyed is his attitude of self-congratulation, which deprivation from the respect and support of the church is likely to bring about." Thiselton, *First Epistle to the Corinthians*, 399–400.

118. Verbrugge, "Delivered Over to Satan," 17. One may not find this argument as convincing, but there are linguistic parallels to take into consideration, and one should observe that this is one piece of the cumulative evidence that supports this interpretation of 1 Cor 5:5.

The discipline enacted upon this man is, therefore, restorative in nature and aimed at ensuring the salvation of the offender, hoping he will not remain in unrepentant sin.[119]

In the final two sections of 1 Corinthians 5 Paul's rationale for such a seemingly harsh call to discipline comes into focus. The apostle begins by reiterating that the Corinthians' boasting is not good and asks rhetorically whether or not they know that "a little leaven leavens the whole lump" (1 Cor 5:6). Paul then commands the Corinthians to cleanse out the old leaven,[120] and he grounds this command in the fact that Christ, our Passover lamb,[121] has already been sacrificed (1 Cor 5:7). Thus, they should "celebrate the festival" in the appropriate way (1 Cor 5:8). The Corinthians, therefore, must repent of their sin and celebrate the festival with sincerity and truth by removing this sinful individual, who is considered "the old leaven, the leaven of malice and evil" (1 Cor 5:8).[122]

---

119. See Travis, *Christ and the Judgement of God*, 120–23. This assertion is also affirmed by Rosner, who states, "Exclusion from the community and salvation are linked in 1 Corinthians 5:5b, but the former does not necessarily lead to the loss of the latter. On the contrary, the express purpose of this expulsion is the offender's salvation. Paul's ultimate aim in excluding the man is his own good. . . . Paul assumes (see 6:9–11) that those who persist in flagrant sin have no future with God; in this sense 6:9–11 clarifies 5:5b. Yet he is confident that God's faithfulness will confirm believers 'until the . . . blameless on the day of the Lord Jesus' (1 Cor 1:8). However, future salvation is not a foregone conclusion for one 'who calls himself a brother but is sexually immoral' (v. 11). The passage does not teach that ethical failure results in the loss of salvation, but that assurance of salvation depends in part on ethical progress; cf. 6:11: 'that is what some of your *were*.' Paul does not answer the question of whether the man is currently 'saved.' His point is that so-called brothers who engage in blatant sexual misconduct will be finally saved 'on the day of the Lord' only if 'the sinful nature is destroyed.' According to 5:5b exclusion is undertaken not only to benefit the community and the individual in the present, but also to secure the salvation of the sinner in the future." Rosner, "Exclusion," 474–75.

120. Ciampa and Rosner explain, "Leaven is a little portion of a previous week's batch of dough that had been allowed to ferment. When added to the next batch, the leaven made the bread rise. It carried with it the slight risk of infection, especially if the process was left to go on indefinitely without starting afresh with a completely new batch." Ciampa and Rosner, "1 Corinthians," 708. Paul emphasizes that although in only a "little" part of the church—one person in fact—the evil would inevitably, slowly but surely, spread through the whole community if left unchecked. Thus, Paul is pointing to a pattern of cleansing, which in this case, connotes cleansing the church of sin.

121. Paul assumes not only that his Corinthian readers will understand this symbolism but also that they will identify metaphorically with Israel. Hays states, "Christ, as the Passover Lamb, has already been sacrificed (cf. Exod. 12:3–7), so the time is at hand for the Corinthians to carry out the major part of the festival, searching out and removing all 'leaven' (symbolizing the wrongdoer) from their household (Exod. 12:15)." Hays, *1 Corinthians*, 83.

122. Wall notes that such a removal "delivers the congregation from the threat of

Paul concludes this passage, noting that in his previous correspondence he did not intend for them to judge, and therefore separate themselves completely from those outside of the church who are engaged in sinful practices. Rather, they were to separate from unrepentant offenders from within the church (1 Cor 5:9–13). Regarding the list of sins Paul provides in this particular context,[123] Rosner asserts that a distinct connection can be made between the sins recorded in 5:11 and the OT quotation given in 5:13, saying,

> The representative list of sinners that the church is to judge (5:12b) is in one sense a list of covenantal norms that, when broken, automatically exclude the offender. Paul lists "sexual immorality" first, since that is the issue at hand. But what governs his choice of the next five vices in the catalog? Paul gives a clue in 5:13b: the sins to which the Deuteronomic formula "Expel the wicked person from among you," which Paul quotes, is connected in Deuteronomy form a remarkable parallel to the particular sins mentioned in 5:11.[124]

It appears that Paul is exhorting the Corinthians to deal with the sin in their midst—while allowing God to judge those who are outside the church (1 Cor 5:11–12)—by expelling the unrepentant sinner from their midst. This exhortation is in keeping with an OT pattern of exclusion, as seen earlier from the texts in Deuteronomy, from which Paul is quoting in 5:13.[125]

---

sin and death." Wall, "Reading Paul with Acts," 87. Thus, it is not only the individual sinner, but the spiritual condition of the entire community that Paul is concerned for.

123. Fee notes, "This is the first of the vice lists in the Pauline letters. Such lists were a common feature of Hellenistic Judaism, and they regularly recur in Paul in a variety of contexts (1 Cor 6:10–11; 2 Cor 12:20–21; Gal 5:19–21; Rom 1:29–31; Col 3:5, 8; Eph 5:3–5; 1 Tim 1:9–11; 2 Tim 3:2–5; Titus 3:3; cf. Mark 7:21–22; 1 Pet 2:1; 4:3; Rev. 21:8; 22:15)." Fee, *1 Corinthians*, 225.

124. Ciampa and Rosner, "1 Corinthians," 709. These authors also produce a helpful chart that compares this text with the various citations of the phrase, "Purge the evil person from among you," in Deuteronomy. See ibid. See also Hays, *First Corinthians*, 88; Newton, *Concept of Purity at Qumran*, 95–96; Zaas, "Cast Out the Evil Man," 259–61.

125. For a detailed examination of Paul's use of Deuteronomy in 1 Cor 5, see Perona, "Presence and Function of Deuteronomy," 69–117. This also demonstrates, while there is discontinuity to be noted, the continuity that exists between the OT and NT regarding this topic. Rosner and Ciampa, for example, assert that Paul employs the texts from Deuteronomy cited in 1 Cor 5:13 to point out the threads of covenantal and corporate responsibility that run through the passage and complement his purposes for the church in Corinth. "Once again we see Paul using Israel as an analogy for the church. If God's people in Israel expelled certain sinners, then God's people in Christ should do no less." See Ciampa and Rosner, "1 Corinthians," 710. Seemingly one should affirm that Paul is using this text in an analogous manner and that the themes

Therefore, while God commanded Israel to rid themselves of unrepentant sinners through capital punishment in the OT, he now calls the church to remove the wicked person from their midst by excluding them from the community of faith.[126] What was once dealt with through physical death is now achieved through a declaration of potential eschatological judgment, should the individual under discipline fail to repent. This action serves to exhort the offender and the congregation to persevere in their faith.[127]

Galatians 6:1

In addressing the churches of Galatia, Paul makes a brief admonition to the Christians there to handle the issue of discipline in a fitting manner. Leading up to this point in the letter, Paul dealt with the issue of the Galatians deserting the gospel (1:1–2:21), stating instead that justification was by faith alone, not by works such as circumcision (3:1–4:11). Paul then calls the Galatians to live in freedom, not under the law, but by walking in the Spirit (4:12–5:12). He defines this freedom as walking in love for the sake of others (5:13–15), not by living under the bondage of sin, but in bearing the fruit of

---

of covenant and corporate responsibility are crucial to Paul's argument. However, his purpose seems to extend beyond mere analogy. While God commanded Israel to rid themselves of unrepentant sinners through capital punishment in the OT, he now calls the church to remove the wicked person from their midst by excluding them from the community of faith.

126. South, noting the severity of this measure, asserts, "The ultimate goal of the disciplinary actions which Paul enjoins was not merely the control or purity of the community. Rather, it was to employ such control and purity as a means to the greater end of saving members by keeping them in the community if at all possible.... So it was not simply, or even primarily, the 'purity of the community' which the Pauline churches were to protect through disciplinary measures, at least not as an ultimate end. The intent of such discipline was salvific, for both the individual and the community. Those within the community enjoyed the spiritual benefits of being 'saints' by virtue of being in Christ. To violate Christian norms put one in jeopardy of losing that relationship. If severe enough, the violation could even jeopardize the entire community by inclining others toward unspiritual behavior. Corrective discipline sought to induce repentance in the offender." South, *Disciplinary Practices in Pauline Texts*, 188–90.

127. See Roetzel, who, in commenting on 1 Cor 5:13, asserts, "It hardly needs saying that Paul is calling for these rigorous measures to equip the church to stand in the final Day. The first fruits of the Kingdom are tasted in the present, but these preliminary signs summon the church to special watchfulness." Roetzel, *Judgement in the Community*, 119. See also Schreiner and Caneday, *Race Set Before Us*, 230, who aver, "For Paul, excommunication has a remedial and redemptive objective: 'that they might be taught not to blaspheme.' It would be unwise to suppose, either with the man in Corinth or with Alexander and Hymenaeus [1 Tim 1:20], that Paul pronounced his final verdict over them. Clearly he hoped that apostolic discipline would restore them."

the Spirit (5:16–24). As such church members are to care for and do good to one another in the power of the Spirit (5:25–6:18).[128]

While Paul advocates for justification by faith alone in earlier chapters, he also certainly emphasizes living by the Spirit as of utmost importance. As such, one is saved through faith, but, as has been demonstrated elsewhere, believers are saved to do good works by the power of the Spirit. Paul is advocating that be true in the Galatian churches.[129] In the near context this involves walking according to the Spirit (5:16–25), which, explained more concretely, means not becoming conceited, envious, or provoking one another (5:26).[130] Paul then states that if anyone among them is overtaken in sin, those who are spiritual should look to restore that person in a spirit of gentleness while they watch themselves so they will not also be tempted (6:1). The idea of "overtaken" appears to connote that one has been overtaken by surprise.[131] This is not to suggest that the sinners are unwilling victims; they bear full responsibility for their sins. However, while believers live their lives in the Spirit, sin can still attack in unanticipated ways.[132]

Those who are "spiritual" are the ones called upon to restore the sinner. Paul is not here referring to a group of spiritual elitists,[133] but rather to all Galatian believers who received the Spirit when they heard the gospel (Gal 3:2, 5, 14; 4:6) and are called to continue to walk in the Spirit (5:16, 18, 25).[134]

---

128. This brief outline of Galatians was derived mainly from Longenecker, *Galatians*, c–cix; Schreiner, *Galatians*, 58–59.

129. See Sweeney, who avers that this section of exhortations from 5:16–6:10 was "a pointed reminder to the entire community of their identity as the new covenant people of the Spirit." Sweeney, "'Spiritual' Task of Restoration," 259.

130. Schreiner, *Galatians*, 357.

131. Fee, *Galatians*, 230.

132. Sweeney notes, "This passage highlights an important understanding of Paul's view of the Christian life and further gives us insight into the nature of Paul's eschatology. On the one hand, the Galatians are identified by their relationship to the Spirit. This assumes that they already possessed the Spirit (3:2, 5), a sure sign that the blessings promised to Abraham have been extended to the Gentiles (3:14), and that God had accepted them as his 'sons' through faith in Christ Jesus (3:26). As a result, they had the responsibility to live by the Spirit (5:16), to be led by the Spirit (5:18), and to follow the Spirit's lead (5:25). Paul further reminded them that they had a pastoral responsibility toward their fellow believers, on the one hand, and implied that they were also susceptible to temptation (cf. 1 Cor 7:5; 1 Thess 3:5), on the other. These twin themes, being people of the Spirit and being vulnerable to temptation, illustrate the dynamic of the 'already–not yet' structure that is characteristic of Paul's eschatology." Sweeney, "'Spiritual' Task of Restoration," 260.

133. Ibid., 259.

134. See Gaffin, *Resurrection and Redemption*, 85–86. In light of this reality Schreiner asserts that this text corresponds to Jesus' teaching on church discipline, as he notes, "It seems likely that what Paul describes here generally accords with the first step

This restoration to spiritual health and vitality should be done in a humble manner. Obenhaus agrees and states, "Instead of conceit, competition, and envy (the terms in Gal 5:26 that echo certain works of the flesh in 5:20–21), Paul urges the churches to pursue a life that evidences the fruit of the Spirit by, for example, restoring transgressors with a spirit of gentleness."[135] One who truly loves others and is walking in the Spirit approaches another person with firmness in dealing with sin, and humility in seeking to treat them with gentleness.[136]

Humility and gentleness are crucial aspects of correcting a sinning member of the church, as Paul exhorts the "spiritual" to look to themselves in this process so they will not be tempted. Some believe the temptation is to commit the same sin as the one who has fallen,[137] whereas others argue that the temptation is to become proud.[138] It seems this warning is general enough to include both ideas.[139] Christians should possess an attitude of self-discernment and critical self-appraisal, as Paul is concerned not only with the restoration of the sinner, but also the spiritual health of the one working to restore the sinner.[140]

A call to perseverance in one's faith (i.e. walking in the Spirit) is key to note in this text, both for the sinner and those who are spiritual. Schreiner asserts, "Instead of becoming arrogant and irritating and envying one another, believers should exercise concern and love for others, so that their goal is to build one another up."[141] This effort to build one another up will involve the mortification of sin and the pursuit of righteousness as believers walk by the Spirit. As members of a community, they are to pursue corporate holiness. Essentially, Paul is calling the churches to be watchful for those who fall into sin, looking to take necessary steps of discipline, but always with a view to restoration. As such, the sinner is called to repentance and restoration, and the church is reminded of the need to continually walk in the Spirit in a humble and persevering manner.

---

of church discipline in Matt 18:15–20. One who becomes aware of another's sin should privately speak to the offender in order to restore him or her to fellowship with Christ." Schreiner, *Galatians*, 357.

135. Obenhaus, "Sanctified Entirely," 9.
136. See Schreiner, *Galatians*, 358.
137. Dunn, *Commentary on the Epistle to the Galatians*, 321.
138. Bruce, *Epistle to the Galatians*, 260.
139. Schreiner, *Galatians*, 358.
140. Obenhaus, "Sanctified Entirely," 9.
141. Schreiner, *Galatians*, 357.

2 Thessalonians 3:6–15

One other important text from the NT to consider regarding discipline within the church is found in Paul's second letter to the Thessalonians. When Paul was in Thessalonica, he instructed the church in the basic manner of the Christian life, which included teaching on the Christian ethic of work (1 Thess 4:11; cf. 2 Thess 3:10). The church is to keep away from anyone who is walking in "idleness" (3:6).[142] Paul further instructed the Thessalonians to work with their own hands and also gave them a tangible demonstration of this type of work, leaving the church an example to follow (3:7–9). In spite of this teaching and example, some in the congregation ignored them, possibly due to an over-realized eschatology,[143] and as a result Paul referred to this theme in his first letter (4:11–12; 5:14) as well as the second as the situation deteriorated further (2 Thess 3:11). As such, Paul directly addresses the offenders who were not working, as well as the entire church, apprising them of what their response should be to such people.[144]

The Apostle commands the church in verse six to "keep away"[145] from any believer who does not obey this practice of laboring with one's own hands. Paul gives what appears to be a rather harsh and abrupt command in this instance; however, the Thessalonians had already received the apostolic tradition on more than one occasion,[146] and now in light of their continued disobedience more drastic measures were necessary. Concerning the use of

---

142. Beale asserts, "We have already seen (in the first epistle) that the rendering of *atakōs* as *idle* is misleading (see comments on 1 Thess 5:14) and the same holds true for this passage. The notion that best fits the usage in the ancient world and in the present context is 'unruly' or 'disorderly.'" Beale, *1–2 Thessalonians*, 249. Seemingly idleness could be a direct cause of disorderliness, and thus these ideas may overlap.

143. For two helpful studies on the way in which over-realized eschatology affected the actions of the Thessalonians, and, consequently, Paul's call for discipline, see Canham, "Not Home Yet"; Menken, "Paradise Regained or Still Lost," 271–89. This conclusion is *contra* Russell, "Idle in 2 Thess,"105–19, who believes the problem is not an eschatological, but rather a sociological issue.

144. For further background to this problem in the Thessalonian church see Green, *Letters to the Thessalonians*, 341–42.

145. As noted by Morris, "[Paul's] verb (*stellesthai*) was earlier used for activities such as furling sails. It signifies a drawing into oneself, a holding aloof. But such a withdrawal is not to be made in a spirit of superiority." Morris, *Epistles of Paul*, 144. See also Green, *Letters to the Thessalonians*, 344, who points out that the only other place this verb is used is 2 Cor 8:20.

146. Regarding the meaning of Paul's assertion regarding the tradition in 2 Thess 3:6, Beale contends, "Though the specific issue here is spreading false teaching and not working, it is plausible that Paul would call anyone disorderly who does not follow other aspects of his teaching. Therefore, disorderliness is characteristically disobeying what Scripture commands." Beale, *1–2 Thessalonians*, 259.

the term "brother," Green notes, "As we will see further on, the community should not consider this person to be an 'enemy' or somehow outside the fold but should 'warn him as a brother' (v. 15)." These persons seemingly continue to be members of the family of faith, "although they are subject to the correction and discipline of the community."[147] By ostracizing such persons, the church as a body was able to express its disapproval in a manner that the offender could not lightly dismiss. Ultimately, the goal of the church was to see the errant one repent, return to a Christ-like lifestyle, and engage in the fellowship of believers (vv. 14–15; cf. 2 Cor 2:6–8).[148]

After a brief section wherein Paul points out the example that he set for them in labor (3:7–13), the apostle broadens his exhortation referring to all that he has said previously in the letter, not just the matter of idleness (3:14–15). Paul asserts that the Thessalonians should "not associate" with a person who does not obey his commands (this appears to pick up the earlier command to "keep away" from the disorderly in 3:6). Morris observes,

> The verb ["do not associate"] is used in only one other passage in the New Testament (1 Cor 5:9–11), where it is added that one is not to eat with the offender. . . . Paul is insisting that the erring one be regarded as a brother and treated in such a way as to bring him back. The action is done *in order that he may feel ashamed* (and so brought to a change of mind and conduct).[149]

This disassociation may be defined, for Paul, as not eating with such a person (1 Cor 5:1–13) and even treating this person as an unbeliever (Matt 18:15–20; Rom 16:17–18; Titus 3:10–11).[150] It appears, therefore, that excommunication is in view here as the disorderly have already been warned at least twice (1 Thess 4:11–12; 5:14; 2 Thess 3:6–12) and rejected the correction both times.[151] However, the church is to warn him as a "brother," since the

---

147. Green, *Letters to the Thessalonians*, 344.

148. See Martin, *1, 2 Thessalonians*, 273.

149. Morris, *Epistles of Paul*, 149. See also Green, *Letters to the Thessalonians*, 354–55. Martin, *1, 2 Thessalonians*, 286, agrees and states, "The reason for ostracizing the person is stated in the following clause, 'in order that he may feel ashamed.' The punishment was not intended to alienate the person and make him an enemy of the church but to make the person aware of the wrongness of his actions by demonstrating the church's unanimous condemnation of his behavior. One who had been 'shamed' successfully would have realized the error of his own position and come to respect the truth of the criticism leveled against him (cf. 1 Cor 4:14; Titus 2:8). Such a change of mind should have led the person to repent and genuinely change his ways. Understanding that the intent of the church's action was redemptive, not punitive, is key to understanding the whole of vv. 5–16."

150. This section is derived mainly from Beale, *1-2 Thessalonians*, 261–64.

151. For further details on Paul's exhortation to "admonish the disorderly" in 1

church has a different relationship with that individual than with a pagan. The hope is that this person will come to repentance and demonstrate true faith in Christ.

As such, there appears to be an intentional ambivalence about how this person is to be treated and regarded. In common with Matthew 18, there is a shunning of correction by the church, and thus the need for disciplinary measures. Like the false teachers in the Pastoral Epistles, Paul views these people as perilously close to eschatological judgment (1 Tim 1:19–20; 2 Tim 2:17), but the church should not give up hope about their repentance and salvation (2 Tim 2:25–26), and should warn that person as a brother. Thus, the church is called to disassociate from the unrepentant individual with a redemptive goal in mind, namely, that that person might be shamed to the point of repentance.

Paul then warns the church in Thessalonica not to express hostility toward the disorderly, attacking them because of their lack of conformity to the norms of the group (3:15). Green elaborates, "Although the person is excluded from the community, some contact continues that gives the members of the church further opportunity to 'admonish' him in the hope that such warnings will correct his conduct."[152] Therefore, while these people continue to be warned as "brothers" and not outside the realm of salvation, they are warned to repent and to obey the commands given by God through Paul, lest they demonstrate by their continued unrepentant behavior that they are not truly a part of the community of faith and undergo eschatological judgment. This discipline is administered in order that the offenders might be ashamed. This action taken by the church is not out of enmity or condemnation, but so that positive change might occur, namely, repentance and restoration. As these disciplinary measures are exacted the members of the church are called to "not grow weary in doing good" (3:13) as they continue to persevere in faith and obedience.

SYNTHESIS

While it is helpful exegetically to think through these texts individually, it is also essential to see how they cohere and what significance they possess when viewed in a more holistic manner. As was stated earlier, Rosner conceives of the texts in Deuteronomy that Paul cites in 1 Corinthians 5:13

Thess 5:14–15, see Malherbe, "'Pastoral Care' in the Thessalonian Church," 375–91.

152. Green, *Letters to the Thessalonians*, 356. See also Martin, *1, 2 Thessalonians*, 287, who stresses that this discipline was not intended as a punishment for enemies, but as a restorative measure intended for lovingly confronting the offenders.

as forming distinct motifs. These motifs are noteworthy for rightly understanding the pattern set forth in Deuteronomy, and, consequently, the other aforementioned texts dealing with church discipline.[153]

The first motif that is noted is the idea of corporate solidarity or responsibility.[154] Rosner notes, "Not unlike the pagan sailors who felt compelled to eject Jonah in order to restore a safe passage for their ship, the people of God removed certain offenders as an exercise in corporate responsibility, in order to avoid impending judgment and to protect the felicitous existence of the community before God."[155] Though not cited previously, there is a phrase in Deuteronomy that is similar to the one focused here ("purge the wicked man from among you"), which states, "You shall purge the guilt of innocent blood from your midst" (Deut 19:13; 21:9). In both cases, this phrase expresses the penalty for the crime of murder. That "blood guilt" touches the whole community is made clear in Deuteronomy 19:13, where the motivation for the expulsion is so that it may go well with the nation (cf. Deut 21:8).

Thus, as observed by Ciampa and Rosner, "The notion of 'blood guilt' introduces the motif of corporate responsibility, in which the community is held responsible for the sin of an individual."[156] This reality is evident in the case of a man like Achan, who sinned against God's command by taking riches from Jericho. Not only did Achan suffer, he also brought trouble on the whole nation since there was a corporate solidarity in the sin committed (Josh 7:1–26). This notion of corporate responsibility is carried into the NT as Jesus calls the church to be involved in disciplinary measures if necessary (Matt 18:15–17), and Paul admonishes various churches to deal with discipline in an appropriate manner, knowing the sinful member could affect them all negatively (1 Cor 5; Gal 6:1; 2 Thess 3:6–16; 2 Tim 2:16–18).

A second motif that should be noted in relation to discipline is that of maintaining the holiness of the people of God.[157] Holiness is an overarching

---

153. Rosner asserts that in the OT "offenders are expelled because Israel is the sanctified (holiness motif) covenant (covenant motif) community (corporate responsibility motif) of the Lord, the holy God. These motifs undergird Paul's teaching throughout the passage." Ciampa and Rosner, "1 Corinthians," 706. See also Rosner, *Paul, Scripture, and Ethics*, 61–93.

154. See Rosner, "Drive Out the Wicked," 27–28. See also Roetzel, *Judgement in the Community*, 116, who asserts, "The Old Testament often speaks of the judgement of an individual offender for the purpose of purifying the community, and how the entire community can be implicated by the sin of one of its own members." This pattern can also be seen in the NT (e.g., 1 Cor 5).

155. Rosner, "Drive Out the Wicked," 27.

156. Ciampa and Rosner, "1 Corinthians," 709.

157. Rosner, "Drive Out the Wicked," 28–29.

theme that can be seen throughout the Pentateuch. Israel is the nation whom God has set apart for himself (Exod 19:5–6), and thus they are called to be holy as God is holy (Lev 20:26). Therefore, when blatant, unrepentant sin comes into the community, it must be removed, as these passages in Deuteronomy call for, in order that the nation might remain set apart to the Lord in accordance to his law.

This theme can perhaps be seen most readily in Deuteronomy 13:5, where Israel is told to rid themselves of false prophets because they teach rebellion against the Lord who brought them out of Egypt and redeemed them from slavery. This verse is close in its rendering to Exodus 20:2, where God reminds his people of their redemption and then proceeds to elucidate the law that the people are to follow. This reality is in close connection with Exodus 19:5–6 where Israel is told they will be a kingdom of priests and a holy nation to God. Thus, holiness is hinged upon God's people keeping the law, and when someone breaches that law they are to be purged from the community that the nation may continue on as holy to the Lord.[158] Holiness is a theme that is also upheld in the NT (1 Pet 1:15–16), and it is certainly a driving force in dealing with sin through discipline. Christians are instructed even in the way they should confront a sinning church member, so that they will not likewise fall into temptation and forsake holiness (Gal 6:1).

A third motif to be noted in this context is that of breaking the covenant.[159] People are expelled by these formulas in Deuteronomy for having breached the covenant of God. Deuteronomy 17:2–7 makes this abundantly clear (cf. Josh 7:15; 23:16).[160] The very reason for the execution of this individual is due to the fact that he is transgressing God's covenantal dealings with his people, specifically in the Mosaic law (17:2). NT believers are living under the new covenant, and as such, instead of the people of God being a "mixed entity" as in the OT, the entire community will experience a "circumcision of the heart" (Jer 31:31–34; Ezek 36:25–27).[161] Thus, in quoting the new covenant as seen in Jeremiah 31 (Heb 8:8–13; 10:15–18), the author of Hebrews is bringing God's covenant to bear on NT believers. He exhorts them to have a full assurance of faith (Heb 10:22; cf. Ezek 36:25), while also urging them to help one another as they seek to persevere in their faith (Heb 10:23–25, 36–39).

158. See Craigie, *Deuteronomy*, 223–24, for similar commentary on this section.

159. See Rosner, "Drive Out the Wicked," 29–30.

160. Ciampa and Rosner, "1 Corinthians" 709. So also Rosner, "Drive Out the Wicked," 30.

161. For a more comprehensive treatment of the nature of the new covenant and its implications for understanding the distinctions between Israel and the church, see Gentry and Wellum, *Kingdom through Covenant*, 433–564.

One final motif to be seen in this material is the deterrence of a further breach of covenant among the people of God. Rosner, speaking of this particular motif asserts, "Deuteronomy 19:19b–20a states: 'you must purge the evil from among you. The rest of the people will hear of this and be afraid and never again will such an evil thing be done in Israel.' The dissuasion to further sin is also a reason for expulsion in Deuteronomy 13:12–18; 17:2–7, 12–13; 21:18–21 [cf. Acts 5:1–11; 1 Tim 5:20]."[162] Thus, while the focus of these texts is certainly upon the personal responsibility of the offending sinner, their effect on the community as a whole is never far from view. This is seen plainly in Paul's rebuke of the Corinthians, as he observes that "a little leaven leavens the whole lump" (1 Cor 5:6–8).

These motifs are crucial in rightly understanding and synthesizing the evidence culled from these distinct passages dealing with discipline. God deals with sin in a direct and indirect manner, sometimes bringing consequences upon people himself, and at other times allowing the people of God to mete out discipline. Regardless of the means God uses, his aim is to preserve his covenant with his people, maintain holiness, deal with sin, and preserve his people in their faith.

CONCLUSION

One can see from this chapter that the idea of discipline is not an innovative notion taken up by the church; rather the roots of discipline can be traced back to the OT. The trajectories from the OT that point forward to NT discipline include Adam and Eve's exile from the garden of Eden, expulsion from the camp of Israel for various offenses, and ejection from the land of Israel due to the nation's continual disobedience and breach of the covenant. A shift in redemptive history is brought about through the life, death, and resurrection of Jesus Christ, and thus the church exacts discipline in the NT era, as delineated specifically by Christ (Matt 18:15–20) and the Apostle Paul (1 Cor 5; Gal 6:1; 2 Thess 3:6–16). What was once dealt with in a physical and permanent sense is handled in the NT era from a spiritual vantage point with the hope of the sinner's restoration.

Thus, in both the OT and NT, one can see the concern for the name of God to receive honor among his people, the importance of the holiness of God's people, the repudiation of sin, the exacting of discipline, and the goal of that discipline, namely, repentance, restoration, and perseverance. Discipline, throughout the Scriptures, aims at the ongoing holiness of God's people, and as such he gives loving declarations and warnings as a means

162. Rosner, "Drive Out the Wicked," 30.

to compel his people to be faithful. As such, various themes and motifs can be traced when analyzing these texts in detail, and these themes support the thesis of this dissertation, namely, that church discipline is to serve as a declaration of potential eschatological judgment, to warn offenders of their need to repent, and, as such, is also a means by which church members are called to persevere in their faith.

3

A Historical Analysis of Church Discipline

THIS CHAPTER WILL FOCUS on the historical precedent for viewing church discipline as a warning of potential eschatological judgment, and a means by which church members are called to persevere in their faith.[1] Throughout church history the practice of church discipline has been largely affirmed, though often sporadically applied. Its purpose and significance has also been nuanced in similar, albeit varying ways, often depending on the way in which the church functioned in its particular historical and cultural milieu. One such historical period where the delineation and application of church discipline received an increasing amount of attention was the Reformation and post-Reformation era.[2]

Reformers such as Calvin and Bucer have received ample recognition for their writings about and application of disciplinary action in the

---

1. This chapter seeks to check the interpretation of the biblical material espoused in this work with that of others in church history. It is proper to recognize that we are not the first to read Scripture. Thus, consulting others who have thought deeply about the scriptural principles regarding these topics is appropriate. These three individuals have done so. The fact that they are separated from us by time and culture is a good thing, for any cultural blind spots we possess may be illuminated by them, as they speak from a different culture. Moreover, they highlight valid aspects of discipline that go beyond the thesis of this work, without contradicting it.

2. During the time of the Reformation, "three marks were defined in distinguishing a true church of Christ: true preaching of the Word; proper observance of the sacraments; and faithful exercise of church discipline." Clowney, *Church*, 101.

church.³ Seemingly less attention has been given to other figures, such as Martin Luther. This fact is perhaps due to the massive quantity of writings he produced, and a more concerted focus by scholars on his contributions to issues such as justification. Luther, however, has a great deal to say on the subject, particularly in relation to his dealings with the Catholic Church.

The Anabaptists are better known for their emphasis on moral purity and the practice of church discipline for the preservation of ecclesiastical unity and order, even to the present day.⁴ Balthasar Hubmaier is a key representative of the Anabaptists, and will serve as a useful figure for study in this chapter due to his many writings on the subject. Finally, Jonathan Edwards, while not often noted for his ecclesiology or disciplinary measures, will also receive investigation. Edwards is an important case study, not only because one can observe his particular ecclesiological views, but also because he dealt with a number of documented instances of church discipline. Each of these figures was involved both in articulating the theology of church discipline, and in practicing discipline within differing congregational contexts.⁵ As such, they deserve specific attention in dealing with this subject.

This chapter will begin with a brief survey of the historical background of ecclesial discipline, noting especially the eventual devaluation of the disciplinary process and the system of penance that essentially replaced discipline within the church. Consideration will then be given to the three historical figures previously mentioned: Luther, Hubmaier, and Edwards. These observations will allow one to see the continuity, as well as the distinctives, between these figures in both belief and practice. They will also demonstrate that these men conceived of church discipline as existing for a number of reasons, one of which was to warn of potential judgment and encourage church members to persevere in the faith.

---

3. See, e.g., Burnett, *Yoke of Christ*; Kingdon et al., *Registers of the Consistory of Geneva*.

4. See Roth, "Church 'Without Spot or Wrinkle,'" 15, who states, "The teaching and practice of church discipline has been a central tenet of the Anabaptist-Mennonite tradition for virtually all groups and for most of our 475-year history. Far from being an eccentric obsession of a few conservative groups, the goal of a disciplined, visible church has been at the heart of our self-understanding."

5. One will discern that while Luther, Hubmaier, and Edwards agreed essentially upon the importance of discipline for the unity and purity of the church, the Anabaptists sought to remove the church from state authority in such matters and apply the practice of church discipline to offending sinners more stringently.

HISTORICAL BACKGROUND

While disciplinary action within the church had its controversial and contentious moments, it appears that for the first several centuries the church consistently sought to apply disciplinary measures according to the biblical witness.[6] Indeed, the early church disciplined members both for the propagation of false doctrine and lack of moral purity. It was common practice in the early days of the church to announce disciplinary judgments on Sunday in the context of the church service. Tertullian, describing this event, states, "For judgment is passed, and it carries great weight, as it must among men certain that God sees them; and it is a notable foretaste of judgment to come, if any man has so sinned to be banished from all share in our prayer, our assembly, and all holy intercourse."[7] Tertullian, as well as other church fathers,[8] recognized the seriousness of the disciplinary process.

Most churches recognized two kinds of repentance: a one-time repentance accompanied by faith in Jesus Christ for salvation, and a continual repentance of sin throughout one's life.[9] Christians who sinned had to confess their sin before the church if they wished to be restored to fellowship. Eventually, by the third and fourth centuries, restoration to the church became rather difficult. Undergoing "penitential discipline," those seeking repentance were first required to come to the place where they met for church services, but not enter the place of worship. They were to beg for the prayers of those going inside, and after a period of time they were allowed inside to listen to the service in a designated area. The penitents would eventually be allowed to remain during the entire service, though without partaking of communion. Only after these steps were taken could an individual be restored to full membership. This kind of penitential action, along with the continued peace the church experienced after the reign of Constantine, contributed to a shift in ecclesial discipline.

Church discipline was a difficult practice to keep consistently due to the many challenges the church faced,[10] but dedication to its implementa-

---

6. For accounts of the kind of discipline exacted in the early church, see Ferguson, *Christian Life*; Haslehurst, *Some Account of the Penitential Discipline*; Lea, *Studies in Church History*.

7. Tertullian, *Apology*, 39.4, 175.

8. See, e.g., Augustine, "Letter 185.3.13, The Correction of the Donatists," in *Works of Saint Augustine*, 187; Clement of Rome, *First Epistle to the Corinthians*, in *Ante-Nicene Fathers*, 1:20; Justin Martyr, *First Apology*, in ibid., 1:185.

9. This summary is derived mainly from Wills, "Historical Analysis of Church Discipline," 132–39.

10. This includes the severe persecution the church often underwent prior to the time of Constantine, the changing standards regarding the severity of discipline that

tion was strong at first. According to Greg Wills, however, the practice of church discipline eventually declined in the early centuries of the church. He claims,

> After the fourth century, the system of public confession, exclusion, and penitential rigor fell into disuse. Nectarius, bishop of Constantinople from 381 to 398, apparently played an important role in the change. Since the third century Constantinople and other churches had adopted the practice of appointing a special presbyter in charge of administering the church's penitential discipline. When the public discipline of a deacon at Constantinople for sexual immorality brought considerable public scandal upon the church, Nectarius abolished the office of the penitential presbyter and largely abandoned efforts to administer church discipline among the laity. Nectarius did not repudiate the strict public discipline in principle but he abandoned it in practice.... The process of strict public discipline withered in the Latin-speaking churches of the West just as it did in the churches of the Greek-speaking East. Bishops did not repudiate it in principle but they slowly abandoned it in practice. In its place emerged a system of private confession and individual penance.[11]

This eventual emphasis on penance transformed church discipline largely into a private affair between the priest and layperson, and as such the communal role of church discipline dissipated. Thus, church discipline was largely dispelled, and instead private confession and works of merit were common fare in the days leading up to the Reformation.[12]

Martin Luther, a key figure in the Reformation, is known in the early part of his career as one who had experienced the weight of the penitential system, and as such questioned much of its validity, particularly in the issuing of indulgences. His criticism of these practices as substitutes for true repentance and contrition was a necessary catalyst in precipitating the Reformation. This also allowed for a more biblical comprehension and application of church discipline by Luther, as well as others such as the Anabaptists and later figures like Edwards. With this historical background in mind,

---

a person was to undergo, as well as widespread controversies involving the Donatists and Novatianists.

11. Ibid., 140. See also Socrates, *Ecclesiastical History*, 5.19, in *Nicene and Post-Nicene Fathers*, 2:128; Sozomen, *Ecclesiastical History*, 7.16, in ibid., 386–87.

12. For greater understanding of the development of medieval penitential practices, see McNeill and Gamer, *Medieval Handbooks of Penance*; Hamilton, *Practice of Penance*; Firey, *New History of Penance*.

Luther's delineation of church discipline will come under more specific consideration.

MARTIN LUTHER

While most often remembered as a Reformer, professor, and exegete, Luther was also the pastor of a local church, and as such his theology had ecclesial moorings. His pastoral ministry ensured that whatever thoughts Luther might have regarding church discipline, he would be motivated by a concern for proper ecclesiastical practice.[13] Therefore, three documents written by Luther will receive detailed examination: *A Sermon on the Ban* (1520), *The Keys* (1530), and *On the Councils and the Church* (1539). While other works by Luther are also applicable and will be cited in some cases, these works are foundational to understanding Luther's thoughts on the matter of discipline. As such they will be considered in chronological order.

Sermon on the Ban (1520)

One must understand that Luther often spoke of discipline and excommunication in a polemical sense, as evidenced in all three of these documents. In a Lenten sermon preached in Wittenberg in 1518, Luther had already attacked the misuse of "the ban" as seen in the Roman Catholic Church. He noted, "So far has this childish veneration and holiness gone that they have started this game of excommunication, and the letters are flying about like bats, all because of a trifling thing."[14] Luther believed the Catholic Church had overstepped its bounds in this area. Penance was linked to the power of the keys, and, according to Roman Catholic doctrine, the pope was in possession of the keys to bind and loose as he saw fit. Thus, his *Sermon on the Ban* sought to bring corrective measures to the implementation of discipline and excommunication in the church.

Much of the discussion in this first document stems from Luther's opposition to the Roman Catholic Church and their abuse of papal authority over both "the large ban" as well as "the small ban."[15] Rittgers maintains, speaking on Luther's behalf,

---

13. See the introduction in Luther, "Sermon on the Ban," 5.

14. Luther, "Two Lenten Sermons," 42.

15. Luther maintains that the church has historically understood these two ideas in the following way: "A bishop or pope may exclude someone from this fellowship and forbid it to him because of his sins. This is called putting someone under the ban. This ban was used frequently some time ago, and is now called the small ban. But the ban

Christ had not authorized the clergy to wield power in the temporal sphere. The Reformer maintained that popes and bishops could only use the power of excommunication to restrict access to the Lord's Supper (the so-called small ban), not to influence a layperson's standing in the world (the large ban), which was the jurisdiction of secular authorities alone. A banned person was to suffer no material disadvantage. Luther recognized the legitimacy of excommunication, and instructed laypeople against whom it was used—properly or improperly—to submit to its authority. But the reformer in no way considered a banned person to be automatically severed from fellowship with Christ—only God could accomplish this spiritual excommunication, and he would only do so in response to unbelief.[16]

Luther thus castigates the Catholic Church for using the ban beyond ecclesial bounds: "For the use of the sword belongs to the emperor, to kings, princes, and the rulers of the world and by no means of the spiritual estate, whose sword should be a spiritual one, namely, the word of God, as St. Paul says in Ephesians 6:17, rather than an iron one."[17] The Reformer asserts, instead, that in its discipline the church must be limited and committed to promoting ecclesial fellowship,[18] and walking in obedience according to the mandates of Scripture.

In this work Luther cites Matthew 18:15–17, 1 Corinthians 5:11, 2 Thessalonians 3:14, and 2 John 10–11 as key texts regarding discipline. He asserts that one can readily learn from these texts how the ban should be used. "First, we should seek neither vengeance nor our own gain—as is now the shameful custom everywhere—but rather the improvement of

---

goes even further and forbids burial, buying and selling, trading, a certain kind of life and fellowship among men, and finally even (as they say) water and fire. This is called the large ban. Some people are not satisfied with this; beyond all this they use secular power against those under the ban in order to conquer them through sword, fire, and war." Luther, "Sermon on the Ban," 8.

16. Rittgers, *Reformation of the Keys*, 62.

17. Luther, "Sermon on the Ban," 8. One may wonder how consistent Luther was in keeping this statement later in his career. See, e.g., Luther, *Letters of Spiritual Counsel*, 318–49, wherein one can see how much counsel Luther offered, as a pastor, to various political figures. One can also consider Luther's vehement opposition of the Anabaptists and the degree to which he sought to put down their movement.

18. Luther describes fellowship as consisting of two different kinds for the Christian: there is the inward, spiritual, and invisible fellowship that one has with Christ through the sacrament, and then there is the outward, physical, and visible fellowship that occurs in partaking of the Lord's Supper with a community of believers. Discipline can exclude an unrepentant sinner from this second kind of fellowship. See Luther, "Sermon on the Ban," 7–8.

our neighbor." He continues, "Second, punishment [of the church member] should stop short of his ruin or death, for St. Paul limits the goal of the ban to improvement, that he be put to shame because no one associates with him."[19] As such, to put under the ban does not mean, as some might think, to deliver a soul to the devil and to deprive it of intercession and of all the good works of Christendom; rather, "he who is put under the ban is forced to live without the common sacrament and association with men; nevertheless he is not abandoned on that account by their love, intercession, and good works."[20] With this understanding in mind, it is clear that Luther seeks to advocate discipline in a loving way within the church, not in a corrupt and condemning manner, as was seemingly sanctioned by the Catholic Church.[21]

Luther then seeks to make the point that after a person has gone through the process of Matthew 18 and is finally subjected to the ban due to unrepentant sin,[22] discipline is to be imposed as a sign, a warning, and a punishment. He asserts,

---

19. Ibid., 8–9.

20. Ibid., 9–10. The sacrament of the Lord's Supper played a foundational role in Luther's conception of church discipline as a sign of the community life shared by all saints. Luther claims, regarding discipline and the Lord's Supper, "For its principal, real function and power is to deprive a sinful Christian of the holy sacrament and to forbid it to him." Ibid., 7.

21. Though Luther disagreed with the Roman Catholic Church on the way it had been handling the ban and dispensing punishment upon those who were not guilty and unable to bear the financial burden put upon them by the church, Luther was conciliatory toward the Catholic Church as a whole to submit and come under the ban in a spiritual sense if one was in fact guilty. He asserts, "My dear people, do not be troubled about those who use and hold the power of the ban, whether they are godly or evil, or whether they do you justice or injustice. The power of the ban may not do you any harm, but should always be helpful to the soul, provided you bear and endure it rightly. Their abuse of the ban does not impede its virtue. Or, if it cannot be endured, you should humbly extricate yourself from it, but not with calculation or revenge in word or deed. Do not keep your eyes on them in this matter, but on the dear mother, the church. What do you care whether she lays her scourge or punishment upon you through a godly or through a wicked man? It is and remains your dearest mother's most wholesome scourge." Ibid., 17–18.

22. In *Instructions for the Visitors of Parish Pastors* (1538), which was written by Melanchthon but received a preface from Luther, thus showing his endorsement, Luther contends for a consistent application of Matt 18:17 and 1 Cor 5:1–13 in "not admitting to the Lord's Table those who, unwilling to mend their ways, live in open sin, such as adultery, habitual drunkenness, and the like. However, before taking such action, they should be warned several times to mend their ways. Then, if they refuse, the ban may be proclaimed." Luther, "Instructions for the Visitors of Parish Pastors," 311.

> In this way he who is put under the ban should acknowledge that he himself has delivered his soul up to the devil through his own transgression and sin, and that he has deprived himself of the fellowship of all the saints with Christ. For his mother, the holy church, wants to show her dear son this unbearable damage of sin, by way of the punishment of the ban, and thereby wants to bring him back from the devil to God again. It is just the same as when a natural physical mother threatens and punishes her son when he does evil. She does not deliver him to the hangman or to the wolves, nor does she make a knave of him, but rather she restrains him and shows him by way of this same punishment how he could end up with the hangman. . . . In the same way, when a spiritual authority puts someone under the ban it should keep this in mind: "Look, you have done this and that whereby you have delivered your soul up to the devil, earned God's wrath, deprived yourself of the fellowship of all Christians, and fallen under the inward, spiritual ban before God, and you neither want to stop it nor to return. Well then, I therefore put you too under the outward ban before men. In order to shame you I am depriving you of the sacrament and the fellowship of people until you come to your senses and bring back your poor soul."[23]

The person under discipline has "delivered his soul up to the devil," and the church must act so that the person under the ban can see "how he could end up with the hangman." The church "wants to bring him back from the devil to God again," and escape the wrath of God and come back into the fellowship of the church. Thus, when speaking of the "inward, spiritual ban," Luther is referencing this person's potential status at the final judgment should they not repent. As such, they are put under the "outward ban" as well.

This sounds like a harsh condemnation of an individual, but Luther's intention is fixed on the restoration of the individual to the church. He believes that the ban does not necessarily destroy or condemn. Rather, the church seeks and finds a ruined and condemned soul under the ban to bring it back, since it is the nature and character of church discipline to lovingly correct sin. Luther continues, "That is why it makes no one either worse or more sinful. Instead, when it is justly imposed, it is instituted only to restore the inward spiritual fellowship, and when it is unjustly imposed it is to be corrected."[24] Discipline is always meant for the purpose of restoration, bringing a person back from the error of their ways.

---

23. Luther, "Sermon on the Ban," 10.
24. Ibid., 11. Luther cites from 2 Cor 13:10 and 1 Cor 5:5 to support this claim.

Luther, therefore, sought to help others see the vital nature of the community of the church and the practice of discipline in order to serve as a means by which people would repent and turn to Christ in faith.[25] Luther desired that people submit to this discipline as coming from the church for their own spiritual good, and that the ban would serve as a means of their bearing spiritual fruit.[26] Luther's *Sermon on the Ban* also seeks to make clear his belief that a man is not condemned because he violates some external ecclesiastical law; rather, he is sentenced to discipline on the basis of his own sin and unbelief. Thus, Luther did not reject the ban laid out by the Catholic Church outright, but sought to reinterpret it in light of evangelical principles.

The Keys (1530)

Luther's next work for consideration, entitled *The Keys*, was a polemic against the papal abuse of "binding and loosing," and instruction on the proper way the keys were to be used within the church.[27] This address is rooted in a certain understanding of Matthew 16:19 and 18:18, wherein Jesus tells Peter and his disciples that he is giving to them the keys of the kingdom of heaven for binding and loosing (Matt 16:19). He later links this idea of binding and loosing with church discipline (Matt 18:18). Luther's

---

This statement is in contradistinction to the Catholic Church who, according to Luther, "boast that they have the power to curse, to condemn, and to destroy." Ibid., 12.

25. This is also demonstrated by the fact that Luther sought for those under the ban to come to hear the preaching on Sunday, even if they could not stay for the sacrament of the Lord's Supper celebrated after the sermon. "It does not matter whether someone is justly or unjustly under the ban—no one is to drive him out of the church until the Gospel has been read or the sermon preached. For no one may ban someone or himself be banned from hearing the Gospel and the sermon. The word of God shall remain free, to be heard by everyone. Indeed, those who are under the just ban should hear it most so that thereby they might perhaps be moved to come to their senses and to improve themselves." Ibid., 22. See also Rittgers, *Reformation of the Keys*, 106.

26. In keeping with this statement, Luther avers, "Therefore, let us understand what is to be recognized as the most significant aspect of the ban, namely, that one should bear it without fear or impatience for two reasons: first, the power of the ban is given by Christ to the holy mother, the Christian church, that is, to the congregation of all Christians. Therefore, we should honor and endure our dear mother the church and Christ in this matter. For we should certainly accept, love, and fear in a childlike way whatever Christ and the church do. Second, the fruit and work of the ban are useful and wholesome and never harmful to him who endures them and does not despise them." Luther, "Sermon on the Ban," 16.

27. For an excellent work detailing the changes in doctrine that occurred regarding the power of the keys from 1450 to 1560, see Rittgers, *Reformation of the Keys*.

understanding of the keys and discipline was rooted in the preaching of the gospel, and as such stood in stark contrast with the system of the Roman Catholic Church.[28] The Catholic Church asserted that the pope, as Peter's successor, possessed the keys of the kingdom, and priests were permitted to grant absolution through confession and penance. This was based on their ordination by a bishop who was closely connected to the pope, the one who ultimately possessed the keys.[29] Luther wanted his readers to understand that if the keys were not properly linked to the realities of the gospel, then abuse was sure to occur.

Luther's basic premise in this work is that the Roman Catholic Church is guilty of four different abuses regarding this doctrine. First, Luther asserts that the Roman Church misinterpreted Matthew 16:19 and 18:18 to refer to the making of an ecclesial command or the forbidding of a particular matter; thus it vested this authority in the pope. Second, the Catholic Church asserts that the pope is infallible in his decrees of excommunication and absolution. Third, it claims that the pope has a key of power and a key of knowledge, thus putting himself over "temporal" powers like emperors and kings. And finally, the approach of the Roman Church to banning and absolving is corrupt and not in accord with the standards of Scripture.[30]

In contrast to these claims, Luther demonstrates that the purpose of Christ's binding is to redeem the sinner from his transgressions. "With his 'binding' Christ attempts nothing else but to free and rid the sinner's conscience of sins. It is for this reason that he 'binds' and punishes the sinner so that he might let go of his sin, repent of it, and avoid it."[31] Herein lies the true significance of the keys. Luther refers to them as an office, a power, and a command given by God through Christ to all of Christendom for the retaining and the remitting of the sins of men.[32] And, unlike much of Catholic rhetoric, he seeks to stress both keys so that sinners are not merely brought under the threat of exclusion but also promised the hope of the

---

28. Luther states, "As we have declared already, the ministry of the Word belongs to all. To bind and to loose clearly is nothing else than to proclaim and to apply the gospel. For what is it to loose, if not to announce the forgiveness of sins before God? What is it to bind, except to withdraw the gospel and to declare the retention of sins?" Luther, "Concerning the Ministry," 27–28. In this sense Luther sees acceptance into the church and discipline hinging on the preaching of the gospel to save souls and root out habitual sin.

29. See the introduction to Luther's work on the keys of the kingdom in Luther, "Keys," 323–24.

30. This is the basic outline of Luther, "Keys," 325–77.

31. Ibid., 328.

32. Ibid., 366.

gospel through repentance.³³ Luther stresses the importance of rightly comprehending the meaning of the keys in that its reality is tied into the truths of the gospel. He states, "Christ's keys help in the attainment of heaven and eternal life, for he himself calls them keys to the kingdom of heaven, because they close heaven to the hardened sinner and open it to the repentant one."³⁴ This, seemingly, is why Luther attacks the Catholic conception of this doctrine with such tenacity.

In this work as well, Luther emphasizes the significance of the community of faith in the proper exercise of the keys.³⁵ In opposition to the Roman Catholic's demand for involvement of a bishop or even the pope in disciplinary cases, Luther asserts, "Paul was an apostle, yet he was not willing to excommunicate a person who was living in adultery with his stepmother (1 Cor 5:1). But he called on the congregation to act."³⁶ In keeping with this congregational emphasis Luther believed, based on Matthew 18:15–20, that the discipline done by the church who possessed the keys would be in step with the judgment also rendered in heaven. In describing discipline from God's perspective Luther affirms, "If you bind and loose on earth, I will also bind and loose right along with you in heaven. When you use the keys, I will also. . . . It shall be one single action, mine and yours, not a twofold one. While you do your work, mine is already done. When you bind and loose, I have already bound and loosed. He binds and joins himself to our work."³⁷ Luther states this quite boldly and unapologetically, seemingly offering little possibility that the church could in fact wrongly use the keys. This is due to

---

33. Ibid., 376–77. The papal keys sought to enjoin and command, but Luther saw the keys as a source of threat and promise. In this way Luther distinguishes his view from the works-based righteousness inherent in the Catholic perspective. See ibid., 375. Similarly Luther makes a statement in "Against the Roman Papacy," asserting, "There must be discipline and punishment in the church for the sake of the wild, impudent people; but also hope and consolation for the sake of the fallen ones, so that they do not think their baptism is now invalid, as the Novationists, but even more the pope, have taught" (329).

34. Luther, "Keys," 328.

35. Luther asserts elsewhere that the pope was not in sole occupation of the keys of the kingdom, the church was. He states, "But this office of the keys belongs to all of us who are Christians. . . . For the word of Christ in Matt 18:15 is addressed not only to the Apostles, but, certainly, to all the brethren." Luther, "Concerning the Ministry," 26.

36. Luther, "Keys," 372. Luther condemns anything contrary to involving the whole church in a disciplinary matter when he criticizes the Catholic Church saying, "I call it a devil's and not God's ban, contrary to Christ's command, when people are cursed with the ban sacrilegiously, before they have been convicted in the presence of the assembled congregation." See ibid., 371.

37. Ibid., 365.

the fact that his focus here is less on the sinful tendencies of those who make up the church, and more on the promise given in Matthew 18.

Luther concludes his address by summarizing his views on the office of the keys in the following way:

> In conclusion, we possess these two keys through Christ's command. The key that binds is the power or office to punish the sinner who refuses to repent by means of a public condemnation to eternal death and separation from the rest of Christendom. And when such a judgment is pronounced, it is as a judgment of Christ himself. And if the sinner perseveres in his sin, he is certainly eternally damned. The loosing key is the power or office to absolve the sinner who makes confession and is converted from sins, promising again eternal life. And it has the same significance as if Christ himself passed judgment. And if he believes and continues in this faith he is certainly saved forever. For the key that binds carries forward the work of the law. It is profitable to the sinner inasmuch as it reveals to him his sins, admonishes him to fear God, causes him to tremble, and moves him to repentance, and not to destruction. The loosing key carries forward the work of the gospel. It invites to grace and mercy. It comforts and promises life and salvation through the forgiveness of sins. In short, the two keys advance and foster the gospel by simply proclaiming these two things: repentance and forgiveness of sins (Luke 24:47).[38]

Of all the points Luther makes regarding church discipline, this statement most explicitly supports the thesis of this dissertation. There is stress put on the idea of warning of judgment, as discipline "admonishes [the excommunicant] to fear God." Emphasis is also put on continuing or persevering in one's faith, specifically, in this case, by understanding the binding key to be a function of the law condemning us in our sin and the loosing key as a function of the gospel offering the forgiveness of sins. This law/gospel distinction plays a primary role in Luther's hermeneutic and here it helps the reader determine the functions of the keys in the process of church discipline. Luther clearly states that a refusal to repent indicates that a person will be eternally condemned before God, but, as has already been stated, he also clearly advocated the practice of the ban for the sake of a person's restoration and endurance in the faith. The keys should be utilized for the believer's continual engagement with the need for repentance as a means by which they can remain strong in their faith.

---

38. Ibid., 372–73.

On the Councils and the Church (1539)

According to Gritsch, Luther's final work for consideration, *On the Councils and the Church*, "represents his final judgment concerning the medieval church as well as the first broad foundation for a new doctrine of the church within nascent Lutheranism."[39] The focus here will be upon the third and final part of this work, which deals with the true marks of the church according to Scripture. Luther outlines seven marks, the fourth of which is the proper exercise of the keys.

Luther describes the office of the keys as the duty of the church to reprove a sinning Christian, and if he does not mend his ways he is to be bound in his sin, but if he does mend his ways he should be loosed or absolved (Matt 18:15–20). He maintains,

> Now where you see sins forgiven or reproved in some persons, be it publicly or privately, you may know that God's people are there. If God's people are not there, the keys are not there either; and if the keys are not present for Christ, God's people are not there. Christ bequeathed them as a public sign and a holy possession, whereby the Holy Spirit again sanctifies the fallen sinners redeemed by Christ's death, and whereby the Christians confess that they are a holy people in this world under Christ. And those who refuse to be converted or sanctified again shall be cast out from this holy people, that is, bound and excluded by means of the keys, as happened to the unrepentant Antinomians.[40]

Certainly this is a much more succinct summary of discipline than the preceding two treatises; however, this text allows one to see the consistency with which Luther held to this particular doctrine, and does so in a condensed form. Seemingly, in a rather definitive manner, Luther links discipline with the issue of sanctification, and also stresses the importance of enduring in one's faith by means of discipline. Discipline is a reaffirmation that the church consists of "holy people in this world under Christ," and as such one must endure in one's faith to avoid potential eschatological judgment. The

39. See the introduction to Luther, "On the Councils and the Church," 5.

40. Ibid., 153. Luther makes a similar assertion in his *Smalcald Articles*. He asserts, "The keys are an office and authority given to the church by Christ to bind and loose sins—not only the crude and notorious sins but also the subtle, secret ones that only God knows." From this assertion Luther then maintains, "Because absolution or the power of the keys is also a comfort and a help against sin and a bad conscience and was instituted by Christ in the gospel, confession or absolution should by no means be allowed to fall into disuse in the church—especially for the sake of weak consciences and for the wild young people, so that they may be examined and instructed in Christian teaching." Luther, "Smalcald Articles," 356–57.

true church is in possession of the keys of the kingdom, and as such the community of faith must exercise its authority in an appropriate manner.

From these three documents one can observe Luther's commitment to ecclesial discipline. Unlike the Catholic Church, Luther advocated for the keys of the kingdom to be exercised by the church, rather than by the pope solely. While seeking to correct what he deemed as errors made by the Catholic Church, Luther still maintained the seriousness of the ban, and emphasized that those who come under discipline were warned of potential eschatological judgment should they not repent. This, however, was the point for Luther, as he viewed church discipline as restorative in nature. He also intended for this measure of discipline to serve as a deterrent to sin for others, in hopes that they would persevere in their faith.

BALTHASAR HUBMAIER

Balthasar Hubmaier is one of the better-known Anabaptists advocating a strict discipline in the church. This is due, at least in part, to the amount of writing available to us, and the amount of space Hubmaier devoted to ecclesiological issues. To better understand Hubmaier, it is important to obtain a brief background regarding the Anabaptists as a whole, particularly their ecclesiological views. Brief consideration will also be given to a historic document known as the Schleitheim Confession, a key text dealing with an Anabaptist view of discipline.

The Anabaptists

The Anabaptists were contemporaries to Martin Luther who also protested the corruption of the Roman Catholic Church, particularly regarding penance and indulgences,[41] but went in some different directions than Luther in seeking to implement what they believed to be biblical reforms.[42] This included issues such as believer's baptism, pacifism, and a radical separation between church and state. The last of these categories is pertinent to our discussion of church discipline, in that the Anabaptists sought to apply a purely ecclesial mode of discipline that was free of magisterial interference. Ludwig elaborates,

---

41. Both the Magisterial Reformers and Anabaptists saw that penance, much like the Mass, granted priests, bishops, and the pope inordinate power in retaining and absolving sins. See Finger, *Contemporary Anabaptist Theology*, 208–9.

42. For a helpful overview of this movement see Roth and Strayer, *Companion to Anabaptism and Spiritualism*; Williams, *Radical Reformation*.

The Anabaptist conception of separation of church and state, therefore, called for three radical changes of the sixteenth-century status quo. First, the power and duty to apply discipline in religious matters did not belong to the state but to the church (Matt 18). Secondly, the punitive state actions of persecution and death for religious reasons needed to be replaced by the redemptive church discipline of the ban, which not only allowed for but aimed at restoration. Thirdly, in this way freedom of conscience could be exercised, or perhaps more correctly, exercised again after twelve centuries of European history dominated by the state church system.[43]

Thus, the Anabaptists did not contend for political punishments such as exile or imprisonment; rather, discipline was to be handled by the congregation regarding religious matters.[44]

Also, generally speaking, Anabaptists closely linked the ideas of church discipline and baptism. When sixteenth century Anabaptists were baptized, the act was seen as more than an outward testimony to inward faith—though, of course, it was that—and obedience to a New Testament command. Travis asserts, "In addition, the newly baptized person pledged to live in newness of life in the believing community, placing himself voluntarily under its authority. Baptized believers constituted a holy brotherhood, in which members were subject to discipline by the local congregation."[45] Thus, a church of voluntarily baptized believers was the necessary milieu in which imperfect, but sincere, submissive, and obedient Christians could grow spiritually and find assistance in restraining their sinful tendencies. Every individual Christian was considered to be in need of the help of others to mature and overcome evil. The imitation of Christ and the maturing of the believer were not considered to be feasible as a private matter; only as the brotherhood of believers could the church properly fulfill its corporate task of exhorting one another to sanctification.

Baptism was, therefore, an integral part of the Anabaptists' understanding of the whole Christian life. It signified that one had died to sin and was free from its dominion to walk voluntarily in newness of life under the reign of Christ in the fellowship of a visibly holy community of regenerated believers. Not only was there no salvation outside the universal, mystical church of true believers, there was also no salvation outside its visible

---

43. Ludwig, "Relationship between Sanctification and Church Discipline," 80.
44. See Travis et al., "Perspectives on Church Discipline," 84.
45. Ibid. See also Harder, *Sources of Swiss Anabaptism*, 355.

expression, the local brotherhood, to which the Anabaptists believed Christ had assigned the keys of binding and loosing.[46]

These general principles are essential in understanding an Anabaptist conception of church discipline. With this background in mind we will now look at the Schleitheim Confession. This document supplies crucial background material when considering Balthasar Hubmaier, and gives context to his contribution to the topic of church discipline.

Schleitheim Confession

The Schleitheim Confession is the most representative statement of Anabaptist principles, evidenced by the fact that it was endorsed unanimously by a meeting of Swiss Anabaptists in 1527.[47] Written largely by Michael Sattler—an important leader in the Anabaptist movement who was soon after tried and executed—this work was an attempt to give the Anabaptists a unified foundation and direction. Seven articles are laid out on the doctrines of baptism, communion, separation, the responsibilities of pastors, pacifism, oaths, and, most importantly for our purposes, church discipline.[48]

Commonly referred to as "the ban," Anabaptists agreed upon the following statement regarding church discipline:

> The ban shall be employed with all those who have given themselves to the Lord, to walk in his commandments, and with all those who are baptized into the one body of Christ and who are called brethren or sisters, and yet who slip sometimes and fall into error and sin, being inadvertently overtaken. The same shall be admonished twice in secret and the third time openly disciplined or banned according to the command of Christ (Matt 18). But this shall be done according to the regulation of the Spirit (Matt 5) before the breaking of bread, so that we may break and eat one bread, with one mind and in one love, and may drink of one cup.[49]

Thus, the Schleitheim Confession requires a member who has sinned and broken baptismal vows in a "disciplined church fellowship" to be admonished twice in private, then, if necessary, before the whole congregation.

---

46. Davis, "No Discipline, No Church," 44.

47. See esp. Strayer, "Swiss-South German Anabaptism," 89–92.

48. It is worth pointing out that the ban is the second article listed, after baptism only. This may signify that the issue of discipline loomed large in their thinking.

49. The text quoted here was taken from Yoder, *Schleitheim Confession*, 14.

Though this section of the Confession is relatively brief, there are two points to be drawn from it. First, though not overt, there is a definite recognition of the fact that the ban is to be implemented by the entire congregation.[50] The statement clearly says that when one must be admonished the third time and subsequently banned it will be done "openly." This idea comes out more clearly in other Anabaptist writings,[51] but it is significant, particularly when noting the emphasis Anabaptists put on the church being made up of believers only.

Second, within the Confession, there is a subtle profession of the "visibility" of the true church. In the second article the ban is given enhanced importance as the instituted means of purifying the members of the church before the administration of the Lord's Supper. Williams claims, "In safeguarding the purity of the communion fellowship by means of committing themselves to the discipline of the pre-communion ban, the Schleitheim brethren were clearly breaking away from the Zwinglian view that the saints or the elect are known only to God and that the true Church is invisible."[52] This would prove to be a key difference between the Anabaptists and the Magisterial Reformation, the latter denying that one could possibly know the true spiritual state of an individual, thus advocating for the concept of an "invisible church." Although succinct, this document offers helpful insights into the nascent Anabaptist understanding of church discipline, which is subsequently teased out by various theologians, including Hubmaier.

Hubmaier's Ecclesiology

An influential German Anabaptist leader, Balthasar Hubmaier (1480–1528) was an educated and passionate preacher and teacher of the radical Reformation.[53] In his efforts to enact a restoration of the church, in a different direction from what Luther and other Reformers were attempting, Hubmaier

---

50. The authority to exercise the ban was ascribed to the local congregations as one of the seven basic articles of the Swiss Brethren, and yet it is also interesting to note that there was leadership vested in the pastor in handling disciplinary cases. Note specifically articles two and five in the Schleitheim Confession. In article five it states, "This office [of pastor] shall be to read, to admonish and teach, to warn, *to discipline, to ban in the church*, to lead out in prayer for the advancement of all the brethren and sisters, to lift up the bread when it is to be broken, and in all things to see to the care of the body of Christ, in order that it may be built up and developed, and the mouth of the slanderer be stopped" (emphasis mine). Thus, there appears to be a bit of tension in the Confession itself.

51. See, e.g., Simons, "Explanation of the Apostolic Separation," 244–63.

52. Williams, *Radical Reformation*, 291–92.

53. For a helpful introduction to this theologian see Vedder, *Balthasar Hübmaier*.

endeavored to emulate the quality and the character of the "pristine New Testament Church." This restoration called for a pursuit of ecclesial unity as well as purity.[54]

Hubmaier's ecclesiology basically converged on three practices: baptism, the Lord's Supper, and church discipline.[55] Hubmaier asserts,

> The church is sometimes understood to include all the people who are gathered and united in one God, one Lord, one faith, and one baptism, and have confessed this faith with their mouths, wherever they may be on earth. This then is the universal Christian corporeal church and fellowship of the saints, assembled only in the Spirit of God, as we confess in the ninth article of our creed. At other times the church is understood to mean each separate and outward meeting assembly or parish membership that is under one shepherd or bishop and assembles bodily for instruction, for baptism and the Lord's Supper. The church as daughter has the same power to bind and to loose on earth as the universal church, her mother, when she uses the keys according to the command of Christ, her spouse and husband.[56]

Here one can see that Hubmaier links his definition of the church—a body of believers that assembles to observe baptism, the Lord's Supper, and possesses the power to bind and loose—with the keys of the kingdom. He continues and states that the church has the power of fraternal admonition because of the baptismal pledge, "in which one has made himself subject to the church and all her members, according to the word of Christ."[57] This fraternal admonition can result in an individual undergoing the ban, which, among other restrictions, would include removal from participation in the Lord's Supper.[58] Thus, one can see in Hubmaier's ecclesiology a strong tie between baptism, the Lord's Supper, and the ban.

---

54. The first programmatic Anabaptist ecclesial writing came from Hubmaier in 1525, and it is here that he establishes the necessity of linking the ban to baptism and the Supper, and provided the first essential ecclesial outline for later Anabaptist communities. See Hubmaier, "Summa of the Entire Christian Life," 81–89.

55. See Hubmaier, "Christian Catechism," 354, who states, "In sum: Where water baptism is not reestablished and practiced one does not know who is a brother or sister, there is no church, no brotherly discipline or reproof, no ban, no Supper, nor anything that resembles that Christian stance and nature." See also Snyder, "Swiss Anabaptism," 79.

56. Hubmaier, "Christian Catechism," 351–52.

57. Ibid., 353.

58. See ibid., 353–54.

Hubmaier further maintained, in connection with these doctrines, that Christ assigned to the church two ministerial powers: binding and loosing. This power to bind and loose is linked to the keys of the kingdom, as indicated in Matthew 16:19 and 18:18. It is also crucial to note that Hubmaier associated the keys with the practice of baptism and the Lord's Supper.[59] He asserts, "For in water baptism the church uses the key of admitting and loosing, but in the Supper the key of excluding, binding, and locking away, as Christ promises and gives to it the power of the forgiveness of sins."[60] McMullan elaborates,

> The first key, binding, empowered the church to receive repentant sinners into the congregation through water baptism, and subsequently, by readmitting those who were previously under the ban. The second key, loosing, primarily functioned through the Eucharist, where those who openly professed faith in Christ continually renewed their pledge first made at baptism to live according to the rule of Christ. Subsequently, as to the key to the purity of the church, the second key gave the congregation the authority to exclude obstinate sinners from the fellowship of the Lord's Supper through the ban. . . . Therefore, the proper function of the first key came into use only when the legitimate exercise of the second key, admonition and the Ban, was in place.[61]

In essence, Hubmaier viewed the church as a community of believers, who, at baptism, publicly pledged to live the life of a disciple of Christ, and who continued to pledge obedience to Christ at the Lord's Supper, lest they come under the discipline of the church.[62]

---

59. Hubmaier, "On the Christian Ban," 410–11. McMullan concurs and further describes Hubmaier's view: "[The keys] were intricately related to the doctrines of baptism and the Lord's Supper for Hubmaier, and together they authorized the church to receive repentant sinners into a local congregation and to exclude those same ones if they were unwilling to behave in a morally upright way." McMullan, "Church Discipline," 38.

60. Hubmaier, "Dialogue with Zwingli's Baptism Book," 175. See also, Hubmaier, "Christian Catechism," 341.

61. McMullan, "Church Discipline," 76–77.

62. See Hubmaier, "On Fraternal Admonition," 383–85. Here he states, "So all of those who cry: 'Well, what about water baptism? Why, all the fuss about the Lord's Supper? They are after all just outward signs! They're nothing but water, bread, and wine! Why fight about that?' They have not in their whole life learned enough to know why the signs were instituted by Christ, what they seek to achieve or toward what they should finally be directed, namely to gather a church, to commit oneself publicly to live according to the word of Christ in faith and brotherly love, and because of sin to subject oneself to fraternal admonition and the Christian ban, and to do all of this with a sacramental oath before the Christian church and all her members."

Hubmaier's Theology of Discipline

With this particular ecclesiology as his foundation, as early as 1526 Hubmaier asserted that without the restoration of the proper use of the ban as seen in Matthew 18 there is no real church, even if baptism and the Lord's Supper are observed. He considered this lack of discipline to be a major reason for the lowly condition of the Roman Church and for the failure of the Magisterial Reformation to achieve practical, moral reform.[63] Even adult baptism would be no better than infant baptism had been if fraternal admonition and excommunication did not go along with it. The Anabaptist ban is, therefore, rooted in the voluntary, personal, penitential pledge of submission to Christ's commands in baptism and expressed communally in the loving fellowship of, and submission to, the visible brotherhood of believers. Its goal was both personal and corporate holiness and witness, which the Anabaptists insisted was the New Testament standard.[64]

Hubmaier saw several purposes behind church discipline. He maintains, regarding the ban, that the excommunicant "must be avoided and shunned so that the whole outward church may not be ill spoken of, shamed, and disgraced by fellowship with him or be corrupted by his evil example, but rather that it will be frightened and filled with fear by this punishment and henceforth die to sin."[65] Thus, Hubmaier believed it was needful sometimes completely to cut off the "corrupt and stinking flesh" together with the "poisoned and unclean members" so that the entire body might not thereby be "deformed, shamed, and destroyed."[66] Hubmaier rightly observed that the entire congregation could be affected by a church member's sinful behavior. Discipline was also constructive because it directed other members of the church away from sin.[67] It exposed those who claimed to have faith

---

63. See ibid. Hubmaier went so far as to argue "no discipline, no church." Even if adult baptism and the Lord's Supper are observed in the congregation, without discipline there is no real church. One of the debates of the sixteenth century centered on what the distinctive marks of the church were. Both Luther and Calvin contended for two marks: the word of God correctly preached, and the sacraments rightly administered. Hubmaier added discipline as a third mark: discipline is *esse*, foundational, to the church's very being. See Travis, "Perspectives on Church Discipline," 84. Davis concurs with this sentiment and lays out Hubmaier's "formula" for a proper church in the following way: no voluntary believer's baptism = no voluntary fraternal discipline = no church. See Davis, "No Discipline, No Church," 47.

64. See Davis, "No Discipline, No Church," 47.

65. Hubmaier, "Christian Catechism," 353.

66. Hubmaier, "On Fraternal Admonition," 374.

67. See Hubmaier, "On the Christian Ban," 411.

but did not perform works in accordance with that faith.[68] Finally, banning could be productive for those banned in drawing them to repentance.[69]

This final purpose appears to be especially important to Hubmaier's understanding of the ban, as he desires the sinner, as well as members of the church, to respond in a fitting manner to discipline and, accordingly, to persevere in their faith.[70] As seen above, Hubmaier desires members of the church to "be frightened and filled with fear by this punishment and henceforth die to sin."[71] The expectation of the ban was to produce fear and assist church members in dying to sin. Hubmaier's belief was that church discipline would serve as a warning and a means by which the church members could persevere in their faith (i.e. "die to sin"). Similarly, regarding the individual under the ban, Hubmaier asserted that the church was obliged by the command of Christ to expel the person from the assembly "so that we might not become participants of your [the excommunicant's] sins and might not be eternally punished and damned together with you."[72] Thus, it appears that Hubmaier viewed those under excommunication as being outside the Christian faith. His desire, however, was that those under the ban would repent, return to the fellowship of the church, and fully renounce their sin.[73] Hubmaier's hope and aim in discipline and his overarching ecclesiology was to continually admonish church members to walk in obedience to Christ throughout their lives.

Understanding Hubmaier's ecclesiological foundation and purposes for discipline allows one to see that he links the ideas of church membership, the ordinances, discipline, salvation, and sanctification tightly

68. Hubmaier, "On Fraternal Admonition," 376, 383.

69. See ibid., 380. Hubmaier says excommunication is "done for the good of the sinner, that he may examine himself, know himself, and desist from the sin." Hubmaier, "Christian Catechism," 354.

70. See Hubmaier, "On the Christian Ban," 411, 416–17. Regarding Hubmaier's connection of discipline with his soteriology, Goncharenko asserts, "It seems clear that in pursuing biblical foundation for his soteriology, Hubmaier achieved two things. First, he was not willing to absolve men of all responsibility for their salvation as his Magisterial counterparts inadvertently did with their predestinarian grace and forensic justification. Second, unable and unwilling to endorse the sacramental system of the Catholic church, Hubmaier guarded against lax living, which often characterized the churches and societies of the Magisterial Reformers, with his usage of church discipline as an integral part of the salvation process." Goncharenko, "Importance of Church Discipline," 95–96. See also Hubmaier, "On the Christian Ban," 411.

71. Hubmaier, "Christian Catechism," 353.

72. Hubmaier, "On the Christian Ban," 417.

73. See ibid., 423–24. See also Hubmaier, "Christian Catechism," 354, wherein he asserts that discipline "is done for the good of the sinner, that he may examine himself, know himself, and desist from sin."

together.⁷⁴ Hubmaier asserts, "Where [church discipline] is not instituted and used according to the orderly and earnest command of Christ, there nothing reigns but sin, scandal and vice."⁷⁵ He also maintained that baptism is a commitment made publicly to God before the congregation where the baptized person renounces Satan and all his works. Hubmaier asserts, "He also vows that he will henceforth set his faith, hope, and trust solely in God and regulate his life according to the divine Word, in the strength of Jesus Christ our Lord, and if he should fail to do so, he thereby promises the church that he would dutifully accept brotherly discipline from it and its members."⁷⁶ Baptism, the Lord's Supper, and the ban are key components to a proper church filled with genuine believers. Thus, Hubmaier held that incorporation into the community of a local church was a necessary component of a believer's sanctification.⁷⁷ Goncharenko asserts,

> The whole idea of discipleship became the overarching theme of the Anabaptist soteriology. What safeguarded one's growth in discipleship or salvation process, to state it in Hubmaier's terminology, was his ardent commitment to and faithful practice of church discipline. Having spent a lifetime entrenched in Catholic theology, it is no surprise to find Hubmaier's theological nomenclature very Catholic-sounding although his understanding progressed far beyond his mother church. This explains how his doctrine of church discipline replaced the Roman idea of sacraments as important to Hubmaier's soteriology, though without containing salvific elements.⁷⁸

As such, the ban was an essential component of Hubmaier's overall theology. His conception of this doctrine gave order to the functioning of the church, served as a warning of eschatological judgment, and was a means for church members to continually persevere in their faith as a community dedicated to purity in doctrine and life.

---

74. Hubmaier tied together the doctrines of the essence of the church, baptism, the Lord's Supper, and discipline in a way that sought to promote the expected, ongoing purity of the church, expressed by an individual at baptism, reaffirmed at the Supper—which served as a reminder of believers' baptismal vows—in conjunction with a believer's church, and maintained by the practice of discipline for the sake of a persevering faith. See Goncharenko, "Importance of Church Discipline," 149–52.

75. Hubmaier, "On the Christian Ban," 410.

76. Hubmaier, "Christian Catechism," 350–51.

77. Goncharenko, "Importance of Church Discipline," 97.

78. Ibid., 152–53.

JONATHAN EDWARDS

While Luther and Hubmaier ministered as contemporaries, arguing against the Roman Catholic Church in relation to penance, the keys, and the authority to practice discipline, Jonathan Edwards served in an American context two centuries later.[79] Piety in early American religious life was a preeminent concern and shaped the policies and practices of early colonial life. As Bezzant notes, "The Puritan experiment in the New World was more than a Calvinist adventure in pure doctrine. At heart, it was founded on a pious vision for pure worship, which was constrained by pure congregational life."[80] In order to maintain and preserve this kind of holy living, observance of a rigorous ecclesiastical discipline was consistently maintained. While the practice of church discipline contains both high and low points in American life, one era of special interest to examine in tracing its application and effectiveness is the Great Awakening, particularly in the ministry and context of Jonathan Edwards.[81]

Edwards, the renowned theologian and pastor of Northampton, has received a great deal of scholarly attention, and deservedly so. Often referred to as America's greatest theologian, Edwards's contributions to metaphysics, soteriology, revivalism, the Trinity, and a host of other topics, make him a figure worthy of study. However, as Sweeney observes, "Despite his lifelong labors in pastoral ministry, Edwards's doctrine of the church has gone largely unnoticed by scholars."[82] While work has been done in this area since Sweeney's publication,[83] more specific investigations are merited, particularly in the area of church discipline. Edwards's context was somewhat unique, particularly as he found himself within a time of revival, handling matters of discipline from within that context. One can observe that Edwards's practice of church discipline was quite exacting and rigorous in relation to much of his historical context, within which church discipline was largely on the decline. This keen application of discipline is so largely

---

79. Though Edwards comes after many of these disputes, he no doubt agreed that doctrines such as penance and papal authority were to be renounced. See, e.g., Edwards, *Apocalyptic Writings*, 192–93; Edwards, "Glorious Grace," in *Works*, 10:394.

80. Bezzant, "Orderly But Not Ordinary," 1.

81. For examples of more thorough studies of church discipline in early American life, see Cooper, *Tenacious of Their Liberties*; Wills, *Democratic Religion*.

82. Sweeney, "Church," 167.

83. See, e.g., Bezzant, "Orderly But Not Ordinary"; Pauw, "Jonathan Edwards' Ecclesiology," 175–86; Sairsingh, "Jonathan Edwards and the Idea of Divine Glory."

due to his ecclesiological and soteriological beliefs, which became more pronounced in the midst of revival.[84]

Edwards's Historical Context

The early settlers of New England sought to exact a fairly strict practice of church discipline,[85] though, unlike Calvin's Geneva, there was typically a separation of church and state in the enacting of disciplinary measures.[86] Most churches in Massachusetts Bay followed similar standards for censuring their members in the seventeenth and early eighteenth centuries. In 1644, John Cotton explained that church discipline represented the "key of order." Such a key "is the power whereby every member of the Church walketh orderly himself . . . and helpeth his brethren to walk orderly also." In 1648, Puritan minister Thomas Hooker explained the necessity of church discipline: "[God] hath appointed Church-censures as good Physick, to purge out what is evil, as well as Word and Sacraments, which, like good diet, are sufficient to nourish the soul to eternal life." Hooker explained that church members must watch over one another, "each particular brother (appointed) as a skillful Apothecary, to help forward the spiritual health of all in confederacy with him." Disciplinary practices helped to ensure that the Puritans stayed on their godly paths.[87]

Throughout the first three generations in New England, Puritans consistently emphasized discipline. However, churches could only discipline full members. During the founding years of the colonies this posed no problems, "as most everyone who made the journey across the Atlantic became members. However, as full membership declined during the second generation, congregations had to confront the growing number of residents who fell outside the power of church discipline."[88] This was a distinct dilemma,

---

84. The length of this section is noticeably longer than that devoted to the previous two figures. This is so due to the lack of substantive treatment of Edwards's doctrine of the church, particularly his view of ecclesial discipline.

85. For general discussion of church discipline and deviance leading up to and in colonial New England, see Bozeman, *Precisianist Strain*; Erikson, *Wayward Puritans*.

86. This is generally true, though for a time in 1638 the Massachusetts General Court was encouraged to order fines, imprisonment, banishment, or further for whoever stood under excommunication for more than six months without seeking restoration. This lasted only a brief time as pastors, such as John Cotton, asserted that connecting civil power to the church would only bring corruption. See Hall, *Faithful Shepherd*, 133–36.

87. This section was derived from Fitzgerald, "Drunkards, Fornicators," 41–42.

88. Ibid., 45.

since in the first generation a document in Massachusetts had been ratified (1646-1648), known as the *Cambridge Platform of Church Discipline*. Led by John Cotton, local churches adopted this treatise as a sort of ecclesiastical constitution. Regarding discipline, this document asserted,

> The censures of the church are appointed by Christ for the preventing, removing, and healing of offenses in the church; for the reclaiming and gaining of offending brethren; for the deterring others from the like offences; for purging out the leaven which may infect the whole lump; for vindicating the honor of Christ, and of his Church, and the whole profession of the gospel; and for preventing the wrath of God.[89]

Thus, according to the *Cambridge Platform*, ministerial responsibilities included the examination of candidates for membership, the reception of "accusations brought to the Church," the preparation of disciplinary cases, and the pronouncement of "sentence with the consent of the Church."[90]

First and second generation Puritan ministers emphasized the importance of church discipline for maintaining a holy community. If the church did not recover or "purge out" the sinner, he could "infect" the whole community, whence God could send his wrath down on the town in judgment. Fitzgerald notes, "Maintaining social order was critical for a godly community, and ministers argued that every Puritan had a responsibility for personal piety and public duty."[91] Thus, church discipline was not the sole domain of pastors. Every stage of the disciplinary process depended heavily upon lay participation. Disciplinary measures in churches revolved around a system of lay "collective watchfulness," where members of the congregation agreed to oversee the moral behavior of fellow congregants,

---

89. *Cambridge and Saybrook Platforms of Church Discipline, with the Confession of Faith of the New England Churches, Adopted in 1680*, 54-55. For helpful background on the Cambridge Platform, see Hall, *Faithful Shepherd*, 93-120.

90. See Cooper, *Tenacious of Their Liberties*, 25. Fitzgerald notes, "Congregations censured men and women for a wide variety of sinful behaviors. This included: dishonoring the Sabbath, child or spousal abuse, lack of deference, immodesty, absence from church, stealing, false witness, cursing, contempt for church, idleness, witchcraft, entertaining sin, lying, fornication, and drunkenness. Censure represented the only judgment or punishment Puritans could instigate against one another within the church; they could not fine, jail or execute a sinner. An accused sinner could be found innocent, forgiven, admonished, suspended from the Lord's Supper, or excommunicated. An admonishment, suspension, or excommunication would hang over the sinner until the congregation determined that the sinner had adequately confessed and repented." Fitzgerald, "Drunkards, Fornicators," 46-47.

91. Fitzgerald, "Drunkards, Fornicators," 46.

resulting in the enactment of discipline if necessary.[92] Failure to exercise "watch" over a fellow churchgoer "represented breach of covenant—itself a grave, punishable violation—with the wayward sheep, whose soul stood in danger, and with the church, which stood to suffer corruption should sin seep in undetected and remain unpunished."[93] This procedure, followed by the lay people, was an application of their understanding of Matthew 18:15–20.

However, as previously stated, by the end of the seventeenth century a gradual decline in the practice of church discipline was evident.[94] Cooper maintains, "Many churches exercised church discipline only in the most obvious of cases in the 1720s and 1730s, a development that in part reflected a decline in commitment to mutual watch."[95] Part of this decline in rigorous discipline may be attributed to the adoption of the Halfway Covenant by a number of New England congregations, particularly Solomon Stoddard, Edwards's grandfather. This covenant allowed the children of full members who had not experienced conversion to enjoy partial church membership.[96] Under this covenant all halfway members assumed the benefits and responsibilities of mutual watchfulness incumbent upon those engaged in church covenant, but did not enjoy the privileges of voting or participation in the Lord's Supper—though Stoddard later retracted this restriction and allowed halfway members to participate in communion as a "converting ordinance"—until they experienced conversion and became full members. "Hailed as a perfect compromise, the measure thus brought the children

---

92. See Cooper, *Tenacious of Their Liberties*, 127, who notes, "Just as concern for the offender's soul outweighed a desire for punishment in disciplinary decisions, so the maintenance of church purity still superseded the members' heightened concern with individual privacy or 'reputation.' Church discipline maintained its unique status as the only institution that in public assembly probed into the most personal details of a member's life."

93. Ibid., 36. See also Walzer, *Revolution of the Saints*, 221.

94. So Bezzant, who states, "From the end of the seventeenth century, the practice of excommunication was severely challenged. The establishment of the Dominion of New England after 1684 with more intrusive royal control, and the pursuant royal charter of 1691 guaranteeing religious toleration to all Protestants, were signs of seismic shifts in New England polity." Bezzant, "Ordered Ecclesiastical Life," 2. However, Holifield does note that between 1690 and 1729, one hundred and fifty-nine ecclesiastical trials are recorded among seven congregations. See Holifield, "Peace, Conflict, and Ritual," 568. Thus, one must seemingly look at this matter geographically, and, for our purposes, it is important to note that the church in Northampton under Solomon Stoddard saw a dramatic decrease in the number of disciplinary cases in his later ministry. See Oberholzer, *Delinquent Saints*, 261–62.

95. Cooper, *Tenacious of Their Liberties*, 195.

96. For a thorough study of the Halfway Covenant, see Pope, *Half-Way Covenant*.

into the covenant and under the disciplinary 'watch' of the church without corrupting church purity."[97] Mutual watchfulness, however, began to become less important and thus, while not universal, the practice of discipline came into decline at least partially due to increased laxity in ecclesiology. It is important to keep this background in mind as one considers the views and practice of church discipline as seen in the ministry of Edwards.

Edwards's Ecclesiology

Before looking specifically at Edwards's view of church discipline, it is crucial that one understand his ecclesiology, which more broadly explicates the foundation of his viewpoint. For Edwards it is important to note that his ecclesiology is rooted in his doctrine of God.[98] For example, Edwards asserts,

> The Father appoints and provides the Redeemer, and himself accepts the price and grants the thing purchased; the Son is the Redeemer by offering up himself, and is the price; and the Holy Ghost immediately communicates to us the thing purchased by communicating himself, and he is the thing purchased. The sum of all that Christ purchased for man was the Holy Ghost.... What Christ purchased for us, was that we have communion with God in his good, which consists in partaking of the Holy Ghost, as we have shown. All the blessedness of the redeemed consists in their partaking of Christ's fullness, which consists in partaking of that Spirit which is given not by measure unto him. The oil that is poured on the head of the church runs down to the members of his body and to the skirts of his garment (*Psalms 133:2*). Christ purchased for us that we should have the favor of God and might enjoy his love; but this love is the Holy Ghost. Christ purchased for us true spiritual excellency, grace and holiness, the sum of which is love to God, which is but only the indwelling of the Holy Ghost in the heart. Christ purchased for us spiritual joy and comfort, which is in a participation of God's joy and happiness; which joy and happiness is the Holy Ghost, as we have shown.[99]

---

97. Cooper, *Tenacious of Their Liberties*, 91.

98. See Bezzant, "Orderly but Not Ordinary," 59, who affirms, "The work of Father, Son and Spirit provides the grammar within which Edwards's doctrine of the church can be viewed."

99. Edwards, "Discourse on the Trinity," in *Works*, 21:136.

The very essence of the church is seen through the work of the Trinitarian God. Bezzant elaborates, "Edwards's conflation of the themes of the immanent and the economic Trinity, which becomes a 'hallmark of Edwards's theology,' serves our understanding of his ecclesiology well. His dynamic and ordered conception of Trinitarian relations has its echo in the dynamic yet ordered life of the church in the world."[100] Schafer likewise asserts that any effort to understand Edwards's doctrine of the church as a part of his system of thought must begin with the question, "Why did God create the world?"[101]

Edwards answers this question briefly in the following way: "That which more especially was God's end in his eternal purpose of creating the world, and of the sum of his purposes with respect to creatures, was to procure a spouse, or a mystical body, for his Son."[102] One may note, particularly from Edwards's essay *The End for Which God Created the World*, that the triune God created the universe ultimately for the emanation of his own glory, and Edwards would argue that this is also for the good of the creature.[103] The church is the point in the created realm wherein the glory of God became prominently visible.[104] In this way, Edwards links his ecclesiology with his understanding of the Trinitarian God.

In defining the essence of the church, early in his career Edwards described the church more generically as "the body of Christ, [the] mystical body of Christ."[105] However, in May 1741, at the height of the Great Awakening, Sweeney notes that Edwards began to define the church more specifically. He asserted that "the church of Christ is the whole society of true saints," and further, in April 1744, he maintained that the church "is that company of men that is by the grace of God effectually called out from this fallen, undone [world] and gathered together in one in Christ Jesus, through him to worship God and have the peculiar enjoyment of him."[106] Therefore,

---

100. Ibid., 65.

101. Schafer, "Jonathan Edwards' Conception of the Church," 52–53.

102. Edwards, *"Miscellanies,"* vol. 23 of *Works*, 178 (no. 1245).

103. Sweeney notes, "Basic to Edwards' understanding of the nature of the church was his belief that God has 'elected' the church *in Christ* for God's own glory." Sweeney, "Church," 169 (emphasis original). See also Schafer, "Jonathan Edwards' Conception of the Church," 54.

104. See McClymond and McDermott, *Theology of Jonathan Edwards*, 452–53.

105. Edwards, "Living to Christ and Dying to Gain," in *Works*, 10:566. See also Edwards, *"Miscellanies,"* vol. 18 of *Works*, 336 (no. 710), wherein he says, "The church is Christ mystical."

106. Sweeney, "Church," 168–69. Sweeney is citing here from unpublished sermons on Rev 22:16–17 and Col 1:24, respectively.

the church, according to Edwards, includes within its (true) membership only those who are born again, who have died to their old ways and risen with Christ through faith to a new pattern of life.

Stoddard and Edwards, thus, had their differences when it came to a proper ecclesiology. Stoddard maintained that whether someone had experienced a saving work of the Holy Spirit was not necessarily discernable by others. Because the saving work of the Holy Spirit could be undetectable, Stoddard taught that persons who agreed with the doctrines of Christianity and were moral in their conduct could be part of the church and partake of communion, whether they professed such a saving work or not.[107] Edwards, however, believed only true believers were part of the church, and as such only they should partake of the Lord's Supper. He states,

> In order to men's being regularly outward members of the Christian Church, they should be visible Christians, or visibly Christians. Now by being visibly Christians nothing else can be understood but being in appearance Christians, appearing really Christians, true Christians. When we say "true Christians in appearance," it can't be understood that it is meant that he should appear so to a prejudiced, and weak, and unfair uncharitable judgment. . . . Nor . . . that he should appear so in the eye of every particular man. . . . Therefore to be a visible Christian is to appear to be a real Christian in the eye of a public Christian judgment and to have a right in Christian reason and according to Christian rules to be received and treated as such.[108]

Edwards called for a regenerate church membership, particularly when it came to partaking of the Lord's Supper. Strange concludes, "Thus Edwards ultimately disagreed with his grandfather that a profession of a true saving work of the Holy Spirit was unnecessary in coming to the Lord's Table,

---

107. Stoddard, *Doctrine of Instituted Churches*, 18–22.

108. Edwards, "*Miscellanies*," vol. 13 of *Works*, 412 (no. 335). See also ibid., 415 (no. 339), wherein Edwards similarly asserts, "There is abundance of talk in the world about 'the Church' and 'the true Church'; but it is a very difficult thing to me to know what they mean by it. By the Church, in Scripture, is certainly meant nothing else but God's people or Christ's people, either really, or at least externally and in appearance. . . . I can therefore think of no other sensible meaning of the phrase 'true Church' or 'truly God's Church,' than either those that are truly and really God's people and Christ's people, or those that truly have those outward appearances of being God's people, that they are so in the eye of a Christian judgment and, according to gospel rules, are to be looked upon, respected, and behaved towards as such. And, by a particular true church, must be meant a society of men that are visibly God's people, or so, really, in the eye of Christian judgment, and that are indeed joined together in the Christian holy public worship."

teaching instead that those who come to the Lord's Table ought to do so professing to have experienced such a saving work."[109]

In this sense Edwards did not call for an arduous process whereby the potential communicant is subjected to congregational questioning and the articulation of a conversion that followed a particular pattern; neither was he willing to allow "halfway members" the same rights and privileges as that of true saints.[110] Bezzant contends that, by preserving its strengths and adapting its expression, Edwards "repristinates an ossified New England ecclesiology."[111] Bezzant is arguing that while Edwards was indeed "not ordinary" in that he emphasized individual affections and immediate conversion, he was nonetheless "orderly" in his conception of the church as God's ordained instrument for carrying the gospel to the world. Rather than return to an outdated Old Church model, Edwards brought the old and the new together into a synthesis that addressed the concerns of his day.[112] Thus, it is crucial to note in Edwards's ecclesiology, specifically relating to church discipline, an emphatic strand of belief in regenerate church membership that is derived from his views of God and the make-up of the church.

Edwards's View of Discipline

Though not the most thoroughly treated area by Edwards, "It cannot be maintained that Edwards was prompted to form his mind on the value of excommunication after the failures of later awakenings."[113] In November 1722, Edwards asserts regarding excommunication, "So excellently is this sort of punishment contrived that when it is just it is exceedingly to be dreaded as a punishment from heaven." He continues, "And thus it is that whosoever sins are justly retained, are retained in heaven. . . . What man doth is only for himself, to keep himself free from sin; but the punishment is Christ's, who is the sole head of the church."[114] In October 1730, Edwards states, "They

---

109. Strange, "Jonathan Edwards on Visible Sainthood," 98.

110. This trajectory of ecclesiological views in early America is described well in ibid., particularly 100–106.

111. Bezzant, "Orderly but Not Ordinary," iii.

112. Elsewhere he states, "Edwards does not merely re-impose seventeenth century assumptions on congregational life in the eighteenth century, but importantly refashions ecclesiology in New England in his own day. His ecclesiology was generated by superimposing revivalist conditions and social aspirations onto Reformed convictions (sometimes with the revivalist strand eclipsing his patrimony), making it innovatively evangelical rather than generically Protestant." Ibid., 210.

113. Bezzant, "Ordered Ecclesiastical Life," 3.

114. Edwards, *"Miscellanies,"* vol. 13 of *Works*, 172 (no. q). Specific dates for these

that are regularly and justly excommunicated, they are bound in heaven; the wrath of God abides upon them."[115] Edwards goes on to assert that one can be restored, and that a church can even be mistaken in a disciplinary case, but the church has the authority of Christ to rule in such matters according to Matthew 16:19.[116] In 1733, Edwards speaks regarding discipline in a treatise concerning the visible church. Here again Edwards takes up Matthew 16:19 to demonstrate that what is bound and loosed in the church is also done in heaven, and when a church member is excommunicated, "they are cast out of God and are treated by him as those that have proved treacherous and unfaithful to him."[117]

This final remark is a very strong statement on Edwards's part, but interestingly he ties in this understanding of excommunication with the perseverance of the saints. He asserts, based on Ezekiel 3:20, that people can have the appearance of righteousness but may at a later time fall away from the faith. This is not a loss of salvation, but a revelation of who these kinds of people really were all along.[118] Thus, discipline, as we will see in his later remarks, may root out those who are not true believers, but its ultimate intention is to bring them to repentance, restoration, and ultimately perseverance in their faith.

Another major source that allows us to better understand Edwards's view of discipline is found in a sermon entitled "The Means and Ends of Excommunication."[119] This sermon, preached on July 22, 1739, is based on 1 Corinthians 5 and 2 Thessalonians 3:6. Based on these texts, Edwards asserts that a church is called to cleanse out the old leaven, which refers to "visible wicked men."[120] As such, excommunication consists of "being cast off from the enjoyment of the privileges of God's visible people."[121] This includes exclusion from four key privileges: "first, from the charity of the church; second, brotherly society; third, fellowship of the church in worship; fourth, internal privileges of visible Christians."[122] Edwards explicates these four points throughout much of the sermon.

---

three Miscellanies come from Schafer, "Editor's Introduction," *WJE*, 13:92, 107; Chamberlain, "Editor's Introduction," *WJE*, 18:45.

115. Edwards, *"Miscellanies,"* vol. 13 of *Works*, 528 (no. 485).

116. See ibid.

117. Edwards, *"Miscellanies,"* vol. 18 of *Works*, 259–60 (no. 689).

118. See ibid., 260–61 (no. 689).

119. The disciplinary issue addressed in this sermon will be analyzed in the next section; at this point we are looking solely at Edwards's understanding of the doctrine.

120. Edwards, "Means and Ends of Excommunication, " in *Works*, 22:69.

121. Ibid., 70.

122. Ibid., 71. This severity is somewhat tempered in that Edwards believed,

First, those who suffer excommunication are barred from the charity of the church. Edwards maintains that the church can no longer "look upon them as saints or worshippers of God," accordingly excommunicants are cut off from the benevolence and good will of the church.[123] This would have been a distinct punishment to those in need of monetary support coming from the church, but Edwards admonishes the congregation to not deprive these people of love, in hopes they will repent.

Second, those under excommunication are removed from brotherly society. Edwards states, "God's people are not only to avoid society with visibly wicked men in sacred things, but, as much as may be, avoid them and withdraw from them as to that common society which is proper towards Christians." More specifically Edwards asserts, "And particularly we are forbidden such a degree of society with them, or appearance of associating ourselves with them, as there is [in] making them our guests at our tables or being their guests at their tables; as is manifest in the text, where we are commanded to have no company with such, no not to eat."[124] Thus, we see a rigorous application of this text by Edwards, which carried into societal relationships.

Third, those under excommunication lose fellowship with the church. Edwards gives particulars regarding what this lost privilege entails, and claims that those under discipline can have no fellowship with the church in baptism, the Lord's Supper, prayers, or singing God's praises.[125] While

---

"excommunication is used for that end [of ultimate restoration], that we may thereby obtain their good." See ibid., 22:74.

123. Ibid., 72.

124. Ibid., 73. This is consistent with a note Edwards makes regarding 1 Cor 5:11 within his Blank Bible. He maintains, "The Apostle doubtless means not only eating at the Lord's Table, but at any table, by the manner of expression, 'No not to eat,' or 'No not so much as to eat.' The Apostle would not express himself so of eating at the Lord's Table, which is the highest act of communion; but he evidently speaks of some lower act. And that 'tis a common eating will further appear, if we consider that it was the manner of the Jews at that time to abstain from eating with those that they looked upon as unclean. Therefore they would not eat with the Gentiles, as Galatians 2:12. And so they would not eat with publicans and sinners. Hence they found so much fault with Christ for eating with them (Matthew 9:11 and Mark 2:16). But Christ commands that excommunicated persons should be unto us 'as an heathen man and a publican' [Matt 18:17]." See Edwards, *"Blank Bible,"* in *Works*, 24:1041.

125. Edwards, "Means and Ends of Excommunication," in *Works*, 22:76. Interestingly, while this section of the sermon appears to rule out every aspect of public worship from those under excommunication, in a later sermon Edwards allows for the preaching aspect of the service to be heard by such people. He asserts, "There are many who are qualified for some duties of worship, and may be allowed, and are by no means to be forbidden to attend 'em, who yet are not qualified for some others, nor by any means to be admitted to 'em. As everybody grants, the unbaptized, the

an excommunicant cannot join in public worship, Edwards does exhort members of the church to commit the person to prayer and so include him in this way in hopes that the individual will eventually be restored. Finally, Edwards maintains that those who are excommunicated are removed from the internal privileges of visible Christians. He argues that such people are cast out of God's sight, much as Cain was, and thus they are not "in the way of those smiles of providence" as the visible church is.[126]

Edwards then deals briefly with 1 Corinthians 5:5, which speaks of handing one over to Satan. He asserts that it is reasonable to suppose that God is willing to make the devil the instrument of "those peculiar severe chastisements that their apostasy deserves." Those under excommunication deserve more severe chastisement than the unsaved, according to Edwards, and thus are delivered to Satan for the destruction of the flesh, "so we may well suppose either that God is wont to let Satan loose, sorely to molest them outwardly or inwardly, so by severe means to destroy the flesh and humble them." He maintains that God can use this time to bring the sinner back in repentance or to further harden them, "yet whether it shall prove the destruction of the flesh and the eternal and more dreadful destruction of them, is at God's sovereign disposal."[127] While the church declares "ministerially" the binding and loosing of all such persons, God is ultimately sovereign over the matter.

Edwards concludes this sermon noting three particular aims involved in the practice of church discipline.

> *First.* That the church may be kept pure and God's ordinances not defiled. This end is mentioned in the context: that the other members themselves may not be defiled. 'Tis necessary that they thus bear a testimony against sin.
>
> *Second.* That others may be deterred from wickedness. That others may fear.
>
> *Third.* That they may be reclaimed, [that their] souls may be saved. [After] other, more gentle, means have been used in vain,

---

excommunicated, heretics, scandalous livers, etc. may be admitted to hear the Word preached; nevertheless they are not to be allowed to come to the Lord's Supper. Even excommunicated persons remain still under the law of the Sabbath, and are not to be forbidden to observe the Lord's day." Edwards, *Ecclesiastical Writings*, vol. 12 of *Works*, 299–300. It is possible that Edwards's view on such matters changed over time, but he was always consistent with fencing the Table.

126. Edwards, "Means and Ends of Excommunication," in *Works*, 22:76–77.

127. Ibid., 78. Edwards similarly states, "It is at God's sovereign disposal whether it [the process of excommunication] shall be for a person's humbling or their dreadful and eternal destruction, as it always is one or the other." Ibid., 70.

then we are to use severe means to bring 'em to conviction and shame and humiliation, by being rejected and avoided by the church, treated with disrespect, disowned by God, delivered to Satan, his being made the instrument of chastising them.

This is the last means, with concomitant admonitions, that the church is to use for the reclaiming those members of the church that become visibly wicked; which, if it be'nt effectual, what is next to be expected is destruction without remedy.[128]

Thus, Edwards has the good of the church and of the one under discipline in mind when he considers and practices excommunication. He notes the themes of purity, warning, and reclamation of the erring individual. Bezzant notes that one of the most intriguing themes in this sermon is "how much attention Edwards gives to the ethics of love, and how much he expects of his congregation in terms of their own nuanced appreciation of love as expressed in interactions with those being disciplined outside of church."[129] Edwards's hope in this difficult practice of church discipline is that sinners would be turned from the error of their ways while under judgment and repent, and that others may be deterred from sin and persevere in their faith.

Edwards's Practice of Discipline

While Edwards's views regarding church discipline are not necessarily innovative, it is of interest to note how he applied this doctrine in actual church cases, particularly in relation to the time of the Awakening. There are in fact no disciplinary cases noted in Edwards's early ministry, though this certainly changes in the 1740s as a number of members fall under disciplinary measures. Sweeney concludes that it is no coincidence that Edwards worked hardest to align Northampton's polity with his doctrine of the church beginning in the 1740s, the height of the Awakening. By the dawn of the decade he feared many in his own congregation were hypocrites, and that number only expanded in the heat of the revivals. Thus, discipline began to play a

---

128. Ibid., 78–79.

129. Bezzant, "Ordered Ecclesiastical Life," 7. See also Rivera, who observes, "Given the sometimes severe Puritan excesses in this regard, Edwards must be recognized as comparatively restrained in the official exercise of church discipline, in that we only have extant only one excommunication sermon. This was the first excommunication to take place at Northampton in 28 years, dating back to the ministry of Edwards' grandfather, Solomon Stoddard." Rivera, *Jonathan Edwards on Worship*, 64–65.

more pronounced role in Edwards's pastoral ministry around the time of the Awakening in 1740-42.[130]

At this point in his ministry, Edwards was engaging in discipline not only at a corrective level, but also in a formative sense. Rivera observes that with virtually every sermon, Edwards was about the work of church and community discipline, as he writes, "One could not sit in the pews when Edwards preached, over the course of any sustained period, and avoid 'discipline' on not merely external matters such as Mrs. Bridgman's drunkenness, but respecting such inward matters as hypocrisy, greed, lust, and supremely the hardness of an unconverted heart."[131] Thus, as Edwards practiced church discipline in a consistent manner throughout this time, it should not have come as a shock to his church who heard him continually preach in a "disciplinary" manner.

In relation to actual disciplinary cases, the first known occurrence is in 1738 as Edwards's attention is drawn to a Mrs. Bridgman, whose continued drunkenness was known to the community. In July Edwards preached a sermon of censure from Deuteronomy 29:18-21 dealing with the nature of hypocrisy. In this sermon Edwards asserts, "That those that go on in the sin of drunkenness under the light of God's word are in the way to bring God's fearful wrath and a most amazing destruction upon themselves."[132] Edwards actually calls Mrs. Bridgman to "stand forth and distinguish herself" during this sermon, as he notes all the means of grace that have been available to her in the church as well as the fact that she had been admonished both in private and in public. Edwards warns her "in the name of Jesus Christ the great head of the church and judge of the quick and dead and in his presence and in the presence of the holy angels . . . to forsake this wicked practice and to be thorough and final in your reformation." If she will not comply, Edwards declares, "I do now this day in the name of God solemnly denounce unto you that God will not spare you."[133]

Due to an apparent lack of repentance on Bridgman's part, Edwards is compelled to preach a follow-up sermon on July 22, 1739, entitled "The Means and Ends of Excommunication," which outlines his justification to proceed with the first excommunication in Northampton since 1711.

---

130. See Sweeney, "Church," 187.

131. Rivera, *Jonathan Edwards on Worship*, 66. Examples of such sermons can be found in Tracy, *Jonathan Edwards*, 130-34.

132. Edwards, "Sermon on Deut. 29:18-21 (July 1738)," 53:482, available through the Jonathan Edwards Center at Yale University, online: edwards.yale.edu. One can clearly note the themes of warning and potential divine judgment in relation to church discipline, as has been advocated in this work.

133. See ibid.

Though not named, the target of his exposition is once again Mrs. Bridgman.[134] Stout refers to this incident with Mrs. Bridgman as "the first in a spate of excommunications that occurred at Northampton during the Great Awakening."[135]

In June 1740, Edwards led in the founding of a local committee to consider matters of difficulty that would arise in the church, which, in effect, was an institutionalization of his concern to promote the purity of the church.[136] Edwards became increasingly concerned with church "order" in Northampton, as socially inappropriate behavior and speech mushroomed during the Great Awakening.[137] The following month he publicly shamed another parishioner, Hannah Pomeroy, for breaking the ninth commandment in reproaching her neighbor. In August 1741, he excommunicated Pomeroy due to the fact that she would not repent. In 1742, Edwards persuaded his congregation to renew its corporate covenant, pledging again to "seek and serve God" by practicing Christian charity.[138]

In February 1743, he acted as a consultant in the rebuke of Bathsheba Kingsley, an itinerant minister from Westfield who claimed immediate revelations and subsequently neglected her wifely duties in the pursuit of a preaching ministry.[139] Kingsley was ultimately admonished to fulfill her duties in the home instead of

> Almost perpetually wandering about from house to house and very frequently to other towns under the notion of doing Christ's

---

134. Ibid. See also Bezzant, "Ordered Ecclesiastical Life," 4.

135. *Stout, introduction* to "Means and Ends of Excommunication," in *Works of Jonathan Edwards*, 22:66.

136. Much of the following summary of Edwards's disciplinary cases is derived from Sweeney, "Church," 187–88. Sweeney derives some of this information about disciplinary cases from several works not currently published. These include the following: "Records of the First Church of Christ," Northampton, book 1, 25, Forbes Library, Northampton Massachusetts; "Copy of a Covenant, enter'd into and Subscribed, by the People of God at Northampton . . . on a Day of Fasting and Prayer for the gracious Presence of God in that Place. March 16, 1741, 2," Edwards Collection, Andover–Newton Theological School; "Some Reasons briefly hinted at, why Those Rules Exod. 22:16 & Deut. 22:28–29, relating to the Obligation of a man to marry a virgin that He had humbled, ought to be esteemed, as to the substance of them, as moral & of perpetual Obligation; with Hints of Answer to Objections," Edwards Collection, Andover–Newton Theological School (on the Hawley/Root fornication case of 1747/48).

137. See Stout, introduction to "Means and Ends of Excommunication," in *Works of Jonathan Edwards*, 22:66.

138. For further commentary on this process of renewing the covenant, see Tracy, *Jonathan Edwards*, 150–54.

139. See Edwards, "Advice to Mr. and Mrs. Kingsley, February 17, 1743," vol. 39 at edwards.yale.edu.

work and delivering his messages . . . often disobeying her husbands commands in going abroad . . . and taking her husband's horse to go to other towns contrary to his mind. . . . Mrs. Kingsley has of late almost wholly cast off that modest, shamefacedness and sobriety, and meekness, diligence and submission that becomes a Christian woman in her place.[140]

Her husband was also reproved and encouraged to take better care of his wife, given the reference to her emotional frailty encoded in the description of her "weak vapory habit of body" and her "continual tumult like the sea in a storm being destitute of that peace and rest in God that other Christians enjoy."[141]

In June 1743, Edwards excommunicated another parishioner, Samuel Danks, for fornication and contempt of the authority of the church.[142] Although little is known of this case, it appears that Danks would not submit to the church's discipline in relation to his sexual conduct and, as such, came under excommunication.

The most infamous of Edwards's church discipline cases came in 1744 with the "Bad Book Affair."[143] The case was one of the reasons Edwards's Northampton pastorate came to an end. A number of young men in Edwards's congregation (ages 21–29) had been passing around a midwifery manual and subsequently using its contents to taunt young women of the congregation. According to testimony, such behavior had been occurring for as long as five years.

When Edwards learned of this lascivious behavior, he brought the matter before the church. In March, Edwards preached a sermon on Hebrews 12:15–16 as a way of introducing the scandal to the church. At a meeting after the service, he laid the situation before the members and obtained permission to investigate the matter. A committee, consisting of some of the most prestigious men in town, was appointed to conduct the inquiry. After a subsequent Sunday service, he read a list of names of certain youth

---

140. Ibid.

141. Ibid. Interestingly, Edwards maintains that Kingsley's itinerant prophesies and mystical revelations are to be channeled but not stifled, although Edwards will sternly rebuke Moses Lyman for a similar expression of charismatic license shortly after this. So Bezzant, "Ordered Ecclesiastical Life," 5.

142. Northampton Church Records, Book 1, 25. This source was found in Stout, introduction to "Means and Ends of Excommunication," in *Works of Jonathan Edwards*, 22:66n7.

143. This summary is derived mainly from Marsden, *Jonathan Edwards*, 292–302; Chamberlain, "Bad Books and Bad Boys," 61–81. See also Edwards, "Documents Relating to the 'Bad Book' Case," vol. 39 at edwards.yale.edu.

who were to report to his house for a time of investigation.[144] In a tactical error, Edwards did not distinguish between the witnesses and the offenders, and, as such, cast a shadow of suspicion on the innocent, raising the ire of several prominent families. The town was in an uproar, and Edwards sought to defend his actions by noting that this was a public offense and it was his duty as pastor to see to it that order and purity were maintained. The case, in his mind, was one of scandal, and it needed to be dealt with. Edwards connected this incident with his continued struggle over "hypocrites" coming and partaking of the Lord's Supper. He was convinced that he could not offer the offenders the Lord's Supper in that they were living contrary to a life of godliness. Eventually the leaders of the group were compelled to offer public confessions,[145] but the damage to Edwards's pastorate was done.[146]

The final two cases of church discipline in Edwards's ministry in Northampton were issues of fornication dealt with from 1747 to 1749. First, Edwards was involved in the excommunication of Thomas Wait for fornication and denial of paternity in February 1747. Not only did Wait refuse to confess his sin, he also publically denied fathering Jemimah Miller's child and maintained that Miller's word should not be accepted as true without corroboration. The church, however, sided with Miller, and thus Wait was excommunicated, though his appeal against the censure was accepted and later brought before a council.[147]

The second case involved Martha Root and Elisha Hawley, a young military officer and grandson of Solomon Stoddard.[148] Root claimed that Hawley was the father of her illegitimate child (the survivor of a set

---

144. "All but one of the boys on the list were church members, most having joined during the 1734-35 Connecticut Valley Awakening." Chamberlain, "Bad Books and Bad Boys," 63.

145. Chamberlain notes that when the committee met to interview the accused, the youth "compounded their offense by speaking contemptuously of the committee's members and playing childish games during its proceedings, thus bringing upon themselves the further charge of contempt of authority." Thus, as it relates to later confessions, Chamberlain maintains that of the three extant confessions, two address the charge of contempt of authority alone, and only one boy confessed to the original offense of "lascivious speech." See Chamberlain, "Bad Books and Bad Boys," 63.

146. Bezzant notes, "It also appears that Edwards's own frustration with the youth has colored his responses, those very young adults about whom he had written so glowingly just a few years earlier in the revivals when they had shown such spiritual promise." Bezzant, "Ordered Ecclesiastical Life," 6. He notes that several of these young men were converted and shepherded by him during the Awakening, and thus his disappointment and frustration was exacerbated by this event.

147. Edwards, "To the Reverend Robert Breck," in *Works*, 16:221-22.

148. Much of the summary of this case comes from Tracy, *Jonathan Edwards*, 164-66.

of twins). Hawley was part of one of Northampton's wealthiest and most prominent families. While the Hawley and Root families had settled the matter of Hawley impregnating Root privately (with a large sum of money and an agreement they would not marry),[149] soon after Edwards felt compelled to interfere and wrote a letter stating that the couple should be married. Hawley was to undergo excommunication if he did not confess his sin and determine to marry Root, and thus Hawley appealed his case to a council of ministers. The ministers of Hampshire, however, voted that it was not Elisha's duty to marry Martha and told Hawley that he was subject to his own conscience. He was told to confess his sin of fornication, which he seemingly did since his name is on later church records. This episode may have been more painful for Edwards, since the Hawley boys were converted under his tutelage and had shown such signs of promise during the Awakening but now sorely disappointed their pastor and mentor.

Sweeney avers, "In short, Edwards labored long and hard on the purity of the church, especially in the wake of the revivals. He preached quite often on matters of discipline."[150] Although Edwards may be viewed in contemporary terms as being rigid and mean-spirited, he sought to persuade people to repent of known public sin so that they might be restored. One example of this is the disciplinary course taken against the notorious itinerant James Davenport, in which Edwards played a major role, and eventually led to Davenport's recantation and eventual resettlement in the ministry.[151] Also, in a noteworthy letter to Elnathan Whitman, dated February 9, 1744, Edwards pled for liberty of conscience in order to reclaim straying parishioners. When some members of Whitman's church absented themselves from Sunday worship in order to hear New Light preachers, Edwards counseled patience and understanding rather than harsh measures more suited to "contumacious offenders."[152]

Yet, while noting his desire to persuade, it may be clearly seen that Edwards was unrelenting in his pursuit of a pure church, exacting a strict ecclesial discipline.[153] This is seen in the cases previously examined, as well

---

149. "Elisha's brother Joseph was a young attorney eager to make a reputation for himself, and with his assistance Elisha went to great lengths to avoid accepting any financial or moral responsibility for the child." Chamberlain, "Bad Books and Bad Boys," 74. Root, as a result of this action, brought a civil suit against Hawley and was given a monetary settlement of £155.

150. Sweeney, "Church," 184.

151. Claghorn, "Editor's Introduction," 16:11. See also Edwards, "Letter to the Reverend Eleazer Wheelock," in *Works*, 16:145–46.

152. See Edwards, "Letter to the Reverend Elnathan Whitman," in *Works*, 16:127–33.

153. Edwards's own practice of censuring women for drunkenness and men for

as his dealings in 1749 with the communion controversy at Northampton. Though not a disciplinary case *per se*, it is directly connected to the issue of discipline in that Edwards sought to maintain a boundary around the Lord's Table that would include true believers only in partaking of the elements. Those who fell under excommunication would be excluded from the Table.

In answer to a question regarding whether someone must express saving faith and repentance in order to be admitted to the Lord's Supper, Edwards answers in the affirmative.[154] Citing a Jonathan Mitchel—and others—in defense of this notion, he quotes Mitchel as saying that this laxity in obtaining a profession of faith from congregants coming to the Table "will not only lose the power of godliness, but in a little time bring in profaneness, and ruin the churches, these two ways. (1) Election of ministers will soon be carried by a formal looser sort. (2) The exercise of discipline will, by this means, be impossible. And discipline falling, profaneness riseth like a flood."[155] One can see from such a statement that Edwards's view of discipline and the Lord's Supper is shaped by a robust ecclesiology, consisting of regenerate membership. This view demonstrates why Edwards focused so vigorously on conversion, progressive sanctification, and perseverance in the faith.

Edwards's Discipline in Relation to his Soteriology

It seems clear from Edwards's discussion of excommunication thus far, that if a church acts in accord with truth, the person that comes under such discipline is seemingly shown to be an unbeliever and in need of repentance. Edwards also asserts that after one's conversion there is "much need of persons' care and diligence to persevere," and this communal aspect of caring for one another's spiritual growth is a "proper and decreed means of perseverance."[156] Elsewhere he avers,

> Universal and persevering obedience is as directly proposed to be sought and endeavored by us, in Scripture, as necessary to salvation [and] as the condition of our salvation, as faith in Jesus Christ; and a wicked man may properly be exhorted directly to strive to break off his sins and resist his temptations, and to bring himself to a thorough willingness, and fixed resolution

---

fornication was out of step with his own context. See Fitzgerald, "Drunkards, Fornicators," 66, 79.

154. Edwards, "Humble Inquiry," in *Works*, 12:338.
155. Ibid., 340.
156. Edwards, "Perseverance. Assurance.," in *Works*, 13:475.

and disposition of mind, utterly to have done with gratifying his lusts, or allowing himself in any way of sin; with that to enforce it, that if he doth, he shall have eternal life. And he would do prudently, and according to the direction of God's Word, in directly attempting of it and immediately setting about [it], in beginning to deny himself, and resolutely resisting the temptations as they come.[157]

While neither of these sections from Edwards mentions church discipline specifically, it is evident that he took the perseverance of the saints quite seriously. He believed the congregation was to be involved in the process of helping one another to persevere, and that the wicked must repent of their sins and endure in God-given obedience. Thus, there is an implicit kind of connection made between discipline and perseverance in Edwards.

Along these lines, Edwards comments that there were numbers in the NT churches who, after their admission into membership, fell into offensive behavior. The apostles gently exhorted some of these people, while others, that had behaved themselves in an overtly scandalous manner, were spoken of in explicit language to expose their wickedness. Edwards maintains, "The apostle Paul, in his epistles to the Corinthians, oftentimes speaks of some among them that had embraced heretical opinions, and had behaved themselves in a very disorderly and schismatical manner, whom he represents as exposed to censure, and to whom he threatens excommunication." He continues and notes, "Upon occasion of so many offenses of this kind appearing among them that for a while had been thought well of, he puts 'em all upon examining themselves, whether they were indeed in the faith, and whether Christ was truly in them, as they and others had supposed."[158] Again, we see a more explicit connection made by Edwards regarding conversion, excommunication, and perseverance.

In referring to excommunication as a punishment, as evidenced by 2 Corinthians 2:6, Edwards argues that even though discipline is not designed by men "for the destruction of the person that is the subject of it, but for his correction . . . yet 'tis in itself a great and dreadful calamity, and the most severe punishment that Christ has appointed in the visible church."[159] And even though the church is to seek only the good of the person under discipline and their recovery from sin, "there appearing upon proper trial no reason to hope for the person's recovery by gentle means," it is at God's sov-

---

157. Edwards, "Condition of Salvation, Universal and Persevering Obedience," in *Works*, 13:532–33.
158. Edwards, "Humble Inquiry," in *Works*, 12:237.
159. Edwards, "Means and Ends of Excommunication," in *Works*, 22:70.

ereign disposal whether it shall be "for a person's humbling or their dreadful and eternal destruction, as it always is one or the other."[160] Again, we see the connection of discipline and perseverance, and even see the doctrine of sanctification brought in as Edwards demonstrates that this discipline is exacted for their correction, good, and recovery from sin. These are interconnected ideas.

In contrast to those who have never been part of the church, Edwards believes, "The church is to have a greater concern for their [the excommunicated] welfare still than if they never had been brethren, and therefore ought to take more pains to reclaim them and to save them by admonishing them and otherwise than they are obliged to take towards those that have been always brethren." He continues,

> That consideration—that he has been a brother heretofore, and that we han't so finally cast him off from that relation, but that we are still hoping and using means that he may be such an one—obliges us to concern ourselves more for the good of their souls than of those that we never had any concern with, and so to pray more for them and take more pains with them by admonishing them.[161]

Edwards sees a significant role for the church in this process to work to reclaim this person, particularly since they have been a part of the church and were seemingly regenerate. In this discipline, the church must work for the good of the souls of the excommunicant, pray for them, and admonish them, all to the end that they would repent and, this time, persevere in their faith.

This understanding of conversion, discipline, sanctification, and perseverance—as well as who could partake of the Lord's Supper—is rooted in Edwards's understanding of "visible sainthood." Solomon Stoddard saw visible sainthood as distinct from real sainthood, whereas Edwards believed that visible sainthood should, as much as possible, approximate real sainthood. In other words, Stoddard reasoned that since we will never know in this life who the elect are, we should give all who say they believe in Christian doctrine and lead moral lives the benefit of the doubt and receive them as true believers. Edwards argued that we should receive as true believers only those who can credibly testify to the church's leaders that they know the Lord and are walking with him. Strange notes, "Stoddard's practice led to most of the town being admitted to communion. Edwards's position would have excluded more of the town than did Stoddard but not as many as were

---

160. See ibid.
161. Ibid., 74.

excluded under the old practice of requiring a narrative of grace that could withstand close congregational scrutiny."[162] Thus the evidence that Edward sought in ascertaining whether a real work of faith had occurred in a person was a verbal profession of having received the grace of God coupled with ongoing, outward godliness.[163]

When revival came to Northampton in 1735 and in 1740-42, during the Great Awakening, it never ceased to concern Edwards that many clergy and laypersons identified the presence of true revival with a person having had a moving religious experience and being able to relate the same loudly and at length to others. Edwards witnessed that many who claimed to have been religiously affected continued to lead lives that were manifestly lacking in love to God and neighbor. Incidents like the "bad book" affair, the reluctance of the congregation in regards to proper ministerial oversight in discipline, along with the abiding factional warfare among the residents of Northampton gave Edwards pause in this regard. He was convinced that if true religious affections were present in a person, then the same would manifest itself in "Christian practice."[164] He saw significant shortcomings in this regard, which caused him to require more evidence of visible sainthood than merely having participated in the revivals. Edwards wanted those who came to communion to be able not only to testify to the grace of God in their lives, but also in a way that made it clear that their claim of an inner saving work of God's Spirit demonstrated itself in outward godliness. Strange asserts, "Edwards wanted those coming to commune, in other words, to have good grounds for believing that they were truly regenerated and continually

---

162. Strange, "Jonathan Edwards on Visible Sainthood," 116-17. Later in this work Strange elaborates on this middle path Edwards seeks to take. He states, "We see then that Edwards, in attempting to understand assurance and define visible sainthood, sought to steer between the Scylla of Arminianism and the Charybdis of Antinomianism. For Edwards, Antinomianism, which he often called by the name 'Separatism,' was represented by those who insisted on immediate assurance, often associated with an insistence on something like a stylized narrative of grace—a position that played down outward godliness and emphasized the supposed experience of inner grace. By Arminianism, Edwards meant a kind of moralism whereby persons imagined that they might commend themselves to God.... One needs more than mere 'moral sincerity' to come to the Table, one needs a sincere and credible profession of having received the grace of God. This requirement avoided the error of the English separatists who required an outwardly moral life but no narrative of grace. It also avoided the error of those who made a stylized narrative of grace paramount. Edwards taught instead that true religious affections in the heart manifest themselves in a godly life." See ibid., 126.

163. Ibid., 122.

164. Ibid.

walking with the Lord. He wanted some assurance of salvation manifested on the part of those coming to communion."[165]

The ends to which Edwards disciplines—that the church may be kept pure, that others may be deterred from wickedness, and that the sinner might ultimately be reclaimed—revolve around Edwards's understanding of conversion, sanctification, and perseverance.[166] Edwards expects to be able to determine with a fair amount of clarity who has undergone regeneration and expects to see Christian growth and perseverance. For those who falter in an unrepentant manner, he believes that discipline must be maintained to promote correction and purity. This also explains why Edwards went to such great lengths—even to the point of losing his pastorate in Northampton—to protect the purity of the Lord's Supper, seeing to it that only visible Christians were partaking of the elements.[167] Discipline, for Edwards, was a crucial means by which he sought to judge whether someone was truly converted and persevering in their faith as should be expected of a Christian. As such, the function of discipline was crucial to Edwards's ministry in maintaining a regenerate church membership and calling for the perseverance of the faithful.

This understanding of discipline and soteriology held by Edwards is also consistent with his ecclesiology. Schafer notes the continuity of Edwards's ecclesiological vision in relation to the eschatological reality that is to come.

> This unity of the Church's life is manifested in its fellowship on earth, its destiny in heaven, and its triumph in history. Edwards' doctrines of excellence and virtue provide a foundation for the fellowship of the saints, both here and hereafter. . . . The destiny of the saints is a perfect, yet increasing, mutuality and communion with one another in love. . . . God's end in creation is realized inwardly in true virtue but outwardly in the "progress of the work of redemption." The Church, heavenly and earthly, is the kingdom of God.[168]

The church should be increasingly what it will be in God's consummated kingdom and what it already is in Christ. With this particular ecclesiological

---

165. Ibid., 122–23.

166. These ends of excommunication are found in Edwards, "Means and Ends of Excommunication," in *Works*, 22:78–79.

167. A number of works seek to analyze the reasons Edwards was voted out of his church in Northampton. For a helpful popular level explanation, see Dever, "How Jonathan Edwards Got Fired and Why It's Important for Us Today," in *God Entranced Vision*, ed. Piper and Taylor, 129–44.

168. Schafer, "Jonathan Edwards' Conception of the Church," 55–56.

vision, Edwards longed to see a people progressively conformed to the image of Christ. Discipline was a natural corollary of such a view, as Edwards labored to present a bride to Christ that was unblemished and without spot or wrinkle.

Early and late in his career, according to Hall, Edwards struggled to curb a temperamental impulse to judge and exclude others, an impulse he justified as essential to the life of the church and the work of the ministry. Perhaps because of the reactions this impulse provoked, he seems consistently to have imagined himself as surrounded by enemies and in ordination sermons of the mid-1740s likened ministers to Christ in their suffering. But he could also evoke the triumphant Christ and "promise final victory to those who 'maintained the exercise of discipline in the house of God.' In the *Farewell Sermon* he prophesied such a victory for himself at the day of judgment over the townspeople of Northampton."[169]

Such a conclusion seems to be more of a negative analysis than is necessary, though one can certainly understand the struggle to respond to Edwards's scenario in an overly gracious manner. Edwards may have struggled with an impulse to judge others, yet, while more consistent in his discipline than many of his contemporaries, he sought to exercise this practice in a fairly gracious manner, always with a mind to persuade the excommunicant to repent of their sin. Understanding ecclesiology and soteriology as he did, with convictions formed deeply in Scripture, it seems natural that Edwards would treat church discipline with such seriousness, as the eternal lives of his people were potentially at stake.

SUMMARY

With this understanding of church discipline as advocated by Luther, Hubmaier, and Edwards, this section will briefly summarize some differences and a key similarity that exist between them regarding this doctrine. One difference between these figures consists in their understanding of the keys of the kingdom and their relationship to church discipline. Contrary to Luther, who often associated the power of the keys to the preaching of the Word of God, as well as the law (binding) and the gospel (loosing), Hubmaier associated the keys with the practices of baptism and the Lord's Supper. Thus, Hubmaier believed that discipline was essential preparation for the Lord's Supper, but he also believed it was a necessary function of the power

---

169. Hall, "Editor's Introduction," 12:82.

of the keys to exclude those who were not living out their public baptismal pledge.[170]

Edwards did not actually say a great deal regarding the keys of the kingdom and the issue of binding and loosing.[171] He claims, "When persons regularly enter into the visible church, we are not to look on their admission as what is done merely by man. They ben't merely admitted by man, nor are they admitted merely to be treated as some of God's people by man; they are admitted or accepted of God." He continues and states that the officers of the church admit in the authority of Christ, claiming, "To them are committed the keys of the kingdom of heaven; and when they open the door it is to admit not only into their society, but into God's kingdom, into the kingdom of heaven. So that when they act regularly, God concurs with them in admitting, and what they do is done in heaven."[172] Thus, Edwards believes this authority to be in line with the proclamation of heaven as it conforms to the will of Christ. However, admittance to the church does not guarantee one's salvation, as, later on in the same work, Edwards exhorts his readers to persevere in the faith lest they come under excommunication.[173]

One other difference to be noted between these historical figures is the strictness with which discipline was to be maintained. Whereas Luther allowed, and even encouraged, those under the ban to come to the preaching portion of the service, Girolimon notes that the Anabaptists "strictly forbade the banished from frequenting worship services, comparing their exclusion from worship services to the practice of the Jews who prohibited 'the uncircumcised heathen' from their regular liturgical assemblies."[174] Regarding the kind of contact one could have with a person under the ban it would seem then that Hubmaier, and the Anabaptists in general, were more specific and more stringent on this issue than was Luther. This may be due to the fact that Luther sought not to mingle the "large ban" with the "small ban," and this allowed for those under excommunication to interact with others in a fairly typical, albeit somewhat limited, fashion.

---

170. See Hubmaier, "On the Christian Ban," in *Balthasar Hubmaier: Theologian of Anabaptism*, 413–14.

171. It is noted by Lee, "There are no extant sermons on Matthew 16:8, Matthew 16:17–19 or Matthew 17:7." Edwards, *Writings on the Trinity, Grace, and Faith*, 21:518. Matt 16:17–19 is the key text on the keys of the kingdom, and binding and loosing, which are terms seldom referenced by Edwards.

172. Edwards, *"Miscellanies,"* vol. 18 of *Works*, 251 (no. 689).

173. See ibid., 259–60.

174. Girolimon, "John Calvin and Menno Simons," 17. See also Simons, *Complete Writings*, 459.

Edwards was emphatic that a person be banned from the Lord's Supper if they were under discipline. However, as was noted earlier, there appears to be a shift in Edwards's view over time, since earlier in his career he prohibits excommunicants from attending any part of the service, whereas later he allowed them to attend the preaching portion of the worship gathering. As such, the later Edwards agreed more with Luther in this regard, but, like Hubmaier, was more stringent on public contact with those under discipline.

Related to this issue of the degree of separation from persons under discipline is the stringency that must be applied when allowing a repentant person under the ban to return to the church. The Anabaptists felt it necessary to take someone through a rather grueling and extended process to ensure they were in fact repentant. Luther, on the other hand, did not believe one could assess the repentance of a person under discipline in such a manner. Rittgers observes,

> Luther and his fellow reformers quickly reached a consensus about what they wished to remove from the traditional sacrament of penance as they sought to construct a new evangelical rite. They would not allow the traditional interrogation of conscience, nor would they allow the concomitant insistence that penitents make a full or complete confession (i.e., one in which they confessed every mortal sin to their priests). The reformers also rejected the effort to assess sufficient degrees of sorrow for sin along with the assigning of penances. . . . Luther and his fellow reformers saw each of these defining elements of the sacrament of penance as creations of a man-made religion that had oppressed lay consciences by denying them access to the gospel.[175]

Certainly a connection can be made here between Luther's affirmation of the invisible church and his hesitancy to think that he could rightly ascertain whether someone was truly in the faith or not. Hubmaier and other Anabaptists, in opposition to Luther, denied the idea of the invisible church and sought to maintain a believer's church through strict discipline, which is why the practice was so vital.[176] These differences were pronounced in this era as they had not only ecclesiological, but political ramifications as well.

---

175. Rittgers, "Embracing the 'True Relic' of Christ," in *New History of Penance*, ed. Firey, 390.

176. One example of this reality is the fact that whereas Luther interpreted the parable in Matt 13 about the wheat and the tares to refer to a mixed church (see Augustine), Anabaptists, such as Hubmaier and Menno Simons, believed this parable referred to the church and the world. See Girolimon, "John Calvin and Menno Simons

In noting Edwards's ecclesiology, one can observe his dedication to maintaining a believer's church in principle, even if the circumstances of his day did not allow this reality to the degree he desired. Like Hubmaier, Edwards maintained that one could ascertain the salvation of an individual by their fruit, and thus he called for people to a certain standard of living. Thus, while holding high ecclesial standards, like Hubmaier, Edwards was much quicker to readmit people to church membership subsequent to their repentance.

While these differences are present, the similarity seen between these figures is most pertinent for defending the thesis of this dissertation. At a fundamental level these Christian leaders agreed that discipline was to be enacted by the church for someone who was living in unrepentant sin. Further, one can also see that Luther, Hubmaier, and Edwards agreed regarding church discipline and its connection to the potential state of one's salvation. They maintained that only those outside of genuine salvation could be excommunicated, since the person would have responded more affirmatively to the admonition of the local church had they been a part of the universal church.[177] Luther seems to state the matter a bit more cautiously than Edwards, as well as his Anabaptist contemporaries;[178] nevertheless, there appears to be an affirmation that the removal of a person from the church was tantamount to recognizing the fact that they were not truly a part of the kingdom of God. Ecclesial discipline was a sign of eschatological judgment.[179] Ultimately, however, these historical figures also affirmed that discipline

on Religious Discipline," 20.

177. See Luther, "Avoiding the Doctrines of Men," 144; Edwards, "Condition of Salvation, Universal and Persevering Obedience," in *Works*, 13:532–33; Hubmaier, "Christian Catechism," in *Balthasar Hubmaier: Theologian of Anabaptism*, 352; McMullan, "Church Discipline," 85–86. Hubmaier further maintained that Jesus had assigned all of his authority to the Christian church, and thus the church really could then forgive and condemn, so that no salvation existed outside of it. See Hubmaier, "Ground and Reason," in *Balthasar Hubmaier: Theologian of Anabaptism*, 371; Hubmaier, "On the Christian Ban," in *Balthasar Hubmaier: Theologian of Anabaptism*, 411–15.

178. Luther maintained, "A person under the ban could still be in fellowship with Christ, and a person in good standing with the Church might not be in right relationship with his Lord. Exclusion from the Lord's Supper was to serve as a sign to the outwardly unrepentant sinner of his (probable) need for inward reconciliation with Christ." Rittgers, *Reformation of the Keys*, 63.

179. A number of texts have been cited earlier to support this claim. The clearest examples of these three historical figures in support of church discipline as a warning of eschatological judgment can be found in Luther, "Sermon on the Ban," 10; Luther, "On the Councils and the Church," 5; Hubmaier, "On Fraternal Admonition," in *Balthasar Hubmaier: Theologian of Anabaptism*, 376, 383; Edwards, "Miscellanies," vol. 13 of *Works*, 528 (no. 485); Edwards, "Sermon on Deut. 29:18–21 (July 1738)," 53:482 at edwards.yale.edu; Edwards, "Means and Ends of Excommunication," in *Works*, 22:78–79.

was restorative in nature, and each sought the good of the person under discipline. Discipline served as an essential means by which those within the church would persevere in their faith.[180] As such, discipline operated as a warning against ongoing sin, a pronouncement of potential eschatological judgment, as well as an invitation to repentance.

CONCLUSION

In both the Reformation era and the time of Edwards, full of significant cultural and theological shifts, Luther, Hubmaier, and Edwards are helpful guides for rightly understanding the nature, purpose, and application of church discipline. These men saw through the errors inherent in the Roman Catholic view of the keys of the kingdom and its affect on the ban, and as such sought to promote change. Regardless of whether one agrees with Luther, Hubmaier, or Edwards on various theological particulars, there should be gratefulness to each of these figures for seeking to make both theological as well as ecclesial reforms for the sake of the purity of the church. Specifically, for the purposes of this dissertation, their reforms regarding church discipline demonstrate the seriousness with which these men treated the task of shepherding a local church. They unapologetically affirm the reality that church discipline serves as a warning of potential eschatological judgment, and it is a means by which members of the church are called to persevere in their faith.

---

180. Again, a number of sources have been accessed to demonstrate this point, but the clearest examples of discipline being seen as a means of persevering in one's faith, seen earlier in this chapter, can be found in Luther, "On the Councils and the Church," 5; Luther, "Keys," 372–73; Hubmaier, "On the Christian Ban," in *Balthasar Hubmaier: Theologian of Anabaptism*, 411, 416–17; Hubmaier, "Christian Catechism," in *Balthasar Hubmaier: Theologian of Anabaptism*, 353; Edwards, "Humble Inquiry," in *Works*, 12:237; Edwards, "Perseverance. Assurance.," in *Works*, 13:475; Edwards, "Means and Ends of Excommunication," in *Works*, 22:78–79.

4

A Theological Analysis of Church Discipline

THIS CHAPTER WILL TAKE into consideration all of the insights from the previous two chapters and seek to formulate a theological synthesis regarding the relationship between church discipline, eschatological judgment, and the perseverance of the saints. Much of the attention of this dissertation has been directed toward the concept of church discipline in particular, with meager consideration given to its connection to judgment and perseverance. At this point clearer definitions and conceptions will be assigned to these latter categories in order to better demonstrate their connection to the practice of ecclesial discipline. Emphasis will again rest on the fact that while church discipline is a warning of potential eschatological judgment, the main goal of discipline is to call sinners to repentance and to serve as a means of perseverance for the people of God.

This chapter will also take into account how this conception of church discipline highlights the missional nature of the church. As a warning of potential eschatological judgment and a means by which members of the church are called to persevere, ecclesial discipline calls for a church made up of believers in Jesus Christ who are dedicated to God's mission and held accountable to specific standards by fellow members. The chapter will end with answers to potential questions and objections to the thesis of this dissertation and its various entailments.

CHURCH DISCIPLINE AND ESCHATOLOGICAL JUDGMENT

While discipline is only a warning—not a fixed rendering—of eschatological judgment, it is still crucial that one understand the relationship between these two ideas. Oden rightly observes, "The church remembers the justice of the final judgment of God, who beholds the heart and thus judges more justly and finally than any human judge. This eschatological view is the frame of reference for any admonition attempted within the worshipping community."[1] In other words, one should rightly understand the truth of eschatological judgment when implementing the practice of church discipline. As such, this section will describe the realities of the final judgment and then demonstrate the connection it holds with ecclesial judgment in the present.

A Biblical Portrayal of Eschatological Judgment

A time will come when history will culminate and Christ will return to set up his eternal kingdom. When Jesus comes and accomplishes his great work there will be judgment for all of mankind. Indeed, as Thiselton avers, "In the Last Judgment the whole world is accountable and responsible to God. His will be the definitive verdict on all human claims and endeavors."[2] We see this coming day of judgment described throughout the Scriptures, beginning with the OT.[3]

---

1. Oden, *Corrective Love*, 88.

2. Thiselton, *Life after Death*, 167.

3. Due to space constraints and the primary aim of this work, eschatological judgment is seemingly depicted in this section as a single event involving both Christians and unbelievers. It must be acknowledged that for some, particularly dispensationalists, the Last Judgment as seen in Rev 20 is limited to the lost, with the church having already been judged. For believers, judgment will transpire at the rapture, which occurs before the seven-year period of tribulation, as well as at Christ's second coming for those who believe in Christ and survive the tribulation. The Day of the Lord, as understood by dispensationalists, is the transition into the Lord's millennial reign on the earth. For examples of dispensational teaching on the timing of the Day of the Lord and eschatological judgment, see Blaising, "Premillennialism," 157–227; Blaising and Bock, *Progressive Dispensationalism*, 226–31, 262–64; Feinberg, "Case for the Pretribulation Rapture Position," 77–79; Saucy, *Case for Progressive Dispensationalism*, 113–14, 135–38. While there are differences between dispensationalists and those who would espouse covenant or new covenant theology as it relates to the timing of judgment, for the purposes of this work it is important to note that any theological persuasion would affirm that all of humanity will stand before God in judgment at some point, and thus the thesis of this work holds true regardless of the details of timing.

Israel was convinced that there would be a future judgment. This conviction is often expressed in the midst of Israel's apostasy and in the context of evils experienced from hostile nations. The final judgment is often referred to as "the day of the Lord" or "that day" (Isa 2:11–12; Zeph 1:7; Ezek 7:7).[4] One can observe that before Isaiah describes new creation (Isa 65:17–25) he announces the final judgment of God (Isa 65:6–7). God will judge the sin of the people and divide them into two groups who receive his blessing and judgment respectively (Isa 65:13–15). Schnabel asserts, "References to a future judgment of all human beings are rare, but they are unambiguous: 'for by fire the Lord will execute judgment, and by his sword on all flesh' (Isa 66:16; also Jer 25:31; Zech 14:1–12; Mal 4:1–6)."[5] Thus, the OT describes the consummation of all things as the Day of the Lord coming with fury, a rendering of final judgment for all of humanity, and the peace of the final messianic order.

The NT depicts eschatology in an inaugurated fashion, denoting that the kingdom of God has been unveiled in the first coming of Christ, but it has not yet been consummated (Matt 4:17; 6:10; 12:28).[6] The kingdom of God is spreading and growing, but will not attain to its finality until the return of Christ, the judge over all of creation. Jesus associates this final day of judgment with his return to earth. In the Olivet Discourse he provides an extensive description of his coming (Matt 24:29–31) that he then connects with the last judgment (Matt 25:31–46).[7] A time will come when all people stand before the throne of Jesus and receive commendation or condemnation. Additionally, Paul speaks of a future judgment for believers, mostly to encourage them, but also to warn them to take sin and its consequences seriously (e.g., 1 Thess 4:18).

This reality of final judgment is sobering, recognizing that all humanity, both believer and unbeliever, will stand before the judgment seat of Christ (2 Cor 5:10). Brower helpfully elaborates on this final judgment and states, "All human activity is scrutinized to determine its alignment with God's purposes.... The last judgment will confirm the verdict already reached. This includes two sets of people, the first of which are in Christ and are freed from all condemnation (John 5:24; Rom 8:1–3, 33–39)." However, he continues, "Those who are finally impenitent, who put themselves outside the ultimate purposes of God, have no part in God's future.... They suffer

---

4. See Schnabel, *40 Questions about the End Times*, 285.

5. Ibid., 285–86. See also Moore, "Personal and Cosmic Eschatology," 858–64.

6. See Beale, *New Testament Biblical Theology*, 227–354; Ladd, *Theology of the New Testament*, 54–117; Schreiner, *New Testament Theology*, 49–116.

7. Schnabel, *40 Questions about the End Times*, 286.

the fate of those cosmic forces implacably opposed to God, 'the devil and his angels' (Matt 25:41), being separated from the source of light and life (Rev 20:15)."[8] Thus, eschatological judgment will come and all of humanity will stand before the throne, but there will be two distinct groups of people: those who trust in Christ for the forgiveness of their sins, and those who refuse to repent.[9]

More specifically regarding believers and the final judgment, Jesus affirms that those who acknowledge him before others, accept his message, and are loyal to him despite opposition will be accepted by the Father who is in heaven (Matt 10:32–33; Luke 12:8–9). Those who walk the narrow path and stand out from the majority of society (Matt 7:14) will enter the kingdom of heaven (Matt 7:21–23), attain to the resurrection from the dead (Phil 3:10–11), will live in the new heavens and new earth (2 Pet 3:13), receive royal authority (Matt 25:34), and ultimately be rescued from everlasting punishment (1 Thess 1:10).[10] As such, believers, while justified by faith, are judged according to their works,[11] and will give an answer for the deeds they have committed in this life.[12] Sampley concurs and observes that as

---

8. Brower, "Eschatology," 464. See also Pate, *End of the Age*, 232, who notes, "Although Paul does not devote extended treatment to the theme of judgment in his writings, it is undeniably present (cf. Dan 12:1–3; *1 Enoch* 10:8–9; *2 Enoch* 65:6; *4 Ezra* 12:33–34) under two categories: the justification of the saved and the wrath of God on the lost. Once again the overlapping of the two ages shapes his thinking. The saved have already been declared righteous in Christ and found to be not guilty (Rom 3:21–26; 5:1; 8:1, 33, 34; 2 Cor 5:21; 1 Thess 1:10; 5:9). Yet they must still appear before the judgment seat of Christ/God to have their works evaluated for rewards or lack thereof (Rom 14:10; 1 Cor 3:12–15; 2 Cor 5:10; Gal 5:5; cf. Rom 2:7, 10). This combination of futurist and realized eschatology also impacts the lost. They will appear one day before God as recipients of divine eternal wrath (Rom 2:5, 8, 19; 19:22), which has already begun to impinge upon their lives (Rom 1:18; 4:15; 1 Thess 2:16)."

9. See Moore, "Personal and Cosmic Eschatology," 871, who notes, "Paul warns believers that they must appear before the judgment seat of Christ, where their fidelity and service will be tested by the one who sees all (Rom 14:10–12; 2 Cor 5:10)." He continues and states that unbelievers "will find the throne of judgment a horrifying experience of finality, as their unrepentant sins disqualify them from entrance into the kingdom of Christ (1 Cor 6:9–10)."

10. See Schnabel, *40 Questions about the End Times*, 294–97.

11. Ortlund observes that Paul consistently uses διὰ or ἐκ when relating faith to justification (Rom 3:22, 25; 5:1; Gal 2:16; cf. Eph 2:8; Col 2:12) and κατὰ when relating works to judgment (Rom 2:6; 2 Cor 11:15; cf. Rom 2:2; 2 Tim 4:14). Thus, "Justification is *through/by/from* faith; judgment is *according to* works." See Ortlund, "Justified by Faith," 332. Harris explicates this use of terminology and asserts that this distinction points us toward understanding justification by faith as denoting contingency or instrumentality and judgment according to works as denoting congruence or correspondence. Harris, "Prepositions and Theology," 3:1200.

12. Giving commentary on the issue of faith and works, Sampley observes, "Then

each person appears before the judgment seat of God, "There each person will have to 'reckon accounts' individually (Rom 14:12). Recompense will be granted to each person on the basis of 'the things which he has done in the body, whether good or bad' (2 Cor 5:10)."[13] Believers in Jesus Christ will bear fruit (John 15:1–6; Gal 5:22–24) and produce works, by God's grace, that demonstrate the veracity of their faith (Jas 2:14–26). In keeping with this point, Schreiner maintains,

> Those who are justified are declared to be "not guilty" before God. In addition, justification is understood in this essay to be an eschatological reality. Hence, the verdict of "not guilty," which believers receive now by faith, is confirmed at the final judgment before the whole world. Salvation, on the other hand, means that one has been rescued or delivered, and here the focus is on being rescued from God's wrath or punishment on the last day.... Justification is a soteriological term, and thus justification and salvation both address the question of the human being's standing before God on the day of judgment, whether one stands in the right before him or is saved, or whether one is condemned before him or destroyed.... I propose here a solution to the dilemma posed in the teaching of both Paul and James and other NT writings, arguing that works are necessary for justification but they should not be considered the basis or foundation of justification. Instead, they constitute the necessary evidence or fruit of justification.[14]

As such, the verdict of justification has been declared in the present and will be substantiated at the final judgment as believers are declared righteous by faith in Christ alone and judged according to their Spirit-wrought deeds, which give evidence of their justification.[15] This understanding of judgment

---

how can it be that one's fate at the last judgment depends on one's works? Faith, once it is established by God's grace, expresses itself through works. Faith 'works' (*energein*) through love (Gal 5:6). The judgment will not assess one's faith because faith is meted out by God as a gift: if God were to judge faith, God would be judging God's own gift. Judgment, therefore, is based on the works that the individual has done, how these works fit and give expression to one's own measure of faith, and how those works bear on others." He goes on to emphasize that all the works the believer does are "finally and profoundly understood by Paul as enabled and powered by grace." *Walking Between the Times*, 72.

13. Ibid., 70.

14. Schreiner, "Justification Apart From and By Works," 20.

15. Schreiner continues and elaborates on this point: "The saving righteousness of God given to us in Jesus Christ is the foundation and basis of our right standing with God. But if works aren't the basis, what are they? They are surely necessary, for one is not saved without them. But they can't be the necessary basis since God demands

has implications for one's stance regarding church discipline and the perseverance of the saints, as will be seen below.

Regarding the fate of unbelievers at the final judgment, Schnabel asserts that they will be rejected by Jesus (Matt 7:23; 25:12), excluded from the kingdom of God (1 Cor 6:9-10) and the Messianic banquet (Matt 8:12), and sentenced to a fate of destruction (Matt 7:13). This destruction is eternal conscious torment in a place called hell, a place of fire and darkness, referred to as the second death (Matt 8:11-12; 18:8; 25:41-46; 1 Thess 1:10; Rev 14:9-11; 20:11-15).[16] As believers will enjoy eternal life with God, so unbelievers—who are also judged according to works—will endure eternal punishment, separated from God in the lake of fire (Matt 25:46; Rev 20:12-15).[17] This reality is the very thing ecclesial discipline is intended to warn against, as the members of a church exhort one another to flee from sin, to "bear fruit in keeping with repentance" (Matt 3:8; Luke 3:8; cf. Eph 2:10; Titus 2:11-14), and, if necessary, to excommunicate unrepentant members to keep them from potentially experiencing the horrific realties of God's eternal judgment.[18]

Church Discipline in Relation to Eschatological Judgment

Taking this reality of eschatological judgment into account, one can see the seriousness with which the process of church discipline should be taken. As such, Schreiner and Caneday assert, "To distinguish believers from unbelievers and to warn the unrepentant concerning their certain destiny of eternal destruction, Jesus instituted a procedure of church discipline."[19] Ecclesial discipline, particularly the step of excommunication, serves as a warning of potential eschatological judgment. Thus, one must hold in constant tension the reality of discipline serving as a warning, not as a definitive declaration, knowing that the church is fallible and Christ has been given

---

perfection and all fall short of what God requires (Rom. 3:23). It seems legitimate to say that works are the necessary evidence and fruit of a right relation with God. They demonstrate, although imperfectly, that one is truly trusting in Jesus Christ." See ibid., 21.

16. Schnabel, *40 Questions about the End Times*, 299-303.

17. See Horton, *Christian Faith*, 974-84. See also Allison, *Historical Theology*, 702-22, who affirms that the vast majority in church history have held to the fact that "unbelievers will experience eternal conscious punishment in hell."

18. Restoration is the goal of discipline, though Schreiner, commenting on 1 Cor 5:5, contends, "Paul does not guarantee that the man will be saved on the last day. The purpose of the discipline is for the man's salvation, but Paul was not granted a vision of the future." See Schreiner, "Biblical Basis for Church Discipline," 117.

19. Schreiner and Caneday, *Race Set Before Us*, 229.

ultimate authority to judge. Also, however, the authority granted by Christ to the church must be properly respected and seen, when done correctly, as a potential pointer to eternal judgment should the sinner refuse to come to repentance.

In serving as a warning, and not as an absolute declaration, church discipline is held in proper esteem, but also fittingly chastened. Calvin, for example, recognized that his understanding of the final step of church discipline differed from the dominant Roman Catholic view of his day, known as anathema. A Roman Catholic view of anathema takes away all pardon, and condemns and consigns a man to eternal destruction; excommunication, however, "avenges and chastens moral conduct." And although excommunication also punishes the man, it does so in such a way that, by forewarning him of his future condemnation, it may call him back to salvation.[20] There is no final pronouncement from the church; discipline is aimed at restoration and used to warn the sinner of their present state with the hopes that they will repent.[21] Leeman concurs with this assessment and maintains that a key purpose of discipline is to warn. He states, "A church does not enact God's judgment through discipline. Rather, it stages a small play that pictures the great judgment to come (1 Cor 5:5)."[22] As such, the warning aspect of discipline must be taken into account, knowing that God is the ultimate judge of all people.

At the same time, it is also crucial to recognize the reality of the church's judgment and the relationship of these pronouncements by the church to God's final judgment. Jeschke rightly asserts that—especially in light of Matthew 16:16 and 18:19—excommunication is a renewed presentation of the gospel message to impenitent persons in that it confronts them with the truth.[23] As Paul says in 1 Corinthians 6:9, "The unrighteous will not inherit the kingdom of God." Jeschke maintains, "To utter this truth in warning to those who have abandoned the obedience of faith is as consistent with the nature of the gospel as informing people in evangelism that unless they repent and believe the gospel they cannot enter the kingdom of God (John 3:5)."[24] Thus, excommunication, rightly practiced, never cuts people off from

---

20. Calvin, *Institutes*, 4.12.10.

21. See Travis, *Christ and the Judgement of God*, 8, who asserts, "The emphasis on restorative justice is not on 'paying back' the offender, but on positively 'putting right' what has gone wrong between the offender and the victim, and between the offender and the community, and on promoting restoration or healing within the offender's own character and behavior."

22. Leeman, *Church Membership*, 110.

23. Jeschke, *Discipling in the Church*, 88.

24. See ibid. See also Oden, *Corrective Love*, 38–39.

grace.[25] He continues, "On the contrary, its function is to prevent persons from anesthetizing themselves against grace. *Excommunication is the form under which the church continues to extend the gospel to the impenitent.*"[26] When the church disciplines an unrepentant sinner, it extends the gospel to that individual because a pronouncement is made about that person's bearing of fruit or lack thereof (Gal 5:16–24).[27]

This assertion regarding the evaluation of a person's ongoing sanctification and bearing of spiritual fruit is seen in the way in which Paul assessed others through various lists of vices and virtues (e.g., 1 Cor 6:9–11). Paul had a clear idea of what a person saved by grace and indwelt by the Spirit would put off regarding sin. Conversely, Paul was well aware of the sinful patterns adopted by those who did not believe in Jesus Christ. Those in the church who fell into such patterns with no signs of remorse or repentance are to be dealt with in an appropriate manner, since they are not showing proper evidences of salvation.[28] In Paul's thought world, judgment of outsiders is not the task of believers, and judgment of other believers is to be reserved for times when others' actions violate the boundaries situated by the vice lists.[29] Sampley notes, "This violation [of the sinner in 1 Corinthians 5] no doubt accounts for Paul's recitation of a vice list (1 Cor 5:9–13) in which *porneia* plays a prominent role (cf. 2 Cor 12:19–21; Gal 5:19–21). Here one

---

25. Regarding this point, Harper and Metzger maintain, "While Christ's grace is a fierce grace, demanding repentance and life change, it is grace nonetheless. As the gospel of God's grace in Christ is no shallow system of behavior modification, neither is church discipline. Grounded in the gospel, it is always a call to respond to the unconditional holy love of God. Only when church discipline arises out of this foundation can it be redemptive." Harper and Metzger, *Exploring Ecclesiology*, 176–77.

26. Jeschke, *Discipling in the Church*, 88, emphasis original.

27. Leeman notes, in disciplining a person from membership, that this does not involve knowing a person's heart as God does. He claims, "God has not given us X-ray eyes. But God does call churches to consider the fruit of individual lives and a make a judgment call (Paul uses exactly this word–1 Cor 5:12; cf. Matt 3:8; 7:16–20; 12:33; 21:43)." Leeman, *Church Membership*, 113.

28. Lauterbach, *Transforming Community*, 163, notes, based on passages like 1 Cor 6:9–11 and the list of sins contained therein, that excommunication is an act whereby the church removes an unrepentant individual from the communion of the church. He elaborates, "They no longer share its common life in Christ, its fellowship in the Spirit, its gathering as the Temple of God. They are aliens to the people of God."

29. Schreiner likewise maintains, "Vice and virtue lists are quite common in Paul (e.g., Rom 1:29–31; 12:9–16; 13:13; 1 Cor 5:9; 2 Cor 12:20–21; Gal 5:19–23; Eph 4:31–32; 5:3–5; Col 3:5, 8–9, 12–13; Titus 3:3), showing that Paul expected believers to forsake evil and to live in a way that pleases God. Indeed, as we have seen, Paul makes it quite clear that those who give themselves over to evil, those whose lives are dominated by evil will not inherit the kingdom of God." Schreiner, "Justified Apart From and By Works," 13. See also Harris, "Beginnings of Church Discipline," 135.

is dealing neither with the secrets of the man's heart nor with his reckonings of what is appropriate to his measure of faith."[30] While not calling for some kind of moral perfection, Paul utilizes these lists to serve as a benchmark by which churches are to observe their members and exhort those who fall into unrepentant sin.[31]

Horton is helpful in explaining this reality of church discipline and eschatological judgment in a more comprehensive fashion. He maintains that as we live in an era where the kingdom of God has been inaugurated, but not yet consummated, thus, "the church is visible not only as a witness to but also as the semirealized inauguration of the kingdom to come."[32] The marks of the church are bound up with the subject of the keys of the kingdom, as the gospel is proclaimed by the preached word, administered through the sacraments,[33] and maintained through exacting discipline. He further asserts,

---

30. Sampley, *Walking Between the Times*, 67–68. See also Oropeza, who maintains, "The incidents related to the vices in 1 Corinthians 5–6, however, depict a genuine danger of loss of eschatological salvation (e.g., 1 Cor 5:5; 6:10), and some of the Corinthians were committing the sexual immorality that Paul was condemning (5:1ff; 6:15ff)." Oropeza, *Paul and Apostasy*, 212.

31. This point is also argued by Schreiner, "Justified Apart From and By Works," 12, who asserts, "What Paul argues in 1 Cor 6:9–11 is that those who have received the grace of Christ, those who are washed in baptism and who are holy and righteous before God, must live a new way. They contradict their baptism, sanctification, and justification if they practice the vices listed in 6:9–10. The grace received in conversion is not an abstraction separated from everyday life and behavior. . . . Certainly we must beware of an over-realized eschatology since believers live in the period between the already and not yet. Christians still experience in part what Paul describes in Rom 7:14–25. Transformation is not the same thing as perfection, and believers still battle the flesh (Gal 5:13–6:10). Believers are no longer slaves to sin (Romans 6), but there is still a battle with sin (Gal 5:17). . . . Until the day of resurrection believers are not yet perfected and thus they still struggle with sin (Phil 3:12–16). Transformation should not be confused with what is sometimes called 'victorious Christian living' or with a passive 'let go and let God' mentality. The Christian life is a war (cf. Eph 6:10–19; 1 Cor 9:26; 2 Cor 10:4; 1 Tim 1:18; 6:12; 2 Tim 4:7), and there are plenty of failures along the way."

32. Horton, *People and Place*, 242.

33. Moule asserts that the NT doctrines of baptism and the Lord's Supper should be viewed in terms of their relation to the last judgment. He states, "Baptism, for each individual, shares something of the finality and uniqueness which the Incarnation itself possesses for the whole world, and anticipates sacramentally the finality and uniqueness of the ultimate judgment of God. Holy Communion is a means of successive renewals of this sacramental verdict—an opportunity for Christians to reaffirm their baptismal tribunal and entry beyond judgment into the life of the age to come. . . . Apostasy from Baptism or unworthy participation in Holy Communion extrudes a member out of the Body into the realm where the forces of destruction are at work: both alike subject a person to extreme peril. It depends upon the person's response to this situation whether

> Ever since the end of the apostolic era, an indirect calling of ministers through the church continues this representational witness not only to Christ but also from Christ. Through preaching, baptism, and admission (or refusal of admission) to the Communion, the keys of the kingdom are exercised. After all, it may be said that the "binding and loosing" involved in church discipline is at issue in every liturgical absolution, sermon, baptism, and Communion. On all of these occasions, the age to come is breaking into this present age: both the last judgment and the final vindication of God's elect occur in a *semi*realized manner, ministerially rather than magisterially. The church's acts are not final—they do not coincide univocally with the eschatological realities, but they are signs and seals. Christ's performative speech is mediated through appointed officers.[34]

Vanhoozer, speaking similarly on the topic of discipline and excommunication, offers an insightful, "dramatic" explanation of this practice.

> Exercising discipline in the church has nothing to do, however, with a literal repetition of divine wrath.... Historically the church has responded to heresy not with literal "wrath and fury" but with what is perhaps the theological and ecclesiological equivalent: anathema and excommunication.... To excommunicate, then, is formally to recognize that a person has taken himself or herself out of the play of the divine communicative action.... To repeat: those who perform "some other drama" take themselves out of the redemptive action. Excommunication is thus an outward or formal recognition of an inward reality, namely, the fact that the heretic is no longer oriented to the way, the truth, and the life. *Excommunication is a dramatic symbolic action that signifies a person's lack of communion with God.*[35]

It is crucial to note, therefore, that the church does not pronounce final judgment on any sinning individual; rather the body of Christ is to confront, warn, and, if necessary, expel in keeping with the commands of God.[36]

---

it proves to be remedial, and to be a judgment which will prepare him for salvation at last, or whether it plunges him further into a condition of fatal self-concern." Moule, "Judgment Theme in the Sacraments," 480–81. See also Hein, *Eucharist and Excommunication*, 415–16.

34. Horton, *People and Place*, 243.

35. Vanhoozer, *Drama of Doctrine*, 425, emphasis original.

36. So South, who asserts, "If the community is regarded as the exclusive community of the redeemed, then expulsion from it would entail the loss of all associated benefits, especially eschatological salvation (hence Paul's 'so that the spirit may be saved in the day of the Lord' 1 Cor 5:5). But it is clear from 1 Corinthians 5 that it is not the

Understanding ecclesial discipline with this tension between warning and reality of eschatological judgment in mind, Wray claims that in excommunicating a person, the church is not passing authoritative judgment on the offender's ultimate salvation. It is a warning to the offender. However, the keys of the kingdom belong to the church. If such an offender is a true Christian to start with, he will be finally brought to repentance and be saved.

On the other hand the offender's profession may not have been real to start with (Matt 7:21–23; 13:1–30; 2 Cor 13:5; 1 John 2:19; 2 Pet 1:10). In cases such as this, the church, in excommunication, has only finally exposed the hypocrisy or self-deception of the offender. "The example of David stands to remind us how badly a true man of God can fall (2 Sam 2, cf. his prayer of repentance, Ps 51), while the life of Judas reminds us how close a man may seem to be to Christ and yet perish."[37] This is a grave matter, knowing that final judgment will render eternal consequences. Leeman helpfully reminds the church that ecclesial discipline is "a small act of judgment on earth that dimly points to God's final judgment in heaven." This act is performed in the hopes that sinners will repent of their sin before the final judgment comes. He then maintains, "When we get down to it, therefore, I think church discipline is hard to do, because we treat God's final judgment so lightly."[38] Thus, the body of Christ is called to exercise discipline as prescribed in Scripture and do so in a manner that takes into account the gravity of the declaration of potential final judgment, but always in a humble and loving spirit with the goal and hope of restoration.[39]

---

disciplinary measure itself which causes the spiritual loss. In Paul's mind the offender has lost his spiritual status already because of his sin. The community's response is simply a concrete demonstration and ratification of the spiritual reality. In this sense the offender stands to *gain* rather than lose by being disciplined." South, *Disciplinary Practices in Pauline Texts*, 186.

37. Wray, *Biblical Church Discipline*, 16.

38. Leeman, *Church and the Surprising Offense of God's Love*, 322. Similarly, Adams asserts, concerning the link made by Paul in quoting several passages in Deuteronomy in 1 Cor 5:13, "Paul's use of the Deuteronomy formula for the removal of persons from the Corinthian church shows that this act is *judicial*—the New Testament equivalent of stoning—and not merely, or even in the first place, remedial." Adams, *Handbook of Church Discipline*, 84. Adams maintains that this reality sets forth the danger involved in failing to repent when under church discipline, as that can have eternal consequences. See ibid., 85.

39. Schreiner contends that love "cannot be separated from moral norms. For instance, Paul gives specific and concrete parenesis to his churches, instructing them not to get divorced (1 Cor 7:10–16) or to commit sexual immorality (1 Thess 4:3–8; 1 Cor 6:12–20). He admonishes the idle to get to work (2 Thess 3:6–13). The man committing incest must be disciplined (1 Cor 5:1–13). Love for Paul does not float free of ethical norms, but is expressed by such norms." Schreiner, "Commands of God," 95.

CHURCH DISCIPLINE AND THE PERSEVERANCE OF THE SAINTS

In noting the connection between church discipline and eschatological judgment, one can also observe that, in seeking to preserve corporate holiness and bring sinners to repentance, discipline is a means by which the people of God are called to persevere in their faith. The concept of holiness is key to deciphering the relationship between discipline and perseverance. Davis helpfully points out that texts such as Matthew 24:42 are exhortations to persevere in holiness and to be watchful because the Lord will someday come back to set up his eternal kingdom. Therefore, Davis maintains, "Church discipline is an integral part of such preparation. Only of the true Church will it be said, 'His wife hath made herself ready' (Rev 19:7)."[40] Thus, a key component of church discipline is the maintaining of purity within the church body, so that the people of God can continually strive for "the holiness without which no one will see the Lord" (Heb 12:14).[41] Davis continues in affirming this connection, saying,

> The doctrine of holiness is noticeably lacking in the theology of the contemporary church, despite the fact that both the OT and NT have much to say regarding the divine mandate that the people of God be a holy people. "Ye shall be holy, for I am holy" is a recurring theme of the OT (cf. Lev 11:44; 19:2; 20:7, 26). The basic idea in the family of Hebrew words translated "holy" (*qodës, qâdës, qâdôs*) is separateness.... *Hagios* ("holy") and its kindred NT words (*hagiasmós*, "holiness"; *hagioi*, "holy ones," i.e., "saints"; and *hagiazö*, "to sanctify, to make holy") depict a twofold significance: (1) negatively, separation from sin; and (2) positively, consecration to God. The tragic and irrevocable consequence of a low view of the holiness of God is a correspondingly low view of the doctrine of sanctification.[42]

---

40. Davis, "Whatever Happened to Church Discipline," 353.

41. Beale affirms this point and maintains that "all Christians are spiritual Levitical priests (in fulfillment of Isa 66:21)." Thus, our ongoing task is to serve God in his temple in which we always dwell and of which we are a part. He continues, "Our continual priestly tasks are what the first Adam's were to be: to keep the order and peace of the spiritual sanctuary by learning and teaching God's word, by praying always, and *by being vigilant in keeping out unclean moral and spiritual things.*" See Beale, *Temple and the Church's Mission*, 398, emphasis mine. Beale, therefore, affirms holiness as not only a personal, but also a corporate pursuit.

42. Ibid.

Thus, the connection between ecclesial discipline and persevering in faith and holiness must be upheld with rigor, knowing the call in Scripture to be holy as God is holy.

In preserving corporate holiness, discipline is exacted so that the church would not be contaminated, but endure in its faith as it sees the severe warning of judgment brought through discipline. And as the ultimate goal of discipline is to bring the sinning individual to repentance, the warning of potential judgment is issued through discipline so that the person would be restored and subsequently persevere in righteousness. Like the previous section, a biblical articulation of the perseverance of the saints will be sketched out, followed by its specific connection to church discipline.

A Biblical Portrayal of the Doctrine of Perseverance

Grudem succinctly defines this doctrine, saying that all those who are truly born again will be kept by God's power and will endure as Christians until the end of their lives, and that only those who endure until the end have been truly born again.[43] As such, this is not some kind of responsibility that lies solely in our own moral exertion and will power. We work out our salvation with fear and trembling and God works within us (Phil 2:12–13). Keathley highlights both the divine and human aspects of perseverance. In speaking of sanctification and assurance he defines preservation as the eternal security of the believer brought about through the ongoing work of God (John 10:28–29; Rom 8:31–39; 1 Pet 1:5; Jude 24). Keathley continues and delineates perseverance: "The doctrine of perseverance teaches that the

---

43. Grudem, *Systematic Theology*, 788. For other works on the topic of perseverance see Bateman, *Four Views on the Warning Passages*; Pinson, *Four Views on Eternal Security*. It is important to note that this definition would not necessarily comport with other views of perseverance that allow for the possibility of apostasy. In Schreiner and Caneday, *Race Set Before Us*, 21–38, the authors summarize four different views of perseverance, the first of which maintains that it is possible for believers to lose their salvation and apostatize from the faith. Advocates of this view maintain that the Bible's warnings and admonitions make it clear that heirs of God's promise can fail to persevere in faithfulness, and thus forfeit the inheritance of salvation. Current proponents of the "Wesleyan/Arminian" view of perseverance include Marshall, *Kept by the Power of God*; McKnight, "Warning Passages of Hebrews," 21–59. Schreiner and Caneday also document three other views: the loss of rewards view, advocated by Eaton, *No Condemnation*; Hodges, *Gospel Under Siege*; Kendall, *Once Saved, Always Saved*; Wilkin, *Confident in Christ*; the test of genuineness view, taught by MacArthur, *Gospel according to Jesus*; and the hypothetical loss of salvation, advocated by Kent, *Epistle to the Hebrews*; Westcott, *Epistle to the Hebrews*. Further attention will be given below to the question of whether those who advocate a different stance on perseverance can still hold to the thesis of this work.

work of regeneration and sanctification eventually and inevitably manifests itself in the life of every believer. Christians are capable of tragic spiritual and moral failure... but the faith of a genuinely saved person remains."[44] Christians will not become perfectly righteous in this life, but will demonstrate tangible evidences of grace as God preserves them and they persevere in the faith by God's grace.[45]

Thus, as one considers the concept of perseverance, one must note that the call to endure is rooted in God's work to preserve until the end (1 Pet 1:5). A text such as Philippians 2:12–13 is key to rightly understanding perseverance. It denotes both our responsibility and God's ministry of preservation. Demarest notes, "Paul recognized that believers' faithful working is enabled by God's prior working in them."[46] Demarest continues and maintains that genuine believers may stumble morally, relapse spiritually, and dishonor their Lord by grievous sins. But such lapses are temporary and not final or absolute. "The judgment of Scripture is that true believers will not persist in a life of disobedience and debauchery (1 John 3:9–10; 5:18a). God will not abandon erring believers to sin, such that they permanently fall under its dominion (Jer 32:40; Job 17:9)."[47] The grace of God is the foundation that undergirds all of our efforts in sanctification and perseverance.

However, this does not negate the fact that there is effort involved on the part of the Christian as God calls believers to persevere in their faith. This grace is the catalyst by which Christians live for God continually in fleeing sin and pursuing righteousness (2 Tim 2:22).[48] True believers must

---

44. Keathley, "Work of God," 760.

45. In relation to the connection between assurance and perseverance, Schreiner asserts, "Through most of its history the Christian church has been divided as to whether genuine believers will truly persevere. The debate centers particularly on the severe warnings in the NT that threaten judgment for those who apostasize (e.g., Rom 11:22; Gal 5:2–6; 2 Tim 2:11–13; Heb 6:4–8; 10:26–31). Furthermore, other texts refer to those who were part of the church and have since defected (e.g., 1 Tim 1:18–20; 2 Tim 4:10; 2 Pet 2:19–22). Most agree that the problem is difficult and defies facile answers. Preserving the tension between assurance and warnings is necessary to be faithful to the biblical witness. If we abstract assurance from the warning passages, believers are prone to fall into lethargy and a false sense of spiritual security. If the warnings are sundered from assurance, believers may be overwhelmed by fear and doubt. The tension between these two sets of passages should be plotted against the background of NT eschatology, in which believers are *already* saved in this present evil age, but have *not yet* received the perfection promised." Schreiner, "Assurance," 71, emphasis original.

46. Demarest, *Cross and Salvation*, 450.

47. Ibid., 454.

48. Demarest, ibid., 448–49, maintains, "From the human side, believers must apply spiritual resources to maintain their relationship with Christ. Christians have an indispensable role to play in their perseverance unto final salvation [Matt 10:22; Phil

and will persevere in their faith to attain final salvation. Highlighting Acts 14:22–23 and 2 Thessalonians 3:1–5, Schreiner asserts that new Christians "are not told that they will inherit the kingdom of God no matter what they do. Rather, they are urged to remain and continue in the faith."[49] He is not here advocating the possibility of apostasy, knowing that those who do not persevere are demonstrating that there was never genuine belief in the first place (1 John 2:19). Rather, he is stating that the authenticity of one's faith will be manifested tangibly in good works.[50] In other words, persistence in the faith no matter what the circumstances will demonstrate that faith is genuine.[51]

As assistance in this process of perseverance, God has issued warnings in the Scriptures to serve as means by which believers continue in their faith. Schreiner maintains that the warning texts in Scripture "admonish the readers against falling away, for those who do so will be damned forever."[52] Thus, the NT authors use these texts to admonish their readers so that they will not finally fall away. Schreiner continues, "The warnings are prospective, not retrospective. They are like road signs that caution drivers of dangers ahead on the highway. They are written so that the readers will heed the warnings and escape the threatened consequence."[53] The purpose of warnings in the NT, therefore, is redemptive and salvific.

The preserving work and assurance of God must be kept in mind as one delineates the doctrine of perseverance. True believers in Jesus Christ will be kept by God's power and grace, and faithfully endure to the end of their lives in the Christian faith. Peterson strikes a helpful balance in describing perseverance in relation to holiness, saying,

> No Christian should doubt the need to give practical, everyday expression to the holiness that is our status and calling in Christ.

3:12–14; Col 1:23; 2 Tim 2:12–13; 4:7; Heb 10:36; 12:14; 1 John 3:3]."

49. Schreiner, *Run to Win the Prize*, 18.

50. Commenting on 1 Cor 6:9–11, Schreiner, ibid., 34, maintains, "Not inheriting the kingdom means that the unrighteous will not obtain eternal life (cf. Gal 5:21; Eph 5:5). Elsewhere Paul argues that believers who suffer and endure are worthy of entrance into the kingdom (2 Thess 1:5). That entering the kingdom involves eschatological salvation is clear from Paul's confidence about his future, stated in 2 Timothy 4:18.... Those who give themselves over to unrighteousness will not enjoy end-time salvation but will face God's judgment." Such behavior as depicted in this passage, according to Schreiner, is not fitting for those who have new life in Christ, and are washed, sanctified, and justified. The Corinthians must live in accordance with their salvation, and if they follow the way of evil and do not persevere in their faith judgment will be their destiny.

51. See ibid., 19.

52. Ibid., 48.

53. Ibid.

> Only those who trust in his sanctifying work on the cross, and take seriously the warning to "pursue holiness," will "see the Lord" [Heb 12:14].... On the other hand, it is possible to be so zealous for "progress" that one's attention shifts from God's grace to human effort.... Progress may be seen as we exercise ourselves in that godly devotion which issues from a true knowledge of God in Jesus Christ.[54]

Thus, Christians must seek to use all spiritual capacities to endure in our faith, since God has made believers into new creations (2 Cor 5:17). Believers are called to holiness (1 Pet 1:15-16), knowing all the while that it is God who is at work in his people by his grace to accomplish such a work.

Church Discipline in Relation to the Perseverance of the Saints

Believers are called to persevere in a faith that works itself out in love (Gal 5:6), for it is this kind of life that demonstrates true faith (Jas 2:14-26). Conversely, if a church member is not persevering in this kind of faith, and it manifests itself in unrepentant sin, the disciplinary process should be applied. Davis notes that in both the OT (Deut 17:8-11; 19:19-20) and the NT (1 Tim 5:19-20), church discipline was meant to serve as a deterrent to others in sinning. Recognizing that even church leaders are not exempt from discipline, a local congregation would be restrained from evil and encouraged to persevere in the faith.[55] Discipline is adjudicated so that the church will not be contaminated and led astray by the sinning member, and also that the individual under discipline may repent, be restored, and persevere in their faith along with the rest of the church.[56]

First, one should observe the connection between perseverance and church discipline as it relates to the congregation as a whole.[57] Citing pas-

---

54. Peterson, *Possessed by God*, 91.

55. Davis, "Whatever Happened to Church Discipline," 358-59. For further commentary on the discipline of church leaders, see Marshall, "Congregation and Ministry," 111.

56. See Oden, who claims, "Discipline is a part of Christ's ordering of the church, not only for fostering the proximate holiness of the church, but also for the spiritual benefit of the offender." Oden, *Corrective Love*, 83. See also Norman, "Reestablishment of Proper Church Discipline," 207-8.

57. Commenting on 1 Cor 5:6-8, Calvin maintains, "The second purpose [of corrective discipline] is that the good may not be corrupted by the constant company of the wicked, as commonly happens. For there is nothing easier than to be led away by bad examples from moral living." Calvin, *Institutes*, 4.12.5. See also Oden, *Corrective Love*, 84; Wray, *Biblical Church Discipline*, 4.

sages such as Hebrews 12:15, 1 Corinthians 5:2–7, and 1 Timothy 5:20, Grudem maintains that one reason discipline is exacted is so that the sin will be kept from spreading to others and, as a result, they can effectively walk in holiness. Paul wants believers to understand that sin will not be tolerated and is dealt with as the person receives discipline from the church, and, potentially, God himself.[58] Vander Broek concurs and maintains that in 1 Corinthians 5 Paul's primary concern is for the community as a whole, and how the lack of discipline will affect them. He asserts, "The apostle feels that the sinner in their midst is a danger to the life of the community. This leaven, as we have seen, might be interpreted as a compromise to the community's holiness, as an indication that all are responsible for the sin of the one member, or as the threat of further contamination."[59] If the leaven of sin is allowed to permeate the church, as 1 Corinthians 5:6–7 suggests, the Christian community and its distinctive holiness is threatened.[60]

As noted above, one must affirm the preserving work of God while also maintaining the call for saints to persevere in their faith. As the passages previously mentioned suggest (1 Cor 5:2–7; 1 Tim 5:20; Heb 12:15), sin deeply affects others, which is why it must be uprooted so that believers can most successfully endure in their faith. Discussing the context of

---

58. Grudem, *Systematic Theology*, 895. See also Davis, "Whatever Happened to Church Discipline," 355, who asserts, "Paul exhorted the church to exercise discipline in order to prevent the sin from 'spreading through the camp.' Paul demonstrated his recognition of the fact that every local church has a twofold responsibility: (1) to do everything within its power and ability to bring the wayward brother back to God, and (2) to exercise every precaution to make sure that the rest of the church is properly protected. This protective aspect of church discipline involves at least three areas. Every congregation is responsible for protecting the church: (1) from doctrinal error, (2) from moral impurity, and (3) from divisiveness."

59. Vander Broek, "Discipline and Community," 11. Also commenting on 1 Cor 5:7, Thompson notes, "Because the old leaven was subject to impurity, it became a metaphor for an infection that could destroy the entire batch of bread. . . . The identity of the community required that it throw out the old leaven in order to maintain its purity." Thompson, *Moral Formation*, 48.

60. In describing the identity of the church, Poettecker claims, "Theologically, it is God's community of grace and discipleship, the fellowship of 'sinners saved by grace' but also the community of 'the saints striving after holiness.' It is Christ's 'imperfect body' yet it is also to be His 'holy Bride.' Thus it is the disciplined church earnestly seeking to be the holy church." Poettecker, "New Testament Community," 18. Kreider likewise maintains, "Paul in his letter to the church at Corinth has made it clear that a church to be the church of Christ must indeed have standards. There are spiritual and moral standards of life in the church. The church must possess a distinctive Christian quality. It must manifest Christ to men and radiate His Spirit. . . . The witness of the church, the spirit of its members, and the purity of its teachings are real concerns. To this end discipline is needed to restrain us from evil when tempted and to strengthen us for effective service." See Kreider, "Standards with Love," 108.

1 Corinthians 5, Hays maintains that throughout the process of rebuking the congregation and calling for the removal of the unrepentant sinner, "concern for the health and purity of the community remains the constant factor in which more specific norms must be grounded."[61] Paul's concern is for the church to persevere in faith and purity, especially in light of the final judgment, as seen above. Thus, discipline is enacted for the final good of the community.[62]

Second, discipline is undertaken for the sake of sinning individuals, that they might repent and subsequently persevere in their faith. Garrett asserts,

> Paul's ethical admonitions show the relationship of the Christian life to church discipline. Sanctification is defined in terms of abstaining from fornication (1 Thess 4:1–8; 1 Cor 6:9–11, 18–20). Christians as sons of light are to walk in the light rather than in the darkness (1 Thess 5:4–8; Rom 13:12ff.; Eph 5:7–14). . . . A Christian is one who had "put off the old man" and "put on the new man" (Col 3:9; Eph 4:22–24). Yet Paul regretfully reported that many live "as enemies of the cross of Christ," but the "manner of life" of Christians ought to be "worthy of the gospel of Christ" (Phil 3:18; 1:27).[63]

The reason one is excommunicated from the community of faith is because their sinful actions are not correlating with their profession of faith. Since they have been washed, sanctified, and justified by Christ (1 Cor 6:11), and since they are new creations in Christ (2 Cor 5:17), they are to walk in a manner worthy of the gospel (Eph 4:1). If they do not repent, they are demonstrating that they were never truly believers in the first place, in that they are not enduring in faith and holiness. However, the point of excommunication is to turn sinners from the error of their ways back to the kind of ongoing sanctification Garrett describes.

---

61. Hays, *Moral Vision of the New Testament*, 43. Thompson also asserts, regarding the call to morality in 1 Cor 5, "The holy community must maintain boundaries. It has assumed the identity of Israel in its separation from the nations; its identity determines its moral conduct." See Thompson, *Moral Formation*, 49.

62. Jeschke defines church discipline as referring to "the ministry of discipling a Christian brother or sister whose spiritual health and life are endangered by a particular act or attitude." Jeschke, *Disciplining in the Church*, 17. See also Laney, *Guide to Church Discipline*, 14. Thus, Jeschke tightly links discipleship and discipline, seemingly implying that discipline is a means by which we improve a person's "spiritual health," or exhort them to persevere as a disciple of Jesus. See also Best and Robra, *Ecclesiology and Ethics*, 30–31.

63. Garrett, *Baptist Church Discipline*, 7–8.

Thus, Schreiner rightly notes that warnings and admonitions in the Bible have a particular function: "Warnings are one of the means God uses to keep believers running in the race, so that they keep trusting in Christ.... By them believers are warned against departing from Christ and the gospel."[64] As has already been established, ecclesial discipline, particularly excommunication, serves as a warning of potential eschatological judgment. As such, this action undertaken by the church is aimed at moving the sinner back in the direction of repentance, trusting in Christ, and perseverance in the faith.

Explicating both 1 Corinthians 5:5 and 1 Timothy 1:20—passages that demonstrate how discipline functions as a warning and a call for repentance and perseverance—Bargerhuff asserts that in both contexts this process of handing a person over to Satan is remedial, correctional, and restorative so that a person can be saved in the end. Handing someone over to Satan seems to entail placing someone outside the covenant community, and, therefore, outside of the sphere of God's blessing and protection. This is done in order to destroy the flesh, which is the self-sufficient, carnal attitude of the unrepentant sinner.[65] This attitude of unrepentance must be done away with in order that the sinning individual may continually bear fruit in keeping with repentance, and in so doing demonstrate their living faith in Christ.

Discipline, therefore, is both for the community as a whole as well as unrepentant individuals, to serve as a means by which they persevere in the faith. Hein reiterates this point: "Consequently, the early Church's discipline in the New Testament is to be viewed as pastoral rather than penal since it was meant to lead the offender back into the Church as an effective and living member.... The expulsion of a serious offender was also intended to protect the rest of the community from the sinner and his faults."[66] While there are other means to persevere in the faith,[67] it must be affirmed that church discipline may have been overlooked as such a means in the past. It is, however, a crucial dimension of church life aimed at our eternal salvation.

---

64. Schreiner, *Run to Win the Prize*, 112–13.

65. Bargerhuff, *Love That Rescues*, 163. See also Hays, *First Corinthians*, 85; Laney, *Guide to Church Discipline*, 69; Thiselton, *First Epistle to the Corinthians*, 396–97.

66. Hein, *Eucharist and Excommunication*, 417.

67. These measures of growing in one's faith are typically referred to as the means of grace. They are intentional habits utilized by believers to grow as Christians, knowing all the while that it is God who works through such means to continue the good work he began in them (Phil 1:6; 2:12–13). Such means include meditation on Scripture, prayer, confession of sins, Christian fellowship, silence, and solitude. For further details on the means of grace, see Brett, *Growing Up in Grace*; Bridges, *Discipline of Grace*.

Thompson concurs and labors to demonstrate that there should be an eschatological dimension to church life and pastoral ministry, knowing that the goal of church leaders is to present the bride of Christ blameless before the Lord at his return (Eph 5:25–27). As such, Thompson asserts, true church ministry should constantly be leading others into ethical transformation. He maintains, "This ethical transformation means that the task of ministry is not only to communicate God's acceptance of the sinner but also to challenge converts toward transformation."[68] Thus, the church is dedicated to assisting others to persevere in their faith, even if it means disciplining them to root out their sinful habits.

THE INTERRELATEDNESS OF DISCIPLINE, JUDGMENT AND PERSEVERANCE

As one can see, while not always highlighted as related doctrines, ecclesial discipline, eschatological judgment, and enduring faith are intricately connected. White and Blue accurately claim, "Church discipline is anything the body of Christ does to train Christians in holiness, calling them to follow their Lord more closely."[69] While this is a broad definition of discipline, it encompasses the fact that enduring holiness, or perseverance in the faith, is the goal, and at times this will require correction to warn and admonish others to remove the sin in their lives.[70]

Rosner helpfully elaborates on this point, and states,

> Exclusion from the community and salvation are linked in 1 Corinthians 5:5b, but the former does not lead to the loss of the latter. On the contrary, the express purpose of this expulsion is the offender's salvation. Paul's ultimate aim in excluding the man is his own good. How is this purpose to be understood? Paul assumed (see 6:9–11) that those who persist in flagrant sin have no future with God; in this sense 6:9–11 clarifies 5:5b. Yet he is confident that God's faithfulness will confirm believers "until the end ... blameless on the day of our Lord Jesus" (1 Cor 1:8). However, future salvation is not a forgone conclusion for

---

68. Thompson, *Pastoral Ministry*, 157.

69. White and Blue, *Healing the Wounded*, 19.

70. See also Oropeza, who maintains that those within a congregation who practice various kinds of vices (1 Cor 6:9–11) potentially threaten other members who will be influenced to practice them as well. Therefore, for the preservation of the believer, Paul demands that the unrepentant offender be expelled from the community (1 Cor 5:5, 13). Discipline, judgment, and perseverance are thus held together doctrinally and practically. Oropeza, *Paul and Apostasy*, 184.

one "who calls himself a brother but is sexually immoral" (v. 11). The passage does not teach that ethical failure results in the loss of salvation, but that assurance of salvation depends in part on ethical progress; cf. 6:11: "that is what some of you *were*." Paul does not answer the question of whether the man is currently "saved." His point is that so-called brothers who engage in blatant sexual misconduct will be finally saved "on the day of the Lord" only if "the sinful nature is destroyed." According to 5:5b exclusion is undertaken not only to benefit the community and the individual in the present, but also to secure the salvation of the sinner in the future.[71]

Again, one can observe that exclusion from the church does not necessarily mean that final salvation is unavailable.[72] Instead, this judgment is meant to foster repentance and perseverance. However, as Rosner asserts, "assurance of salvation depends in part on ethical progress." Schreiner concurs and notes that most of the texts that refer to an eschatological judgment also emphasize the need for growth in godliness during the present age. "NT writers never consign holiness to the future with the idea that the lives of believers here and now do not matter. Believers are not and cannot be perfected now, but they are to advance in holiness until the final day (1 Thess 3:12–13)."[73] Thus, ecclesial discipline is needed to ensure that, to the best of the church's ability, sin is shunned and righteousness is pursued.[74]

71. Rosner, "Exclusion," 474–75.

72. Rosner notes, "On the one hand, damnation can be perceived as the ultimate 'exclusion,' as a final and retributive exclusion from God's presence (cf. 2 Thess 1:9): in 1 Corinthians 6:9–10, Ephesians 5:5, and Colossians 3:5–6 those who have no future with God are said to be guilty of roughly the same sins that as those who should be excluded from the community according to 1 Corinthians 5:11. On the other hand, there is no hint that the act of excluding people damns them. On the contrary, in 1 Corinthians 5:12–13 such judgment is explicitly said to be God's exclusive prerogative." Ibid., 474.

73. Schreiner, *Run to Win the Prize*, 60. Commenting on 1 Thess 3:11–13, Beale maintains that these verses teach about an increasing love for others that must characterize the life of a Christian. He asserts, "This godly mark becomes a badge allowing exemption from the end-time sentence of condemnation and allowing safe entrance into the kingdom. The badge is an outward emblem demonstrating that one has truly believed in the atoning death and resurrection of Jesus, which makes one blameless in God's eyes (see also 2 Thess 2:16–17)." See Beale, *1–2 Thessalonians*, 110–11.

74. This position is not in any way suggesting that works contribute to our salvation. Ortlund asserts regarding the idea of salvation and works that "obedience is not merely evidential but is rather built into the very fabric of salvation itself, yet without contributing to justification." Justification and judgment are linked not so much in cause-and-effect or linear progression as they are organically unified. This organic bond, says Ortlund, is union with Christ, in which one is not only declared righteous, but also indwelt by the Spirit. "Justification and obedience both sprout from the seed

Though the confrontation involved in church discipline may seem unpleasant, it is necessary and, when done rightly, brings about a greater pursuit of holiness in the life of the church. Laney asserts that a careful study of the New Testament indicates that such confrontation is a Christian duty. He maintains, "Christ desires that the church be 'holy and blameless' (Eph. 5:27). Caring confrontation may be the means God will use in these days to purify the church so that Christ's bride will have 'no spot or wrinkle' at His coming."[75] Thus, church discipline is needful in that it is a warning of eschatological judgment and a means by which the saints are called to endurance in their faith.

CONCEIVING OF CHURCH DISCIPLINE AS MISSIONAL

It is worth noting that, while seemingly counterintuitive, this understanding of church discipline contributes to the discussion on the missional nature of the church.[76] As the redeemed people of God,[77] believers in Jesus Christ are called to articulate the gospel to the world in word and deed. Beale rightly notes, "We, as God's people, have already begun to be God's end-time temple (1 Cor 3:16–17; 6:19; 2 Cor 6:16; Eph 2:21–22) where his presence is manifested to the world, and we are to extend the boundaries of the new garden-temple until Christ returns, when, finally, they will be ex-

---

of union with Christ. For this reason the category of those who are justified by faith is coextensive with those who will be justified on the last day after a whole life of perseverance. Those who are justified will, for reasons other than any kind of earning, do the law." While the church cannot definitively know the state of one's soul, the spiritual fruit of one's life must be examined and, therefore, discipline should be exercised to maintain perseverance and demonstrate the validity of one's justification. See Ortlund, "Justified by Faith," 338.

75. Laney, "Biblical Practice of Church Discipline," 363–64. Also commenting on Ephesians 5:25–27 and the call to the purity of the church, White and Blue assert, "The church is anything but pure. She would be a lot purer if corrective church discipline were revived." They later state, "Only the pure in heart see [God] and our hearts are no longer pure. . . . We ought to be exercising corrective church discipline. It is a matter of life and death." White and Blue, *Healing the Wounded*, 58–59.

76. The works available on the subject of the missional church continue to rapidly proliferate. For a point of entry into this topic, see Ashford, *Theology and Practice of Mission*; Chester and Timmis, *Total Church*; Goheen, *Light to the Nations*; Guder and Barrett, *Missional Church*; Stetzer and Putman, *Breaking the Missional Code*; Wright, *Mission of God*.

77. Images for the church, such as the people of God (1 Pet 2:9–10), the body of Christ (1 Cor 12:27), the temple of the Spirit (1 Cor 3:16; 6:19), and the family of God (Rom 8:15) reveal the fact that regenerate church membership is at the center of a biblical concept for the church. See Ashford and Akin, "Missional Implications," 192–96.

panded worldwide."[78] Thus, the task of the church is to exhort one another to keep the faith, and make the gospel visible to others, warning them of final judgment and calling them to a kind of faith that will persevere to the end. Church discipline, therefore, is a continual proclamation of the gospel to both the outside world as well as its own members.[79]

The saving power of the gospel is a reality in our lives ultimately because of the love of God displayed in the life, death, and resurrection of his son, Jesus Christ (1 John 4:7–10). Realities in the church, such as regenerate church membership and ecclesial discipline, establish proper boundaries for the church community. These actions are not meant to be unloving; rather, God sets up these parameters to make the gospel visible and accessible to others outside of the boundaries. Leeman explains, "Insofar as the gospel presents the world with the most vivid picture of God's love, and insofar as church membership and discipline are an implication of the gospel, local church membership and discipline in fact define God's love for the world."[80] Indeed, regenerate church membership and church discipline are part of God's intention to shape or structure the church in such a way that it complements the gospel and is prepared for missions. First, the doctrines of regenerate church membership and church discipline are based upon the reality of gospel transformation in salvation (Titus 3:4–7). Second, these two practices of the church proclaim and reflect God's love to the world, in that God has the ultimate, eternal good of his people in mind. God's love for the world is on display in the gospel as it is proclaimed and lived out, and regenerate church membership and discipline is one way in which the missional church makes this gospel known.[81]

The church, as a "window" to God and the gospel,[82] makes his name known through regenerate membership and remains unstained through church discipline. Indeed, church membership and discipline make the gospel visible by fostering a God-centered and supernatural view of salvation, gospel-shaped disciples, a gospel-shaped community, and a clear

---

78. Beale, *Temple and the Church's Mission*, 395.

79. See Ashford and Akin, "Missional Implications," 191. The authors further assert, "The church, as a spiritual family, is *sending* a people who are in covenant relationship with other believers and a people who are accountable to others for the way they live their lives. The church is shaped and sent to represent the power of the gospel to transform the lives of people and to represent the sovereign and messianic reign of Jesus Christ. The church is not only the agent but also the product of the same process." See ibid.

80. Leeman, *Church and the Surprising Offense of God's Love*, 17.

81. Ashford and Akin, "Missional Implications," 194–95.

82. For commentary on this imagery, see Wright, *Mission of God*, 127.

and unconfused gospel testimony. In these ways, assert Ashford and Akin, regenerate church membership and ecclesial discipline are profoundly connected to the church's ability to provide a clear and unobstructed window to God and his gospel.[83] As such, a right understanding of church discipline—namely, as a warning of judgment and a means of perseverance—paves the way for the church joining in God's mission in a more effective manner.

ENGAGING POTENTIAL QUESTIONS AND OBJECTIONS

The entirety of this dissertation has been dedicated to proving that one purpose of church discipline is to serve as a warning of potential eschatological judgment, and as such also functions as a means by which the church is called to persevere in the faith. This understanding of the concept, however, raises potential objections that must be answered. Thus, while not in an entirely comprehensive manner, the final section of this chapter is dedicated to answering these questions and, where appropriate, pointing the reader to other helpful resources on these various topics.

Does the Fallibility of Churches Affect this View of Discipline?

Some will question the legitimacy of the church's authority in issuing a warning to unrepentant sinners. If the church is not infallible, will the judgment rendered against a sinning individual always be correct? This is a crucial question to answer, since this view of discipline potentially speaks to a person's eternal state, and because local congregations can err in their judgments.

First, it should be noted that some make this objection, because they believe the church has no authority to judge. This is often based on a misreading of Matthew 7:1, "Judge not, lest you also be judged." Interestingly, in our present day culture, the idea of judging another person is seen as arrogant and narrow-minded, and this verse is often used as ammunition against a concept like church discipline. This, however, would be a misreading of the text.[84] Dever affirms, "We are specifically told to judge one another within the church (though not in the final way that God judges); Jesus' words in Matthew 18, Paul's in 1 Corinthians 5–6, and other passages clearly show that the church is to exercise judgment within itself."[85] Thus, there is

---

83. Ashford and Akin, "Missional Implications," 203.
84. Dever, "Biblical Church Discipline," 29.
85. See ibid.

a sense in which judgment in this context is necessary and appropriate, but it must be done in a certain way, or else it is sinful (cf. Matt 7:2–5; Gal 6:1).[86]

The church is certainly not to condemn others unjustly. The imagery in Matthew 7:1–5 (the speck and log in one's eye) in fact suggests that we must be self-critical when it comes to our own sin, but this is done not for the purpose of excluding the judgment of others altogether, but as a prerequisite to judging.[87] Thus, Jesus has not condemned judging altogether, but has rather called his people to be above reproach in the way they do so by examining their own hearts first.

Second, when considering the legitimacy of such a pronouncement coming from the church, one must take into consideration key passages from Matthew 16 and 18.[88] These deal specifically with the authority given through the keys of the kingdom, as well as the concomitant power granted to the church in binding and loosing (Matt 16:19; 18:18). Commenting on these passages and the authority of the church, Lauterbach states, "[Jesus] does not give *carte blanche* to the church to do as it pleases and assume his blessing on all actions. This is a stern warning to churches not to abuse this principle and practice." The Lord of the church does not endorse discipline over vain rivalries or petty sin; rather, Jesus is giving a promise concerning a very specific situation: the maintenance of the integrity of the body of Christ. Lauterbach continues, "He is building his church and care must be taken in that process. When the church acts according to his will, as

---

86. Carson maintains, "The verb *krinō* ('judge') has a wide semantic range: 'judge' (judicially), 'condemn,' 'discern' . . . Jesus] demands that people 'make a right judgment' (John 7:24; cf. 1 Cor 5:5; Gal 1:8–9; Phil 3:2; 1 John 4:1). All of this presupposes that some kinds of 'judging' are not only legitimate but mandated. . . . Jesus' demand here is for his disciples not to be judgmental and censorious. The rigor of the disciples' commitment to God's kingdom and the righteousness demanded of them do not authorize them to adopt a judgmental attitude. Those who 'judge' like this will in turn be 'judged,' not by men (which would be of little consequence) but by God (which fits the solemn tone of the discourse)." Carson, "Matthew," 183. See also Knuteson, *Calling the Church to Discipline*, 35–36.

87. Bruce Ware brings out this point and helpfully connects it to church discipline: "After Jesus says what is commonly quoted ('do not judge lest you be judged'), he proceeds with instructions precisely about how properly to bring an erring brother to account. Recall that he warns to 'take the log out of your own eye, and then you will see clearly to take the speck out of your brother's eye' (7:5). What is often missed in this is that once the log is removed, one has the obligation then to help remove the speck from his brother's eye. In other words, Jesus expects us to be used in the lives of others to help them advance in holiness, just as they may be used likewise in our lives to help us to grow. Church discipline is, most essentially, the formal structure that grows out of a healthy practice of corporate accountability." Ware, "Perspectives on Church Discipline," 87.

88. For a more detailed analysis of these passages, see chapter 2 of this work.

described in his Word, then he is at work in its actions. Consider it his hand working through the glove of the church."[89] As such, if the church is to possess the authority as stated in Matthew 16:19 and 18:18, the community must act in accord with the truth of Scripture and distinct details of each disciplinary situation.[90]

Thus, when a church—no matter how large and influential or small and seemingly inconsequential—acts in accordance with God's word, its authority is real, albeit mediated. The church possesses a kind of power, wherein, according to Knuteson, there is "the heavenly recognition of earthly transactions when they are handled according to divine directions."[91] Exercising discipline in the church, then, is a most delicate affair. Vanhoozer helpfully summarizes the proper interpretation of these passages, saying, "Ultimately, only God can judge the human heart. At the same time, the church has received a dominical and apostolic commission to preserve the truth and to pursue holiness."[92] As such, the church must humbly and discerningly apply its mediated authority granted by Christ.

Finally, the wording of the thesis of this dissertation must be taken into account. Church discipline is referred to as a "warning" within this dissertation, not a "pronouncement." This is significant in that there is recognition that God is the ultimate judge of all things, not the church. Warning, therefore, connotes a proper tone of serious admonition, while also granting final authority to God. Another key word found within the thesis of this work is "potential." Eschatological judgment is not unerringly certain, due to the fact that the church is filled with sinners. It is, however, a sign of potential judgment, and as such should be taken with all seriousness. Thus, while the fallibility of the church must be taken into account, this particular understanding of ecclesial discipline still holds.

---

89. Lauterbach, *Transforming Community* 201. See also Goulder, "Already?," 29.

90. See Wray, who asserts, "The church is not by this text made infallible, nor is the holy God by it engaged to defend their errors. The only fact to be established at this point, however, is simply that the Lord Jesus Christ *does* indeed intend his church to govern its members even to the extent of disciplinary measures when these become necessary." Wray, *Biblical Church Discipline*, 3.

91. Knuteson, *Calling the Church to Discipline*, 36. He continues, regarding the idea of "binding" and "loosing," and asserts that these terms denote divine ratification of an earthly action in a completed and final state. He states, "God is therefore vitally interested in the disciplinary work within His church. Extreme care, however, should be taken in the exercise of such discipline, lest we do on earth that which heaven cannot ratify." Ibid., 36–37. See also Bargerhuff, *Love That Rescues*, 157; White and Blue, *Church Discipline That Heals*, 97–98.

92. Vanhoozer, *Drama of Doctrine*, 424.

Does This Thesis Hold if a Different View of Perseverance Is Held?

Another important question to grapple with deals with the view of the perseverance of the saints espoused in this work. The view held in this dissertation is that true believers will persevere in their faith until the very end.[93] Those who "apostasize" were never truly believers to begin with.[94] There are a number of warning passages in the NT that serve as a means of assisting believers in enduring in their faith,[95] and church discipline serves in a similar fashion.

There are others, however, who have argued that apostasy is possible for genuine believers.[96] Marshall, for example, suggests throughout his work that the writers of the NT warn against apostasy as a potential threat among the Christian community, and hence there is the need for them to persevere.[97] As such, this view dictates that the warnings in Scripture, such as

---

93. On a broad theological level, one should observe that this view of the perseverance of the saints is grounded in the nature of the new covenant (Jer 31:31–34; 32:40; cf. John 3:15–16, 36; 4:14; 5:24; 6:40, 47; 1 John 5:11–13), Jesus' effectual prayers for believers (John 17:6–19; Rom 8:34; Heb 7:24–25), the unbreakable circle of salvation (Rom 8:29–39), the promise that God would complete the work he began in believers (Phil 1:6), and the Spirit's multifaceted ministry on our behalf (Rom 8:9, 11, 15, 26–27; Eph 1:13). See Demarest, *Cross and Salvation*, 444–48. One must also take into account the verdict that is rendered when a person comes to salvation in Christ. Horton notes, "If there is 'now no condemnation for those who are in Christ Jesus' (Rom 8:1), on the sole basis of Christ's righteousness imputed, then a reversal of the court's verdict is impossible. That verdict has already set into motion the process of inward renewal, as the believer has been inserted by the Spirit into the powers of the age to come [2 Cor 5:17–18; Eph 3:20]." Horton, *Christian Faith*, 681. These kinds of pronouncements made by God regarding the believer are crucial to take into consideration when understanding one's standing as they are united to Christ.

94. For an excellent defense of this view of discipline from an exegetical vantage point, see Schreiner, *Run to Win the Prize*, 25–49. He holds this view in opposition to other theological stances, such as Arminianism, that claim a Christian can apostasize and in effect lose their salvation. One key point Schreiner makes in refuting such a position is that in reading a text like Phil 1:6 or Rom 8:35–39, if one were to take an Arminian reading of this passage, as does McKnight and Marshall, "it drains the verse of virtually all comfort." Comfort is the point of this text, which is precisely why Schreiner argues these warnings are for Christians and are prospective in nature. This allows for comfort to be drawn from these passages as we recognize our perseverance stems from the work of God within us. See ibid., 88.

95. Schreiner asserts, "By heeding the warnings, believers gain assurance in their lives." Ibid., 102.

96. See, e.g., Marshall, *Kept by the Power of God*; McKnight, "Apostasy," 58–60. Those who hold to this view are typically Arminian in their understanding of soteriology.

97. Marshall, *Kept by the Power of God*, 86–88, 106–14, 129, 145, 165–67.

Hebrews 6,[98] be taken as authentic, since the possibility of abandoning the faith is genuine. Others, as has been mentioned previously,[99] hold to a view of perseverance denoting either the loss of rewards or hypothetical loss of salvation. While the assertion of this dissertation is that those whom God has truly saved will persevere to the end, it will here be argued that, regardless of one's position regarding perseverance, key aspects—and often the entirety—of the thesis of this dissertation hold true.

First, regarding the position that Christians can commit apostasy, proponents of this view assert that the warning passages are still intended for the believer in order to prevent potential apostasy and, in turn, eschatological judgment. Marshall avers that "the need for exhortation shows that there is a possibility of failure to work out salvation."[100] Thus, according to the loss of salvation view, the warning texts seen throughout Scripture, particularly in Hebrews, are intended to keep believers from apostasy, lest they incur eschatological judgment.[101] The NT authors do not want believers to apostasize from the faith, and as such, though advocates of this view see these warnings as negative in nature, they are still intended to assist believers to endure in their faith.

Despite these differences, Schreiner notes areas of agreement between those who hold that Christians can commit apostasy and those who do not. He states, "We should observe that both sets of interpreters believe that good works are *evidence* of genuine saving faith, and both argue that good works as a fruit of faith are necessary for eschatological salvation (cf. James 2:14–26)." Furthermore, both groups would agree that obedience

---

98. In dealing with Heb 6, a notoriously difficult passage to contend with when adopting the view of perseverance seen in this work, Grudem maintains, "Careful analysis of the terms used to describe these people before they fell away showed that, while the terms could be used to apply to genuine Christians, they could also be used to apply to people who were not yet Christians but who had simply heard the gospel and had experienced several of the blessings of the Holy Spirit's work in the Christian community." See Grudem, "Perseverance of the Saints," 171–72. See also Carson, "Reflections on Assurance," 261–67. Thus, this passage seems to assert that these people had experienced many of the preliminary stages that often precede conversion, but they had not truly embraced Christ alone for salvation. This understanding, especially of Heb 6:4–6, fits when understanding that the metaphor of the field demonstrates the true barrenness of their spiritual lives (6:7–8). When referring to the "things belonging to salvation," the author is comparing true believers to those who had fallen away, and asserting that while the blessings seen in verses 4–6 are positive, they did not belong in the category of salvation (6:9–12).

99. See n43 of this chapter.

100. Marshall, *Kept by the Power of God*, 100.

101. See Ashby, "Reformed Arminian View," 170–80, for more detailed analysis of the warning texts in Hebrews.

is one indication that a person genuinely belongs to God (1 John 2:3–6; 2 Pet 1:5–11). Schreiner continues, "In both instances assurance is not an abstraction that is realized apart from the work of the Spirit in the lives of God's people."[102] Thus, while the view of perseverance advocated in this work seems warranted,[103] one can still see church discipline as a warning of judgment and a means of perseverance for the church body, even for those who espouse a view of perseverance and assurance that advocates for the possibility of apostasy.

Others hold that lack of perseverance in the faith will lead to loss of rewards, not loss of salvation. Advocates of this view agree that the warnings in the NT address true Christians, but because they believe Christians cannot lose their salvation, the threat of loss in these passages concerns rewards, not eternal salvation.[104] As such, those who hold this view assert that "perseverance in holiness is an indispensable condition," but only for the attaining of future rewards.[105] Thus, while this view would not agree with the link made between perseverance and eschatological judgment, proponents of this position would still see the warning passages in the NT as admonitions to endure in the faith. The aspect of genuine warning to believers is still present, though admittedly it would be for the purpose of attaining rewards, not final salvation.

One final view of perseverance to be considered is the hypothetical loss of salvation. Seeking to avoid the apparent contradiction between biblical warnings and God's promises to secure his own people, advocates of this view maintain that NT warnings threaten Christians with eternal loss if they commit apostasy, but this threat is hypothetical. These passages warn true believers what the outcome would be if apostasy could occur.[106] While not always seeming to do justice to each of the warning texts in conceiving of the matter as merely hypothetical, this view does endorse the thesis of this work in that the warnings are issued so that others avoid eschatological judgment as they are exhorted to endure in the faith. One can thus observe

---

102. Schreiner, "Assurance," 72.

103. It seems that the biblical teaching on assurance is best preserved by acknowledging that those who defected from the church only appeared to be genuine believers. Their leaving of the church demonstrates that their faith was not genuine (1 Cor 11:19; 1 John 2:19). Gundry Volf maintains that those who continually practice unethical behavior are not truly converted in the first place. Alternatively, God may chastise a genuine Christian who falls into sin, but this is not the same as saying that he or she will be eternally condemned. See Gundry Volf, *Paul and Perseverance*, 155–57.

104. See Kendall, *Once Saved, Always Saved*, 49–53.

105. Wilkin, *Confident in Christ*, 116.

106. See Kent, *Epistle to the Hebrews*, 113–14, 206–7; Westcott, *Epistle to the Hebrews*, 165.

how other views of perseverance adhere to key aspects, if not the entirety of the thesis of this dissertation.

What Sins Call for Church Discipline and What Sins Should Love Cover?

Another clarification must be made in regard to the sins for which the church should actually discipline. Some will object to discipline, especially excommunication, since love should cover a multitude of sins (1 Pet 4:8; cf. Jas 5:20), and this is particularly the case due to the thesis of this dissertation pointing toward the potentiality of eternal judgment for those who fall under discipline. The Scriptures speak to grace being extended, as well as discipline being meted out for sin issues, and thus a closer examination of this topic is merited.

First, in relation to love covering over sin, this is not referring to one believer atoning for the sins of another believer, but rather a spirit of love offered in the face of sin, particularly in issuing forgiveness.[107] This loving spirit is also the point of the parable following Jesus' instructions on church discipline; the church must be willing to forgive repentant sinners (Matt 18:21–35). Thus, as Strauch asserts, genuine Christian love is tolerant in that it is forgiving, forbearing, kind (Eph 4:2), humble-minded (Phil 2:1–4), and respectful toward people, who are created in God's image.[108] In the process of discipline as advocated by Jesus (Matt 18:15–20) we go to one another in a spirit of love, looking to forgive and restore.

However, Strauch continues, there is also a legitimate sense in which Christian love is intolerant. He states, "It is not tolerant in the sense of approving or accepting that which is immoral or false as defined by God's Word. Love cannot be tolerant of that which destroys people's lives or spreads lies about the gospel."[109] Discipline must take place for unrepentant sin. More specifically, Wray asserts that excommunication must come for those who unrepentantly go through the entire process of Matthew 18:15–18, form divisive factions within the church (Rom 16:17–18; Titus 3:10), live publicly scandalous lives (1 Cor 5), or reject essential doctrines of the faith (1 Tim 1:19–20; 6:3–5; 2 John 7–11).[110] Davis similarly maintains that there are

---

107. See Schreiner, *1, 2 Peter, Jude*, 212–13.

108. Strauch, *Christian Leader's Guide*, 161.

109. Ibid.

110. Wray, *Biblical Church Discipline*, 8–9. See also Hammett, "Regenerate Church Membership," 42; Kitchens, "Perimeters of Corrective Church Discipline," 211; Leeman, *Church and the Surprising Offense of God's Love*, 319.

four major categories for sins for which church discipline may occur: "(1) private and personal offenses that violate Christian love; (2) divisiveness and factions that destroy Christian unity; (3) moral and ethical deviations that break Christian standards; (4) teaching false doctrine."[111] Grudem more generally classifies examples of discipline in the NT, which include divisiveness (Rom 16:17; Titus 3:10), sexual sin (1 Corinthians 5), laziness (2 Thess 3:6–10), disobedience (2 Thess 3:14–15), blasphemy (1 Tim 1:20), and teaching false doctrine (2 John 10–11). Nonetheless, he, along with the aforementioned works, would maintain that "a definite principle is at work: all sins that were explicitly disciplined in the New Testament were publicly known or outwardly evident sins, and many of them had continued over a period of time."[112] Discipline, therefore, is exacted not for trite matters over difference of opinion or personal slights, but for the issue of unrepentant sin.

Thus, love can cover a multitude of sins, but there are other times when love compels a church to act, even to the point of excommunication. Leeman maintains, "Formal church discipline or excommunication is warranted when an individual seems to happily abide in known sin. There's no evidence that the Spirit is making him or her uncomfortable, other than the discomfort of getting caught. Rather, obedience to sin's desires are *characteristic*."[113] Passages such as Matthew 18 and Galatians 6 seem to signify and approach to discipline that is thoughtful, patient, and loving. However, repentance is the goal and, thus, while love does signify that we quickly address and forgive sins at times, the church is also called to walk through the process of discipline if necessary.

---

111. Davis, "Practical Issues of Church Discipline," 173. Keach, "Glory of a True Church," 73–84, offers a similar list for discipline, which includes private offenses, scandalous immorality, heresy, divisiveness, and disorderliness. For similar reasons given for the practice of church discipline see Griffith, "Short Treatise," 106–7; Jones, "Treatise of Church Discipline," 153–56; Mell, "Corrective Church Discipline," 422–25; Savage, "Manual of Church Discipline," 487–88.

112. Grudem, *Systematic Theology*, 896. See also Norman, "Reestablishment of Proper Church Discipline," 206–7.

113. Leeman, *Church Discipline*, 50, emphasis original. Elsewhere Leeman maintains, "Formal church discipline from the entire congregation is reserved for sins of such significance that the church no longer feels able to affirm a person's profession of faith. . . . So the church removes its public affirmation by barring him from the Lord's Table. It takes away his passport and announces that it can no longer formally affirm his citizenship in Christ's kingdom." See Leeman, *Church Membership*, 112.

What Is the Process for Restoration after Discipline?

One final question deals with the procedure for restoring people to church fellowship after they have been disciplined. Is this an immediate reinstatement, or is there some kind of probationary period? As churches become more faithful in implementing the process of discipline, this question will become increasingly relevant and therefore demands thoughtful attention.

Restoration can be defined as the forgiveness of an excommunicated individual by the church after they have repented and also a reaffirmation of his or her "citizenship" in God's kingdom.[114] There is no timetable given in Scripture as to how long a church should take in restoring the person to church membership.[115] Sound wisdom must be present with each case, as various details will have to be factored into the discussion.[116] However, while some time may be taken to sort out the various issues concerning disciplinary cases and restoration to membership, Jeschke asserts, "The perennial temptation of the church is to demand more for restoration than for baptism, to make the conditions for restoration more rigorous than for joining the body of Christ originally."[117] If one looks at the parable Jesus tells immediately after the teaching on church discipline in Matthew 18, one can see that forgiveness of a genuinely repentant individual is paramount.

Thus, it would seem that while restoration and forgiveness should be extended to individuals under discipline, the key is ascertaining to the best of the church's ability the genuineness of the person's repentance. Once that

---

114. See ibid., 79–85.

115. In the early years of the church there was a struggle over of those who lapsed in their faith. This was seen specifically with the Novationists and Donatists, two groups who protested the restoration of those who abandoned the faith during times of persecution. Others, such as Basil of Caesarea and Gregory of Nyssa, advocated for certain periods of time passing before a sinner was restored to the church based on what the offense was (e.g., twenty years for murder, eighteen years for adultery, nine years for fornication). See Basil of Caesarea, "To Amphicolus, Letter 217," 8:256; Gregory of Nyssa, "Canonical Epistle to Letoius, Bishop of Melitene," 188–98. This kind of process sought to ensure continuing righteousness on the part of the offender, though such measures are not found in Scripture. For further details see Wills, "Historical Analysis of Church Discipline," 131–39.

116. After years of pastoral experience, Lauterbach advocates for a one-year period for restoration, wherein the person seeking restoration meets with a team each week, receives help in reestablishing spiritual disciplines, prays with the team and continually confesses sin, and, upon their acceptance into church membership, work gradually back into ministerial functions within the church. Lauterbach, *Transforming Community*, 204. Regardless of how long a process this is, the key is to see the person's repentant heart and set up a plan to avoid this kind of sinful pattern in the future.

117. Jeschke, *Discipling in the Church*, 101.

occurs, forgiveness, restoration, and concentrated discipleship must take place.[118] Davis asserts, regarding restoration as seen in 2 Corinthians 2:6–8,

> Therefore, when an excommunicated sinner repents and comes back to the elders of the church and expresses a desire for reinstatement, the elders should examine the individual thoroughly to determine if genuine repentance has occurred. The repentant sinner should plainly repudiate the sinful acts that led to the excommunication and be willing to say so in front of the whole church. Before the individual speaks to the church, the elders should investigate the life of the person, asking relevant persons—friends, family, neighbors, coworkers, other church members—for evidence of the individual's repentant life. Having thus ascertained the genuineness of the repentance, the individual should ask for the church's forgiveness ... and express sorrow over the sins that led to the excommunication. The church should then reinstate the individual ... and express in many ways the delight they have at what God has done to restore this person. It would also be wise for an elder to be assigned to meet with the individual regularly for concentrated discipleship and counseling after that person has been reinstated.[119]

Again, the timeframe is not specifically expressed, but these principles should be maintained in any scenario wherein a person under excommunication is seeking restoration to their local church.

---

118. See Adams, *Handbook of Church Discipline*, 91–97, who asserts, based on 2 Cor 2:6–8, that restoration requires three factors: the repentant offender must be forgiven, he must be assisted to avoid that sin in the future, and he must be reinstated in love. He gives no timeframe for this process, but it would certainly take some time to work through it all effectively. See also Driscoll and Breshears, *Vintage Church*, 166–70.

119. Davis, "Practical Issues of Church Discipline," 179. Davis here mentions the role of elders in church discipline, which is another question that arises, particularly in congregationally governed churches. He maintains, "The elders are in the best spiritual position in the church to act both as witnesses against the sinning church member and (even more importantly) as mature shepherds of souls, skillfully wooing one of Christ's wandering sheep back to repentance." Davis explicates the "toolbox for skillful shepherding" as including encouragement, instruction, exhortation, comfort, warning, rebuke, and excommunication. Ibid., 170–72. For works that advocate a leading role for elders in a congregational context, see Merkle, *40 Questions about Elders and Deacons*; Merkle, *Elder and Overseer*; Newton, *Elders in Congregational Life*.

CONCLUSION

This understanding of discipline has serious ramifications for the life and well-being of a church. John Dagg noted perceptively and correctly, "It has been remarked, that when discipline leaves the church, Christ goes with it."[120] Rightly understanding the theological intricacies regarding ecclesial discipline is crucial in articulating a particular doctrine and applying it to present-day disciples of Jesus. In this particular instance, an accurate comprehension of Scripture's teaching on church discipline dictates that we earnestly consider the words of Dietrich Bonhoeffer: "Nothing can be crueler than the tenderness that consigns another to his sin. Nothing can be more compassionate than the severe rebuke that calls a brother back from the path of sin."[121] Thus, the call to discipline, and, if necessary, to exclude is necessary for the health and vitality of the church, particularly as it relates to warning the unrepentant sinner of potential eschatological judgment and exhorting church members to persevere in their faith.

---

120. Dagg, *Manual of Church Order*, 274.
121. Bonhoeffer, *Life Together*, 107.

5

Implications of This Study and Conclusion

THE FINAL CHAPTER OF this dissertation will conclude with four practical implications this study yields for local churches. First, this chapter will take into consideration how church membership factors into this understanding of ecclesial discipline, specifically noting the responsibilities incumbent on those who become part of a covenant community to exhort one another to avoid sin and pursue righteousness (cf. Heb 3:12–13; 10:23–25). The exercise of faithful discipline demands that a particular culture is set up within the church, wherein regenerate church membership is taken seriously, members care for one another deeply, and rightly understand their responsibility to hold one another accountable.

Second, pastors of local congregations must also recognize, in light of the understanding of church discipline espoused in this dissertation, that they are stewards of the gospel and also stewards of the members of their church. Therefore, they must shepherd the church effectively. As such, pastors are called to teach and lead their people, and to faithfully practice ecclesial discipline. As stewards, pastors must be dedicated not only to exercise corrective church discipline, but also formative discipline. This stewardship also includes faithful preaching and teaching, leadership, as well as the proper administration of regenerate church membership.

As shepherds, pastors must also exercise faithful oversight over their congregations. Personal attention must be directed toward all members within the church in order to assess their spiritual vitality and provide them with proper shepherding. Pastors should not just take the lead in discipline, but should watch out for those who may be heading into dangerous areas and forestall the need for discipline (Acts 20:28). Several practical issues will be addressed in this section, including the difficulty of oversight in megachurch and multi-site models, and the need for a plurality of elders in effective oversight.

Finally, one other practical implication involves one's understanding of the ordinances. Historically, baptism was a necessary step in joining a church, playing a key role in guarding the "front door" of the church and upholding regenerate church membership. Undergoing excommunication meant that, among other things, one was excluded from the Lord's Supper. And yet, in our contemporary church culture, this hardly seems like punishment. If the thesis of this work is correct, one should acknowledge that greater significance must be vested in the ordinances. It is hoped that this study will inspire such measures so that scholars, as well as pastors and church members, will rightly comprehend that church discipline is a warning of potential eschatological judgment, and as such is a means by which believers in Christ are compelled to persevere in their faith.

FAITHFULLY MAINTAINING REGENERATE CHURCH MEMBERSHIP

The first practical implication of this dissertation is the reestablishment of regenerate church membership in local churches. It is crucial to observe the relationship that exists between church membership and ecclesial discipline.[1] Hammett notes, "Church discipline and regenerate church membership are related in that the former can be effectively practiced only by a congregation composed of the latter, and that the latter can be maintained only if the former is consistently practiced."[2] As such, in order for either to be effectively maintained, care must be taken to uphold regenerate church membership and a thoroughgoing practice of church discipline.[3]

---

1. For a helpful study of church membership and discipline and their relationship to one another, see Leeman, *Church and the Surprising Offense of God's Love*.

2. Hammett, "Regenerate Church Membership," 30. This point is also affirmed by both Benjamin Griffith and Benjamin Keach, who assert that regenerate church membership is a prerequisite to the proper exercise of church discipline. See Griffith, "Short Treatise," 71; Keach, "Glory of a True Church," 99.

3. Ashford and Akin, "Missional Implications," 194, assert, "Through regenerate church membership and church discipline, the church has a way to designate those who are truly God's people. While, on this side of eternity, we will never know for sure the state of another person's soul, we must keep diligent watch over the church, discipling and disciplining toward the goals of faithfulness and holiness. The natural

The Warrant for Regenerate Church Membership

Before delving into the practical ways one can pursue a regenerate church membership in a local church context, it is important to observe briefly the theological basis for membership. Lauterbach maintains, "Membership in a local church is rooted in the dynamic of shared life in the Spirit. Communing members are born of God, and their fellowship is with the Father and with the Son, Jesus Christ."[4] Church membership goes beyond mere attendance at a weekly gathering; it is participation in a divine reality. Thus, it is a high privilege to assemble with God's people and participate corporately in communing with God and ministering to one another.

Church membership can be defined simply as a formal commitment or covenant between an individual and a local church.[5] God calls for his people to gather corporately (notice, for example, that most of the NT epistles are addressed to specific churches), to submit to qualified leadership (1 Tim 3:1–7; Titus 1:5–9), to come under the teaching of the Scriptures and faithfully partake of the ordinances (Acts 2:37–47; 1 Cor 11:23–26; 2 Tim 4:1–2), and to exercise the authority Christ has given to them (Matt 16:19; 18:17). Leeman further asserts, "In Matthew 16, 18, and 28, Jesus gave the apostles and the apostolic church the power of the keys. This authorized the church to guard the gospel, to affirm credible professions, to unite such professors to itself, to oversee their discipleship, and to exclude hypocrites."[6] As the people of God under the new covenant a local church is committed to the reality that God is identifying them as a people for himself, distinguishing them from the world, calling them to righteousness, making them his witness, using them to display his glory, identifying them with one another,

---

complement to regenerate church membership is church discipline. . . . In the practice of church discipline, members who are living a life contrary to the transforming power of the gospel (regeneration) are called to repent and live in accordance with the gospel or else be separated from the church. In order for regenerate church membership to be maintained in the church in any viable sense, church discipline must be exercised as well."

4. Lauterbach, *Transforming Community*, 163.

5. Merkle, "Biblical Basis for Church Membership," 32. See also Hammett, *Biblical Foundations for Baptist Churches*, 117–20; Hammett, "Regenerate Church Membership," 34–37; Dever, *Nine Marks of a Healthy Church*, 160–65. Leeman, *Church and the Surprising Offense of God's Love*, 217, also helpfully defines church membership as a covenant union between a particular church and a Christian, consisting of the church's affirmation of the Christian's gospel profession (Matt 16:19), the church's promise to give oversight to the Christian, and the Christian's promise to gather with the church and submit to its oversight (Heb 3:12–13; 10:24–25; 13:17).

6. Leeman, *Church and the Surprising Offense of God's Love*, 177. See also Tidball, *Ministry by the Book*, 24.

and rendering accountability and protection for members.[7] Thus, a local church gathers for a specific purpose and they do so as the people of God who have been redeemed through faith in Christ (Col 1:13–14).

While church membership is not explicitly demonstrative within the NT, there are certainly pointers to the necessity of its existence within a local church. Highlighting Hebrews 13:17 and 1 Thessalonians 5:12–13, Merkle demonstrates that the kind of accountability spoken of demands a commitment made by an individual to formally join a local church. He states, "In order for Christians to give respect and recognition to their leaders, they must place themselves under the authority and accountability of those who will shepherd them. . . . Church membership provides the God-ordained means of providing accountability that all sheep need."[8] Merkle also makes the simple point that church discipline as advocated in Matthew 18 and 1 Corinthians 5 cannot be properly carried out if a church does not have an official membership role.[9]

Church members also have particular responsibilities toward one another, most generally that they love each other (John 13:34–35). This love includes watching over one another and holding each other accountable (Rom 15:14; Gal 6:1–2; Phil 2:3–4; 2 Thess 3:15; Heb 12:15).[10] These commands to care for one another are given in order that believers would not be hardened by sin, but instead would corporately pursue perseverance in the faith (Heb 3:12–13; 10:24–25).[11] From this evidence one can thus observe the implicit reality of church membership.

---

7. See Leeman, *Church and the Surprising Offense of God's Love*, 236–70.

8. Merkle, "Biblical Basis for Church Membership," 36–37.

9. Ibid., 40. In Matt 18:15–20 we see that the keys of the kingdom (Matt 16:19) extend to the local church. As a result, Leeman, *Church Membership*, 61, asserts that "the local church has heaven's authority for declaring who on earth is a kingdom citizen and therefore represents heaven."

10. Newport asserts, "The church is not a chance collection of people but a community of believers called and united together by the grace of God—a covenant people. Christian believers therefore accept responsibility for each other and agree to exercise such discipline as is necessary to remain faithful to God's covenant. The church should take seriously the Bible's many injunctions to warn, rebuke, exhort, encourage, and build one another up in love." Newport, "Purpose of the Church," 28.

11. See Dever, "Church," 793. See also Peterson, *Possessed by God*, 114, who aptly observes, "Practical holiness means working out in everyday life and relationships the moral consequences of our union with Christ." In short, church membership demands that we exhort one another regularly so that we will not be hardened by the deceitfulness of sin (Heb 3:12–13).

Recovering Meaningful Membership

People are brought into the membership of a local church based on their profession of faith in Jesus Christ and baptism, and thereby they become a part of a particular group of people who strive together, by the grace of God and the power of the Spirit, to live in obedience to him.[12] Church discipline is a means by which the congregation can hold one another accountable to keeping the commands of God; and excommunication, therefore, is a loving way to warn the offending sinner of potential judgment due to their continual sin and lack of repentance.[13] Leeman maintains, therefore, "Remember, to be a church member is to be a Jesus representative. Discipline, then, is the appropriate course of action when the character of a person's representation brings shame on Jesus' name."[14] Thus, membership and discipline are tightly linked, as we are called under the new covenant to be a people who are forgiven and persistently obedient to God (Jer 31:31–34).

---

12. Banks further maintains that Christians are to see themselves as members of a divine family. Family terminology is utilized by Paul to demonstrate the kind of membership one inhabits when joining the church as a member (Rom 16:13; Gal 6:10; Eph 2:19; Col 4:7). In viewing the church as family, emphasis is also put on the responsibilities that church members have to one another. One responsibility toward fellow members includes discipline. Banks asserts, "If one of the members succumbs unwittingly to a course of action harmful to himself, those who have not fallen into it should 'restore him in a spirit of gentleness,' looking to themselves, however, lest they 'too be tempted' (Gal 6:1). When an action detrimentally affects the life of the community, anyone aware of this should bring the matter to the community's attention: however there must be at least two, if possible three, involved so that it may be substantiated by more than one witness. . . . Both nurture and discipline within the congregation should then arise spontaneously from the concern of every member for the quality of its life and the involvement of every member in decisions affecting the whole." See Banks, *Paul's Idea of Community*, 54–57.

13. Hamilton gives a helpful and rather stark summary of membership and its relationship to discipline. "God is holy. He really is. Jesus gave instructions for putting people out of the church. He really did. The early church followed these instructions (1 Cor. 5:1–13; 2 Cor. 2:6–7; 1 Thess. 5:14; 2 Thess. 3:6–15; Titus 3:10–11; 2 John 1:7–10; 3 John 1:9–12). They obeyed Jesus and enacted God's holiness. Corrective church discipline is enacted against unrepentant people because people who have been born again repent of their sin. Those who refuse to repent show that they have never been born again. Only those who have been born again are united to Christ by faith and are truly members of his body, the church; so when it becomes evident that someone has not been born again (by their refusal to repent), they are to be removed from church membership. This action is for the salvation of those who are expelled from the church (cf. 1 Cor. 5:5; 1 Tim. 1:20). The church is telling the unrepentant that they need the gospel; they need to believe in Jesus. The church is hoping they will trust in Christ, repent of their sin, and be reconciled to God." Hamilton, *God's Glory in Salvation*, 567–68. See also Dever, "Church," 807; Hamilton, "Church Militant and Her Warfare," 76.

14. Leeman, *Church Membership*, 109–10.

Due to the tight link that exists between church membership and ecclesial discipline, and because of the significance of church discipline as seen in the thesis of this dissertation, it is imperative that one considers the practical steps that must be taken in regaining a meaningful church membership.[15] First, churches must be committed to faithful gospel preaching. Pastors must be clear in proclaiming the realities of a holy God, sinful humanity, and the substitutionary death and bodily resurrection of Jesus Christ. There must be a strong call for repentance and faith. This kind of preaching will clearly demarcate the boundaries between those who believe in Christ and have joined in membership, and those who have not. Clear lines should be drawn in a loving manner through faithful preaching.

Churches should also have an agreed upon statement of faith and church covenant. Statements of faith unite a church doctrinally, while church covenants guide a church in its conduct.[16] Membership in a local church means that one takes on certain responsibilities, both to know and to guard the doctrine of the church, as well as the overall behavior of its members. Without such documents, membership loses a certain amount of authority. Churches should discuss who and what they are as a church, and what the Bible demands of them as Christians. Churches can then work to personalize a specific statement so that the covenant is owned as their covenant, not as one imposed upon them.[17] Thus, church membership must include a clear notion of what the local church believes and how they will live as believers in community and in the world.

Regaining meaningful membership should also include some form of membership classes and interview.[18] Membership classes can vary in length and content, but should include teaching on the statement of faith, the church covenant, the history of Christianity and of that particular local church, the expectations of members, and the way in which the church operates, including the process of church discipline. Before admission into membership an interview should also be conducted to personally ascertain the candidate's understanding of the gospel, their conversion experience,

---

15. Many of the practical steps advocated in this section are derived from Dever, "Regaining Meaningful Membership," 57–61; Hammett, *Biblical Foundations for Baptist Churches*, 114–26.

16. For a historical account of the application of church covenants and pertinent examples, particularly in Baptist contexts, see Deweese, *Baptist Church Covenants*.

17. For a helpful outline of practical steps that need to be taken for the preparation and implementation of a church covenant, see Deweese, *Community of Believers*, 28–40.

18. For an article that offers historical warrant for membership classes, looking specifically at the catechumenate in the early church, see Arnold, "Early Church Catechesis," 39–54.

and to ensure that they have been baptized as a believer.[19] Taking these steps prior to looking for congregational approval of candidates for membership will further ensure the integrity of the membership process.

Care should also be taken for those members already within the church to know one another and pray for each other consistently. One practical way that this can be accomplished is by keeping an updated church directory. Pastors must continually teach and model for their people the importance of praying for one another and caring for each other in specific ways. This type of application will cultivate a family spirit within the church as members can confidently know that people are praying for them and looking out for their interests.

One final step toward recovering a meaningful church membership is to create a culture of discipleship within the church. This happens through faithful preaching and teaching, intentional small groups, and individuals pursuing means by which they may grow. Members must be encouraged to give of themselves in love toward one another. As members they are called to care for one another in specific ways, not living the Christian life in isolation.

This reality is described in texts such as Hebrews 3:12–13 and Hebrews 10:23–25. Both of these passages assume that one is part of a local church and under its authority. Hebrews 3:12–13 warns of an evil, unbelieving heart leading any in the church to "fall away from the living God," and as such the author admonishes the church to exhort one another so they will not be "hardened by the deceitfulness of sin." Commenting on this passage, Davis avers that we must live together in close community with such wisdom and spiritual attentiveness that we can see if a brother or sister is developing an "evil, unbelieving heart that departs from the living God." The passage says that sin is deceitful and that it has a gradual hardening effect on our hearts. Thus, Davis maintains, "A healthy church will be filled with people who care about the spiritual well-being of fellow church members, and who 'encourage each other daily,' warning about the effects of sin."[20] For the community addressed in Hebrews struggling with the problem of spiritual drifting, hardening of the heart was a real danger. Thus, mutual exhortation to flee from sin and pursue righteousness was essential.[21]

---

19. More will be said regarding baptism below in the section dealing with the ordinances. Aside from the biblical arguments for a credobaptist position, one must understand that the pursuit of meaningful regenerate church membership demands that believer's baptism be the norm, since baptism is a necessary step prior to formally joining a church.

20. Davis, "Practical Issues of Church Discipline," 162.

21. See Guthrie, *Hebrews*, 130. One can also observe that this call to exhortation

Similarly, Hebrews 10:23–25 contains an exhortation to God's people to meet together continually and to consider how they can "stir up one another to love and good works." Neither of these texts has excommunication in mind directly; however, such passages seemingly depict the early stages of discipline (Matt 18:15–17) and function as a means of keeping God's people from sin and entering into the latter part of discipline, namely, excommunication. This is the point of discipleship, to flee sin and pursue righteousness. Leeman further maintains, in relation to Hebrews 10:24–25, "Further, if church membership consists in the church's public affirmation of an individual's profession of faith, nonattendance renders the church incapable of fulfilling its responsibility. The church can no longer claim with integrity to oversee one's discipleship. Therefore, excommunication effectively sets the record straight."[22] Thus, this kind of rigorous discipleship seen in church membership is, at least partially, intended to be one of the means of maintaining the people of God in a state of perseverance, as it relates to their faith.

Guthrie affirms this understanding of the text when he states,

> In Hebrews' conception, unbelief and disobedience go hand in hand (3:12, 18–19). Unbelief leads to sin, and sin leads to a hardened heart that does not believe in the living God (3:13). Assurance of one's relationship with Christ, therefore, results from perseverance in holding firmly to one's posture of belief and a life characterized by obedience to Christ.[23]

The people of God are called, therefore, to exhort one another continually in a local church context in order that we might be holy as God is holy (1 Pet 1:16; cf. Lev 11:44).[24] If an individual stumbles and becomes involved

---

sounds much like the first step of the disciplinary process as advocated by Jesus (Matt 18:15). As such, concerning the seriousness of disciplining church members, Hays asserts, in regards to Matthew 18:15–20, "The final step of expulsion of the unrepentant sinner from the community (18:17) indicates how seriously the imperatives of righteousness are to be taken. One cannot be an unrepentant sinner and remain within the community of Jesus' disciples." Hays, *Moral Vision of the New Testament*, 102. See also Garrett, *Baptist Church Discipline*, 5.

22. Leeman, *Church Discipline*, 106–7.

23. Guthrie, "Hebrews," 956. Elsewhere Guthrie elaborates on this point and notes that, "Whatever the reason, the author sees their discontinuance of common fellowship and worship as fatal for perseverance in their faith." Guthrie, *Hebrews*, 345.

24. Owens maintains, "The biblical answer for maintaining a godly witness of a pure church to the world is the practice of church discipline.... A recovery of proper stress on sanctification would soon yield a recovery of proper, biblical church discipline." Owens, "Doctrine of Sanctification," 195. Leeman, *Church Discipline*, 28–29, also helpfully notes, regarding Matt 18:15–20, that the deeper conviction underlying

in continual, unrepentant sin, the church must lovingly confront and, if necessary, remove those who refuse to repent.[25] This ongoing, communal process of discipline must take place,[26] but a robust culture of discipleship will prevent many of these extreme cases. As such, churches must be dedicated to encouraging honesty and mutual exhortation in corporate gatherings, smaller classes, small groups, and one-on-one settings. This may mean a change in the way things are currently done in our churches, but the changes will be worthwhile as seek to better accord our ways with texts such as Hebrews 3:12–13 and 10:23–25. In these ways, churches can better implement meaningful regenerate church membership and take the process of church discipline more seriously.

THE PASTOR AS STEWARD AND SHEPHERD

A second practical implication that this understanding of church discipline brings about is the kind of pastoral care that must take place within the church. The thesis of this dissertation states that discipline serves as a warning of potential eschatological judgment for the sinning individual. As such, it is a means by which the members of the church are called to persevere in their faith. As leaders of the church, pastors are held accountable for the spiritual condition of their people (Heb 13:7, 17).[27] This reality regarding

---

the disciplinary process is that the church should look different than the world. In other words, Christians are not to live as "Gentiles or tax collectors," church members should live differently than the world.

25. The reader is rightly reminded by Leeman, *Church Discipline*, 67, that "public accountability [in church discipline] should be the outgrowth of what's already going on in the private lives of church members." Leeman elsewhere notes, "Again and again Christians are told to keep one another out of harm's way and to bear one another's burdens (Gal 6:1–2; also 1 Cor 4:21; Jude 22–23). . . . The love of Christian accountability best occurs under the authority of the local church, where the ordinances can be distributed in a disciplined manner." See Leeman, *Church and the Surprising Offense of God's Love*, 264.

26. See Lauterbach, who asserts, "Church discipline is not something we 'do' to someone in sin. Church discipline is the constant activity of a church where holiness and love are pursued. We should always be watching over each other, encouraging each other daily against the possibility of a hardened heart, stimulating each other toward love and good works." Lauterbach, *Transforming Community*, 20.

27. It should be noted, as was implied above, that while pastors exercise the primary duties in oversight, church members are responsible for one another, and thus they must continually exhort one another to pursue godliness. Davis, "Those Who Must Give an Account," 207–8, asserts that all Christians are stewards, and at the final judgment they will have to give an account (Rom 14:12; 2 Cor 5:10) of everything God has entrusted to us, including our physical blessings, spiritual blessings, and our relationships with others. Thus, by implication, church members will be held accountable regarding the

church discipline demands that pastors function as faithful stewards of their local congregation and shepherd their people effectively. Effective stewardship and shepherding are essential in that pastors must care for the souls of their congregation before they reach the dangerous stage of discipline where they must be excommunicated. While pastors cannot prevent every case of church discipline, they can ensure that the instances are less frequent.

A variety of titles and images are used in the Scriptures to describe those who commit their lives to serve in pastoral ministry. Those who are called to such a vocation are described as shepherds or pastors (Eph 4:11), elders (1 Pet 5:1–5), overseers (1 Tim 3:1), and stewards (Titus 1:7), which are all terms replete with meaning and significance.[28] Through these various titles we receive a more full-orbed understanding of what the role and function of a minister truly is. This is due to the fact that words like steward and shepherd can function as metaphors, describing the realities of pastoral ministry.[29]

Terms such as "steward" and "shepherd" are not always appreciated or utilized in our contemporary milieu to describe pastoral ministry. However, it is important to observe that elders are responsible as stewards for rightly proclaiming the gospel of Jesus Christ, and they function as shepherds for overseeing the souls of the people in their local church.[30] If this is true, implications exist for modern-day pastors as they seek to watch over the spiritual condition of the people within their congregation, knowing they will have to give an account to God as stewards.[31] As such, these images give greater

---

stewardship of their church relationships in holding one another accountable, disciplining the unrepentant, and encouraging one another to persevere in the faith.

28. Throughout this section I will be using the terms of pastor, elder, and overseer interchangeably (cf. Acts 20:17–35; 1 Pet 5:1–5). For a recent argument in favor of elder and overseer being one office in Scripture, see Merkle, *Elder and Overseer*. See also Dever, "Church," 800–5; Hammett, *Biblical Foundations for Baptist Churches*, 159–89; Newton, *Elders in Congregational Life*; Waldron, "Plural-Elder Congregationalism," 212–21. This list is certainly not comprehensive, but gives the reader an ample starting point for further research.

29. For a helpful discussion of metaphors in Scripture, specifically in regards to shepherding, see Laniak, *Shepherds After My Own Heart*, 31–41.

30. Thomas Oden uses similar terminology when defining the pastoral office: "'The Pastor,' concisely defined, is a member of the body of Christ who is called by God and the church and set apart by ordination representatively to proclaim the Word, to administer the sacraments, and to guide and nurture the Christian community toward full response to God's self-disclosure." Oden, *Pastoral Theology*, 50.

31. Ferguson, *Church of Christ*, 276, comments on this biblical understanding of stewardship, looking at its implications for ministry: "The language of stewardship refers to the practice in the ancient world of giving to a trusted slave or employee the administration of the owner's property or business. . . . The biblical theme of stewardship

depth and clarity to the role and function of one who serves in pastoral ministry. Care must be taken to shepherd and steward a congregation well, so as to keep members from getting to the point of excommunication. Pastors cannot always prevent this from happening, but greater diligence would seemingly be applied in their oversight if they understood church discipline to be a warning of potential eschatological judgment. It is therefore essential to first briefly understand the teaching of Scripture regarding these concepts, and then draw out practical implications for church ministry.

The Biblical Basis of Stewardship and Shepherding

First, regarding stewardship, in the NT era of the first century, absentee landlords dominated the landscape. These wealthy landowners typically lived in the city and visited their farm estates only occasionally. As a result, these landlords utilized people known as stewards to inspect, certify, manage, oversee and report on the household and its accompanying land.[32] Responsibility belonged to the steward to faithfully maintain what was under their care. Thus, the terms οἰκονόμος and οἰκονομία have a tangible background to draw from in elucidating how stewardship was conceived of in that time.

The idea of stewardship is depicted in a literal manner in several places throughout the NT (Matt 24:45–51; Luke 12:42–48; 16:1–13; Rom 16:23;

---

derives from the premise that God creates all and so owns all (Gen. 1:1; Deut. 10:14; Ps. 24:1). His claims as creator are enhanced by his redemptive activity, his saving plan itself referred to as a 'stewardship' or 'administration' (Eph. 1:3–5, 9–10; 3:9). Hence, human beings are accountable to God for their use of what he placed at their disposal (Gen. 1:26–30)." Ferguson goes on regarding stewardship, specifically in reference to Titus 1:7, and states, "The church is presented as the family or household of God the Father (1 Tim. 3:15); the stewards take care of its affairs for him. Since a steward took care of what was not his own but belonged to another, he was expected to be prudent (Luke 12:42) and above all faithful (1 Cor. 4:1–2), for he would have to give an account to the owner (Luke 16:2; cf. Heb. 13:17)." Ibid., 323. Similarly, Hammett maintains, "As it is a position of considerable trust, the key requirement of a good steward is faithfulness to the master." Hammett, *Biblical Foundations for Baptist Churches*, 164.

32. So Tomlinson, "Purpose and Stewardship Theme," 75–77. See also Rengstorf, 'Hupēretēs', 8:539. He states, "The steward is an assistant to another as the instrument of his will." Additionally, Tidball defines the relationship between the steward and his master in the following way: "[The steward] completely identifies with the aims of his master and knows how his master would wish his desired objectives to be brought about. Moreover, his master has put all the necessary resources for their achievement at his disposal. The relationship between master and steward is close and it gives the steward a certain independence from the criticisms and designs of others. He is, however, unlikely to abuse his master's trust, for the steward knows that accountability is another mark of their relationship." Tidball, *Skillful Shepherds*, 105.

Gal 4:1-2),³³ however, as it relates to pastoral ministry, the metaphorical uses are more relevant for this study. Of all the NT writers, the Apostle Paul uses these terms the most extensively (1 Cor 4:1-2; 9:17; Eph 3:2; Col 1:25; Titus 1:7; 1 Tim 3:15), though they can also be found in the writings of Peter (1 Pet 4:10). In several of these passages one can observe that Paul considers himself to be a steward of the gospel. As such, Paul is compelled to preach the truth regarding Jesus Christ faithfully so that the grace of God can be revealed to both Jew and Gentile. Paul refers to elders as "stewards of God" (Titus 1:7) who must faithfully oversee the church, which is God's household (1 Tim 3:15).³⁴ This is the task of a steward. Thus, the concept of the "steward of God" cited in Titus 1:7 is given greater clarity when one understands the connection to household imagery.³⁵ The elder is the steward of God overseeing his household, the church, through the means of preaching, teaching, and leadership.

33. In summarizing the literal usage, the οἰκονόμος, who was typically a slave himself, held responsibility over the properties belonging to his master, was accountable for the other slaves of that particular estate, performed administrative duties in caring for the estate, at times may even have been involved in the upbringing and education of the children of their master, and would have to give an account for his actions. All of these literal uses of this particular word in the NT give us a helpful interpretive lens to better understand its metaphorical usage. See esp. Tooley, "Stewards of God," 74–86.

34. Knight gives helpful commentary regarding the relationship between οἶκος and ἐκκλησία in the Pastoral Epistles: "The standards of conduct prescribed are no mere rules of etiquette, they are standards for the house/household that is none other than God's. They provide directions for conduct in his temple, where he dwells by his Spirit, and they provide directions for relationships among his people. . . . An analogy had already been drawn between οἶκος and ἐκκλησία at the first occurrence of both in 1 Timothy (3:4, 5). Now what was implicit is made explicit: God's οἶκος is his ἐκκλησία. The three occurrences of ἐκκλησία in the PE (all in 1 Timothy: 3:5; 3:15; 5:16) provide a description of the church similar to what we see elsewhere in Paul and the NT. 3:5 depicts the church as a family under the oversight of the ἐπίσκοπος, 3:15 depicts it as the house/household of God and on that basis calls for godly conduct on the part of those who are the possession and locale of the living God and the structure undergirding God's truth, and 5:16 depicts the church as the caring community (next to the actual family itself). Since the whole letter is about the church, it would be inappropriate to restrict the description of the church in it to the three occurrences of ἐκκλησία, but the emphasis on order and oversight, on godly conduct and on God's people upholding his truth, and on caring for those in need is striking and noteworthy." Knight, *Pastoral Epistles*, 180–81.

35. See Towner: "Theological description of the church is most evident in 1 Timothy where household imagery provides the dominant components. The church is God's household (3:15; Gk. *oikos theou*). This phrase ties together related concepts in key places to describe God's rule in life in terms of household order (1:4; Gk. *oikonomia theou*), and the overseers' leadership in terms of household management (3:4–5)." Towner, "Pastoral Epistles," 334.

Regarding shepherding, one may observe key details in relation to pastoral ministry in Acts 20:17–38 and 1 Peter 5:1–5. In Acts 20 Paul calls the elders at Ephesus to meet with him (20:17), though these men are later referred to as overseers (20:28).[36] The elders are exhorted to "care for the church of God" (20:28). The term ποιμαίνω (*poimanō*) is a verbal form of the term ποιμήν (*poimēn*, which is the idea behind our English word "pastor" (cf. Eph 4:11). The verb ποιμαίνω in this verse carries the idea of serving as a herder of sheep, protecting, caring, leading, and nurturing.[37] "The metaphor of shepherding the flock of God takes up a familiar OT picture of God's people under their rulers (Ps. 100:3; Isa. 40:11; Jer. 13:17; Ezek. 34) and applies it to the task of caring for and directing the church."[38] Therefore, the elders, in continuity with OT leadership, function as overseers who are to care for the people that God has entrusted to their care.[39]

Acts 20:28 is quite similar to the exhortation Peter gives to his fellow elders in 1 Peter 5:1–5. They are told to "shepherd the flock of God that is among you, exercising oversight" (5:2).[40] Laniak elaborates and offers the following assessment of these two passages:

> The elders are to shepherd (*poimanō*) God's flock under their care. Only here and in Acts 20:28 is the imperative form of the verb used in this way.... In both contexts the association between shepherding and careful oversight is clear. In Acts the "overseers" (*episkopoi*) are expected to guard or pay close attention to (*prosechō*) the needs of the flock (in the context of wolves; v. 29). Similarly, leaders in Hebrews 13:17 "watch over" (*agrypneō*) your souls as they serve the "great Shepherd of the sheep" (Heb. 13:20). In 1 Peter 5:2 the elders are to oversee (*episkopeō*) the flock. This is the flock of the "Shepherd and Overseer (*episkopon*) of your souls" (2:25). Watching, noted frequently in this study, is a comprehensive summary of

---

36. It seems safe to conclude, therefore, that elders and overseers are two different designations for the same office. See Schreiner, *New Testament Theology*, 693; Merkle, *Elder and Overseer*, 129–35.

37. BDAG, s.v. "ποιμαίνω."

38. Marshall, "Acts," 596.

39. So Bock, *Acts*, 629–30; Bruce, *Commentary on the Book of the Acts*, 415–16.; Polhill, *Acts*, 426–27.

40. Regarding the participle ἐπισκοποῦντες, Schreiner notes, "The participle is missing in some early manuscripts (א, B, 323), but the majority of manuscripts witnessed include it, and we should not put much confidence in B, which also wrongly omits v. 3. The corrector of Sinaiticus includes the participle, and it may have been omitted by some scribes because they distinguished the offices of elder and overseer and thought the text was mistaken in correlating them." Schreiner, *1, 2 Peter, Jude*, 234.

shepherding tasks. It is the vigilant attention to threats that can disperse or destroy the flock.[41]

Therefore, the elders are to watch over the church of God, which is the flock entrusted to them by the Chief Shepherd (1 Pet 5:2, 4). Pastors are the stewards of God's gospel message, as well as the shepherds of God's people, and thus they must labor to see the members of their congregations living lives that are worthy of the gospel of Christ (Phil 1:27).

The Practical Implications of Stewardship and Shepherding

Having examined the relevant texts in this study it would seem that the concepts of stewardship and shepherding are paradigmatic for rightly understanding the task of present-day pastors. God has given pastors a tremendous amount of responsibility, and those who serve in ministry should feel the weight of this calling. It must be noted, therefore, that elders are not simply taking on some unimportant leadership position in a local church; rather they are called to faithfully preach and teach the word of God and oversee the members of their local church.

Proper Stewardship

With this understanding in place, we must now look at the practical ways in which the metaphors of stewardship and shepherding will specifically affect a pastor's conception of his ministerial task in the present. First, like Paul, pastors are responsible as stewards of the gospel to faithfully preach and teach the whole counsel of God. As such, practically speaking, pastors should proclaim biblical truths as accurately as possible, which means that exposition through entire books of the Bible would be the primary way in which Scripture would be communicated.[42] This type of preaching will focus most intensely upon the actual words of Scripture, and as such serves as the greatest possible means to being a faithful steward of God's word.

---

41. Laniak, *Shepherds After My Own Heart*, 232–33.

42. See Vanhoozer, who writes, "To preach is to address people in God's name, an address 'directed to men with the definitive claim and expectation that it has to declare the Word of God to them.' This is precisely why preaching ought to be an exposition of Scripture, the objective or written form of God's Word. To be sure, the ultimate authority over church proclamation is God in triune communicative action, and those who proclaim the word are not able to coerce the Spirit to accompany it so that it will unfailingly achieve its purpose. Nevertheless, we are responsible for preserving as much of the communicative action in Scripture as we can." Vanhoozer, *Drama of Doctrine*, 74.

Included in faithful exposition is clear proclamation of the gospel of Jesus Christ. This does not simply mean that a preacher tags the gospel onto the end of any sermon he preaches without making previous reference to it; rather, Christ will be the culminating focus and aim of every exposition, regardless of the text being preached.[43] The gospel must be brought to bear on the lives of listeners so that unbelievers can be exhorted to repent and place their faith in Christ, and believers can continue to pursue sanctification based on their identity in Christ.[44]

As stewards, pastors must not only preach and teach faithfully, they must exercise proper leadership within their local church. Leadership is exercised through sound, biblical preaching, but pastors can also lead by overseeing the entire teaching ministry of the church. Pastors should determine what is being taught in the church's children's ministry, student ministry, adult classes, small groups, and other teaching venues. If proper stewardship is to take place, this is a necessary component. Leadership should also be given in developing a specific scope and sequence that will equip people across all age ranges in pressing forward in their walk with Christ.[45]

Pastors should also lead in overseeing the process of taking in new members, as well as the administration of the ordinances. Details have already been given above regarding regenerate church membership, but it should be noted here that as stewards, pastors should take a leading role in overseeing the process. Regarding the ordinances, while more will be said below, one should here observe that stewardship demands a faithful accounting of who enters into the covenant community by baptism, and who the church acknowledges to be part of the people of God through the partaking of the Lord's Supper.[46] Thus, preaching, teaching, and leader-

---

43. For works that seeks to equip preachers to make Christ central in every sermon see Chapell, *Christ-Centered Preaching*; Goldsworthy, *Preaching the Whole Bible*; Johnson, *Him We Proclaim*.

44. See Horton, *People and Place*, 253., who asserts, "Preaching is not only doctrinal and moral instruction (although it includes these); it is also God's living and vivifying voice, through which the Spirit creates and sustains Christians and churches in their union with Christ." Pastors must rightly conceive of their stewardship of God's word, knowing that by rightly proclaiming the truths of God, his people, under the sovereignty of God, will be transformed progressively into the likeness of Christ (cf. John 6:63; Acts 10:44; 12:24; Phil 2:14–16; 2 Tim 2:9; Heb 4:12; 1 Pet 1:23).

45. See, e.g., the core seminars offered by Capitol Hill Baptist Church to adults in their congregation, online: http://www.capitolhillbaptist.org/we-equip/adults/core-seminars/.

46. Moore and Sagers elaborate helpfully on this point: "When the church is gathered together in a covenant community, with the Word of God faithfully proclaimed, Jesus is present as King (Matt 18:20; 1 Cor 5:4). The ordinances are themselves a continuation of the preaching ministry of the church. . . . The church proclaims 'the Lord's

ship—also known as formative church discipline—are key components to being a faithful steward, and if formative discipline is properly maintained the cases of corrective church discipline will be significantly reduced.[47]

Effective Shepherding

Pastors, however, must not only be faithful stewards, they must also shepherd their people in such a way as to watch over their lives and assist them in pursuing godliness on a personal level.[48] Pastors must have a knowledge of each member within their church in order to honestly claim that they are faithfully stewarding the church God has given them. Commenting on Acts 20:28 and Hebrews 13:17, Leeman states that "the plainest way to read these two passages is to say that the elders of a church, collectively, should be able to pay careful attention to every member of the flock, because they will give an account for every member of the flock before God."[49] Davis argues that pastors are accountable for knowing the identity of their flock and

---

death until he comes' (1 Cor 11:26), a death that was overcome in resurrection, and a triumphant return that is certain. Partaking of the Lord's Table is no light matter (1 Cor 11:27–32), and unbelievers or those in persistent sin are not to partake of this church ordinance (1 Cor 5:6–13). The Lord's Supper, then, is to look forward to the marriage supper of the Lamb, when all the redeemed of all the ages will eat with a slain and resurrected King Jesus of Nazareth seated at the head of the table (Rev 19:6–9). But until that day, the church eats together of the broken bread and the fruit of the vine in anticipation of the Kingdom to come and in celebration of the Kingdom at hand. No doubt many Baptists have misunderstood the sign nature of the Lord's Supper and baptism, translating the ordinances into hyper-Zwinglian terms. Baptists are right to deny sacerdotalism, but we would not speak of the baptismal waters or the Eucharistic bread and wine as 'just symbols' any more than we would speak of the Bible preached as 'just words.' All of these are proclamations—the voice of Jesus announcing an invading Kingdom through the first stage of the invasion force, his church. Where Jesus speaks, he is *there*. And he is there as King and Lord." Moore and Sagers, "Kingdom of God and the Church," 80–81, emphasis original.

47. For an excellent article on the practice of formative church discipline, see Cox, "Forgotten Side of Church Discipline," 44–58.

48. Bucer insists on both public and private ministry as being priorities for the minister: "Christian doctrine and admonition must not be confined to the assembly and the pulpit; because there are very many people who will take what they are taught and admonished in the public gathering as being of only general application, and consider it to apply more to others than to themselves. Therefore it is essential that people should also be instructed, taught and led on in Christ individually in their homes." See Bucer, *Concerning the True Care of Souls*, 181.

49. Leeman, *Church and the Surprising Offense of God's Love*, 308. This is also a pragmatic argument for a plurality of elders serving in a local church, particularly as churches grow.

understanding their physical and spiritual condition.[50] Merkle elaborates on Hebrews 13:17 and also maintains that pastors are given the crucial task of keeping watch over the souls of the congregation. Pastors will give an accounting for how they shepherd those under their care, which likely refers to an account being given at the eschatological judgment.[51]

Shepherding and oversight of church members can readily be applied in several areas: first, regular pastoral visitations should be taking place in the homes of the members in the church. While this practice is not typical in today's culture, it seems logical, if not essential, if pastors have an understanding of the teachings of Hebrews 13:7, 17.[52] They must have a proper awareness of the condition of their people and act accordingly if they are to stand before God someday and give an account of their oversight. Shepherding can also take place through pastoral counseling. Pastors should use these opportunities to gauge a person's spiritual vitality and to assist them in their ongoing sanctification. Oversight can also take place over meals in the pastor's home. This is an excellent opportunity to better acquaint members with their pastors and allow proper exhortation to take place.[53] This is done in order to watch out especially for those who may be heading into dangerous territory and potentially merit church discipline.

While discipline is a congregational matter, particularly in the step of excommunication, this understanding of shepherding seemingly demands pastors to take a leading role in the process. Going through the steps of church discipline involves a concerted effort to assess accurately and effectively the lives of the members and deal with unrepentant sin as it arises.[54] The disciplinary process involves confronting someone who has sinned against you, and even taking witnesses along with you if they refuse to repent the first time (Matt 18:15–16). If repentance still does not take place, the matter must be brought before the entire church (Matt 18:17). The church must strive for maturity in these matters, knowing that Paul instructed "those who are spiritual" to undertake this responsibility gently, with the goal of restoration (Gal 6:1). However, there are times when a person will not come to repentance, and thus they must be excluded from the

---

50. Davis, "Those Who Must Give an Account," 210–15

51. Merkle, "Biblical Basis for Church Membership," 37. See also Lane, *Hebrews 9–13*, 555.

52. For an excellent historical example of shepherding being done within each member's home, see Baxter, *Reformed Pastor*. Baxter believed that this meticulous kind of shepherding was just as crucial in the lives of his members as was his preaching.

53. For an excellent text on the significance of meals in relation to ministry, see Blomberg, *Contagious Holiness*.

54. This section was derived in part from Allison, *Sojourners and Strangers*, 190–92.

church and treated as an unbeliever. This usually happens after the process described in Matthew 18 takes place, although there are occasions of public, scandalous sin that call for immediate action if repentance is not present (cf. 1 Cor 5:1–13).

Throughout this process, one can see that as shepherds, the elders—while not the exclusive practitioners of discipline—should have a leading role, as they are responsible to oversee church members. Davis maintains that pastors should be made aware of a sin issue after a person has personally confronted the sinning member and there was no repentance. The leaders of the church are in a good position to know one or two reliable witnesses to send along with the person the next time (the witnesses could even be two or three of the elders of the church). Prayer should be made by the elders and the whole church to seek this person's restoration. While the church must take opportunity to confront and ask questions of the offending member, the pastors can offer helpful guidance throughout the process.[55] Thus, shepherding involves the admittance, the edifying, and, when necessary, the exclusion of persons from the local church. This must be done if the overseers are to oversee the people of God in a responsible fashion. The goal is to see that, to the best of their ability, their people persevere and avoid eschatological judgment.

It is difficult to press on this issue too definitively and say that no oversight can be delegated to lay ministers such as small group leaders, but it should at least be conceded that every mediating step placed between the elders and a believer moves that individual one step further away from careful shepherding. Thus, seemingly the church should receive oversight, not just from a senior pastor, but also from a plurality of elders who are committed to their spiritual well being.[56] No specific number of elders in a local church is advocated in Scripture, though it should be acknowledged that they are often spoken of in plurality (Acts 14:23; 20:17; Jas 5:14; 1 Pet 5:1).[57] The issue is having enough qualified, called, and gifted men to serve in this capacity to ensure that effective shepherding in that congregation is taking place.

This concept of shepherding via a plurality of elders is especially pertinent for megachurch and multi-site models of ecclesiology that, with increasing membership, may find it difficult to oversee their people effectively. The multi-site model has come under intense scrutiny and debate, as some emphasize the need to oversee each member and be in one location

55. See Davis, "Practical Issues of Church Discipline," 173–75.

56. For a convincing argument on the church being led by a plurality of elders and governed by the congregation, see Waldron, "Plural-Elder Congregationalism," 187–221.

57. See Hammett, *Biblical Foundations for Baptist Churches*, 177–89.

as the gathered body, while others underscore the call for evangelism and outreach.[58] Regardless of what position one takes on this issue, churches will need to carefully consider how they can oversee members in megachurches and multi-site churches if pastors are to fulfill their roles as the stewards and shepherds of God.

Thus, the dual concepts of stewardship and shepherding demand a particular role and function for those who would serve as elders in a local church. They must recognize that God has granted them a responsibility in giving them the Scriptures and a people to watch over. These are gifts that must be handled faithfully, for they will one day give an account to their master (Heb 13:7, 17).[59] This kind of work is summarized by Thompson, who defines pastoral ministry in the following way: "Ministry is participation in God's work of transforming the community of faith until it is 'blameless' at the coming of Christ."[60] Certainly, even when a pastor faithfully does

---

58. For an example of constructive engagement with both sides of this issue, see the 9Marks ejournal, May/June 2009, online: http://www.9marks.org/journal/multi-site-churches. Here one can see articles from Gregg Allison and J. D. Greear defending the multi-site model, while others, such as Grant Gaines, Jonathan Leeman, Bobby Jamieson, and Thomas White offer critique of the model. See also Allison, *Sojourners and Strangers*, 310–17; Driscoll and Breshears, *Vintage Church*, 243–66; Frye, "Multi-Site Church Phenomenon"; Surratt et al., *Multi-Site Church Revolution*; Surratt et al., *Multi-Site Church Roadtrip*. While there are advantages to the megachurch and multi-site models as it relates to resourcing and the potential for expansion and evangelism, it does seem virtually impossible to exercise oversight in the way in which someone like Baxter did. One must, therefore, take the passages mentioned regarding shepherding and oversight into consideration when taking a position on such ecclesiological matters.

59. It must be noted that the term ἡγέομαι is used in Heb 13:7, 17 to conceive of the church's leadership rather than the more commonly used words (elder, overseer, pastor), and the question must be asked as to whether this text refers to pastoral leadership. This word was used in Greco-Roman culture to refer to civic leaders, while later Jewish sources often associated this word with elders who looked after the affairs of the community. See BDAG, s.v. "ἡγέομαι." Thus, it is a more generic term, but the author also places qualifications on who this leadership consists of: they have spoken the word of God to the people and possess a faith that is imitatable (13:7), and keep watch over the souls of the congregation (13:17). In regards to the term ἀγρυπνέω in 13:17 Guthrie states, "The same verb is used in Ephesians 6:18 in an injunction to keep alert in prayer. The task of the leaders is to maintain constant watch over those committed to their care. This is reminiscent of Paul's care of all the churches (2 Cor 11:28) and of Peter's injunction to the elders to tend God's flock (1 Pet 5:2), which is itself reminiscent of the words of Jesus to Peter (John 21:15ff.)." Guthrie, *Letter to the Hebrews*, 276–77. Thus, the leadership described here appears to be that which is carried out by pastors, and this assertion is further supported by the author's reference to Jesus as the great Shepherd of the sheep in 13:20 (cf. 1 Pet 5:1–4). See also Allen, *Hebrews*, 624–25; Guthrie, *Hebrews*, 438–42; O'Brien, *Letter to the Hebrews*, 529–30.

60. Thompson, *Pastoral Ministry*, 20. Thompson spends the rest of the book teasing

his work there will be seeming shortcomings in his congregation, preaching, and his own life, but no matter what the results may be, God calls for his stewards to be faithful to their calling.

This understanding of ministry necessitates the pursuit of faithful discipline—in a formative and corrective sense—within a local church context. Pastors must recognize that the individuals within their church will stand before God someday to give an account of their lives (2 Cor 5:10). Part of the elders' responsibility is to shepherd their people faithfully in such a way that the moment of judgment has a positive outcome. As such, faithful stewardship and shepherding must take place,[61] and this includes discipline if needs be, knowing it is a warning of potential eschatological judgment, and as such is a means by which the members of the church are called to persevere in their faith.

THE SIGNIFICANCE OF THE ORDINANCES

One final practical implication that is derived from the thesis of this work relates to how we understand the importance of the ordinances of baptism and the Lord's Supper. If church discipline is a warning of potential eschatological judgment and a means of perseverance, then churches must be diligent to guard entrance into the covenant community by means of baptism, which correlates with the understanding of regenerate church membership given above. Care must also be taken to ensure that those who partake of the Lord's Supper are not living in unrepentant sin. A careful practice of the ordinances will ensure, as much as humanly possible, that the membership is made up of believers, and only those living consistently as believers are partaking of the Lord's Supper.

First, baptism as a formal act[62] is the public profession of one's conversion, and, concurrently, involves a local church recognizing that person's

---

out that thesis in a convincing fashion by concentrating specifically on the apostle Paul.

61. While careful oversight is required of pastors, one must also be careful not to cross into "heavy shepherding." This terminology is derived from instances when leaders exert overt psychological control over members of the congregation, and is most often associated with cults. Because churches are often not used to shepherding at any level they may deem intentional oversight as "heavy shepherding." Pastors must be sure not to overstep proper boundaries while also seeking to offer faithful guidance and exhortation.

62. Jeschke, *Discipling in the Church*, 88, shows a link that can be seen between baptism and excommunication. He claims, "If we should not call excommunication a formal act, it is logical to infer that baptism and receiving someone into the body of Christ also should not be recognized as a formal act. For excommunication, like baptism, is an official church act concerning membership. Excommunication is, in

confession of faith and welcoming them into the membership of the church.[63] Therefore, churches must work diligently to see that those they baptize and bring into membership are in fact truly believers in Jesus Christ.[64] Baptism is vested with symbolism and purpose, not some act empty of meaning, and thus churches must be thorough in their examination of membership candidates.

Hammett asserts that baptism is best understood as a rite of commitment, identifying oneself with Christ. It can also be a means of grace, "not in the sense that it saves, but in the sense that it is the occasion where God acts to seal and confirm the blessings and promises of the gospel."[65] Akin maintains that baptism signifies several key truths: we are now identified with Christ, not Adam (Rom 5:12–21); we are now dead to sin (Rom 6:1–2); we are identified with Christ in his death (Rom 6:3); we are identified with Christ in his resurrected life (Rom 6:4–5); we are no longer enslaved to sin since the old man is dead (Rom 6:6–7); we have confidence that the life we have in Christ is a life that will never end (Rom 6:8–10); and, finally, baptism signifies the basis for our daily mortification of the flesh (Rom

---

effect, the reverse of baptism. It officially ends someone's church membership in the way baptism officially begins it. We must therefore also recognize the formal act of excommunication, because baptism and excommunication are correlatives." See also Davis, "Whatever Happened to Church Discipline," 360.

63. It is outside the purview of this work to discuss the merits of credobaptism as opposed to paedobaptism. The discussion of membership above along with this section concerning baptism will fall under a credobaptist viewpoint. For an excellent defense of this position see Schreiner and Wright, *Believer's Baptism*, especially Wellum, "Baptism and the Relationship between the Covenants," 97–161. Dever, "Church," 787, also gives four reasons that baptism is exclusively meant for those who already believed in Christ: "First, those who evangelize are only commanded to baptize those who repent and believe (Matt 28:18–20; cf. John 4:1–2). Second, the only clearly recorded subjects of baptism in the book of Acts are individuals who have repented and believed (Acts 2:37–41; 8:12–13, 36–38; 9:18; 10:47–48; 16:15, 33; 18:8; 19:5). Third, Paul's letters demonstrate the twin assumptions that those who have believed have been baptized and that those who have been baptized believe (Rom 6:1–5; Gal 3:26–27; Col 2:11–12). Finally, Peter associates baptism with salvation, not as a cause of salvation but as a roughly contemporary occurrence (Acts 2:38; 1 Pet 3:21)." Regardless of one's stance on this issue, baptism and church membership must be taken very seriously, knowing that the incidences of church discipline will inevitably lessen in churches that guard membership carefully.

64. No church can be infallible on this point, but they can certainly do better if they take steps such as the ones offered in the section above on bringing people into the church's membership. Questions also arise concerning the baptism of children. This is a complex topic, with good arguments on both sides. For further thoughts on the matter, see Allison, *Sojourners and Strangers*, 360–62; Dever, "Baptism in the Context of the Local Church," 344–50.

65. Hammett, *Biblical Foundations for Baptist Churches*, 267.

6:11–14).⁶⁶ Baptism also serves as a sign of our communion with the triune God (Matt 28:19).

Baptism, therefore, while certainly symbolic is also vested with meaning in the Scriptures, particularly regarding one's identification. People are taking a step to commit to the membership of a local church, and are also testifying to their new birth in Jesus Christ. If understood in this way baptism is a serious step for an individual as it makes clear to them their commitment to live for Christ and live in covenant with the church. Pastors and churches, therefore, must take this step very seriously so as to ensure, to the best of their ability, a regenerate church membership. This can be done through an interview with several elders regarding their conversion, as well as having the candidate give their testimony directly before their baptism, either live or via video. In so doing, churches will likely avoid a number of cases of discipline as believers encourage one another to persevere in their faith.

The Lord's Supper also holds similar significance as an ordinance. Scripture speaks of the Lord's Supper as a commemoration and proclamation of Christ's death and the establishment of the new covenant (Matt 26:26–29; Mark 14:22–25; Luke 22:14–23), a participation in Christ and all his salvific benefits (1 Cor 10:14–22), an expression of unity (1 Cor 11:17–34), and the anticipation of an eschatological feast with the triumphantly returned Messiah (Rev 19:6–9).⁶⁷ Unlike baptism, which is a one-time initiatory rite, the Lord's Supper is an ordinance that is observed repeatedly. Hammett maintains that baptism can be pictured as a wedding ceremony wherein a believer publicly professes his or her commitment to Christ, and the Lord's Supper is similar to an anniversary celebration where the wedding vows are renewed.⁶⁸ As a memorial⁶⁹ and continual renewal of the vows, Hammett avers, "The Lord's Supper proclaims the gospel message of Christ's death as

66. See Akin, "Meaning of Baptism," 66–79.

67. Allison, *Sojourners and Strangers*, 394–95.

68. Hammett, *Biblical Foundations for Baptist Churches*, 277.

69. This term is used in contradistinction to those who conceive of the Lord's Supper as transubstantiation or consubstantiation. For helpful works on this topic, see Armstrong, *Understanding Four Views on the Lord's Supper*, especially Moore, "Baptist View: Christ's Presence as Memorial," 29–44; Schreiner and Crawford, *Lord's Supper*. One other view of the Lord's Supper that has been held since the time of Calvin is the Reformed view or spiritual presence view. Essentially this view affirms that, while Christ is not present in any physical way, the body and blood of Christ are present spiritually and appropriated by faith during the observance of the Lord's Supper as a means of grace. While this view is somewhat unusual to see in contemporary Baptist life, it was taught in the Second London Baptist Confession. See Lumpkin, *Baptist Confessions of Faith*, 293.

the sustenance of the Christian life."[70] This ordinance is a continual testimony of God's grace in the lives of those who partake.

As it relates practically to church life, there are several considerations one should take in the observance of the Lord's Supper in light of the view of discipline espoused in this work. First, only believers are to partake of the Lord's Supper (1 Cor 10:16–21). Beyond that, in order to ensure that those who are partaking of this ordinance do so in a worthy manner, it seems wisest to allow only those who are baptized members of the congregation to participate in the Lord's Supper. Historically this position has been referred to as "closed communion," which is in opposition to "open communion," wherein the Lord's Supper is open to be received by all believers in attendance.[71] In holding the position of closed communion one is not saying that those in attendance who cannot participate are not in fact believers. Rather, the church is simply trying to have integrity as they offer the elements to those whom they have affirmed as believers in Jesus Christ.[72]

Another consideration is the preparation one takes in coming to the Table. The severe discipline enacted by the Lord upon those who partook of the Lord's Supper in an unworthy manner merits careful attention (1 Cor 11:17–34). First, it should be understood that no one is worthy to participate in the Lord's Supper if we understand it to mean perfection. All are unworthy participants, and that is the point of the Lord's Supper, to remind us again of the justifying work of Jesus Christ on our behalf. The issue is unworthy participation wherein unrepentant sin is present in individual members. Self-examination,[73] therefore, is needed prior to partaking of this ordinance, particularly the sin of disunity as is seen in the context of 1 Corinthians 11.[74] Hammett encourages churches to prepare in advance for

70. Hammett, *Biblical Foundations for Baptist Churches*, 281–82.

71. See Wills, "Sounds from Baptist History," 285–312. In this chapter Wills argues that closed communion has been the majority position in Baptist history up until approximately the last fifty years.

72. For support for this position, see ibid., 283–88. Others affirm what is known as "close communion." This practice allows baptized members in good standing in another church to participate in the Lord's Supper. For advocates of this view, see Allison, *Sojourners and Strangers*, 404–6; Van Neste, "Lord's Supper," 378–86. While there is no problem to be found with this view theologically, there still seem to be practical reasons to hold to a closed communion position in order to ensure as best as possible that partakers of the elements have been confirmed by the congregation as believers.

73. For an excellent study on the topic of self-examination in relation to the Lord's Supper, see Church, "Self-Examination as Preparation."

74. See Allison, *Sojourners and Strangers*, 406–7, who believes that this self-examination is specifically for dealing with broken relationships, division-causing behavior, disrespect, and mistreatment of brothers and sisters in Christ. He maintains that sin as a general pattern should be confessed and repented of immediately, though, if this

participation in the Lord's Supper by emphasizing the significance of the ordinance in renewing one's repentance, faith in Christ, and love for one another.[75]

A third application relates to how frequently a local church observes the Lord's Supper. Hamilton notes, "From what Paul says in 1 Cor 11:17–34, it seems that the church partook of the Lord's Supper when they 'came together,' and from 1 Cor 16:2, it seems that the Corinthian church 'came together' on the first day of the week."[76] Thus, the pattern of the early church seemed to include celebrating the Lord's Supper when they gathered for worship. While there is no hard and fast NT imperative to celebrate the Lord's Supper every week, it seems that this would be a wise choice on the part of the church. Hamilton continues, "If it is objected that this would diminish its significance, my reply is that those who make this argument typically do not claim that weekly observance diminishes the significance of the preaching of the Word, the prayers of God's people, and the singing of Psalms, hymns, and spiritual songs."[77] The same practices and attitudes that keep weekly preaching, praying, singing, and perhaps even baptism from having their significance diminished could also be applied to the Lord's Supper.

The mood and atmosphere within which the Lord's Supper is taken is another consideration. Too often, seemingly, the Lord's Supper is a time where a church comes together to castigate themselves for their sins and partake of the elements in a cautious and somber manner. While this ordinance is a remembrance of Christ's death and should be taken with care, knowing the potential consequences of unworthy participation, it is also proleptic in anticipating the coming marriage supper of the Lamb.[78] Moore asserts, "Often Lord's Supper services characterized by a funeral atmosphere, complete with somber, droning organ music as the ministers or deacons distribute the elements to the congregation." In contrast, Moore continues and maintains that churches "must recapture the vision of the eschatological messianic banquet—and seek to recover the joyfulness and triumph of this event."[79] Thus, the Lord's Supper is to depict Christ's triumph over Satan, sin, and death in a celebratory manner, while also maintaining a serious

---

does not happen consistently, the Lord's Supper may certainly encourage one to do so.

75. Hammett, *Biblical Foundations for Baptist Churches*, 288–91.

76. Hamilton, "Lord's Supper in Paul," 100–101.

77. Ibid., 101. See also Van Neste, "Lord's Supper," 370–74.

78. For further detail on the Lord's Supper as celebrating both Christ's death and the marriage supper of the Lamb, see Vickers, "Celebrating the Past and Future," 313–40.

79. Moore, "Baptist View," 33.

note regarding Christ's sacrificial death on our behalf.[80] Believers should recognize what was accomplished on their behalf in the past and anticipate their eternal destiny with the one who accomplished that salvation.

Finally, the relationship between the Lord's Supper and church discipline should be clearly understood. Historically those who underwent excommunication were barred from the Table.[81] In our present-day culture it seems that many times if a person were to be disciplined and banned from the Lord's Supper, they would think this to be an insignificant event. This is due to an insufficient view of the Lord's Supper.[82] Though not exhaustive, if one were to adopt the view of the Lord's Supper as advocated in this section, churches would understand the significance of this ordinance. Partaking in the Lord's Supper signifies that as a community of faith the church is committed to renewing the vows made at their baptism to renounce sin and live for Christ in all things, a result of one's new birth (2 Cor 5:17). Christians must not be living in unrepentant sin, as this does not correlate with the message that the Lord's Supper is seeking to convey. As discipline is a warning of potential eschatological judgment, and the Lord's Supper is the celebration of an anticipated eschatological feast, the exacting of discipline in barring an individual from the Lord's Supper is a potentially significant statement regarding that person's salvation.[83] In this way, the Lord's Supper takes on greater importance in relation to the view of ecclesial discipline advocated in this dissertation.

CHAPTER SUMMARY

This chapter has highlighted several key implications for the church in light of the view of church discipline espoused by this dissertation. First, regenerate church membership must be maintained to the best of the church's ability. Hamilton rightly asserts, "In order to understand what it means to be the church, we must be clear on how people become part of the church, and we must devote ourselves to preserving the purity of the church. In other words, we must understand the nature of the new birth, and we

---

80. See Allison, *Sojourners and Strangers*, 408–09.

81. See Wills, "Historical Analysis of Church Discipline," 131–48, who gives many historical examples of this reality.

82. This levity with which the Lord's Supper is held may also be due to the infrequency with which we observe the Lord's Supper. If the Lord's Supper were a weekly occurrence in our worship services it may bolster the significance of this ordinance in the minds of those under discipline as they are excluded from the Supper each week.

83. For a similar viewpoint, see Moore, "Baptist View," 42–43.

must practice church discipline."[84] Thus, the establishment of a regenerate church membership and the enactment of proper church discipline is key to the overall health of the church. Lauterbach claims that most churches are indifferent as to how the church is supposed to function in these matters. He maintains, "Their attitude to matters of government and discipline is pragmatic: whatever works. The point is this: local churches are to look like this, a new people, a corporate identity as a body, with all members functioning."[85] As such, regenerate church membership is key to ensuring the purity of the body.

Second, pastors must understand that they are to function as stewards of the gospel and shepherds of God's people. They are caretakers of the good news of Jesus Christ, and thus must preach, teach, and lead in an appropriate manner. Beyond that they must also exercise oversight and see to it that their congregation is healthy spiritually. As responsible stewards and shepherds, pastors are also called upon to exercise church discipline when necessary. However, if pastors work diligently to preach, teach, lead, and exercise oversight, the instances of discipline, particularly excommunication, can be significantly lessened.

Finally, churches need to consider the importance of the ordinances of baptism and the Lord's Supper. Baptism, which is connected with pursuing a regenerate church membership, is the initiatory rite in identifying oneself with Jesus Christ and with a particular local church. The Lord's Supper is the commemoration of Christ's death and the anticipation of the eschatological feast we will one day enjoy with him. These two ordinances are key in ensuring that those who are members of the church are in fact believers in Jesus Christ who have made a public profession of their faith, and that they persevere in their faith and do not succumb to unrepentant sin. Churches would do well to note these implications and make the necessary adjustments, knowing that church discipline is a warning of potential eschatological judgment, and as such is a means by which the saints are called to persevere in their faith.

AREAS FOR FURTHER RESEARCH

There are several areas for further research that can build off of the arguments presented in this dissertation. First, additional study could be devoted to the OT trajectories leading up to NT church discipline. While chapter 2 discussed the themes of exile from Eden, expulsion from the camp, and

---

84. Hamilton, "Church Militant and Her Warfare," 72.
85. Lauterbach, *Transforming Community*, 33–34.

ejection from the land, greater detail could be elucidated on these three trajectories that point to NT church discipline. Most discussions of church discipline focus mainly—if not exclusively—on the NT data, and it has been demonstrated from chapter 2 that work devoted to the OT realities that point forward to the contours and nuances of church discipline can yield profitable results.

Another area of potentially fruitful inquiry would be further study on various historic figures, and their view and practice of church discipline. Luther, Hubmaier, and Edwards received focused attention in chapter 3, but an entire dissertation could certainly be dedicated to Edwards's view and practice of ecclesial discipline, for instance. Studies of this nature have been undertaken,[86] and works dedicated to historical figures and time periods can help to illumine how theological truths—such as the thesis defended in this dissertation—are put into practice in a specific ecclesial context.

Finally, further research could be devoted to the way in which church discipline is connected to other areas of theology. Within this work, effort was devoted to showing how discipline is related to eschatological judgment and the perseverance of the saints. More work could be done on how ecclesial discipline connects to the doctrine of God,[87] the realities of sin, or other ecclesiological concerns.[88] One other specific doctrine that could be elaborated in relation to church discipline is sanctification. While perseverance speaks to progressive sanctification, more detail could be given regarding one's identity in Christ and the reality of growth in one's faith that must be present in church members. Certainly discipline is related to this theological reality as we are already sanctified, but not yet completely so, and as such the process of ecclesial discipline is crucial for continued growth into who we are already are, namely the people of God, united to Christ, indwelt by the Spirit.

CONCLUSION

This dissertation has shown that one purpose of church discipline is to serve as a declaration of potential eschatological judgment, both to warn offenders

---

86. See, e.g., Burnett, *Yoke of Christ*.

87. Work has been done in this area by Bargerhuff, *Love That Rescues*, who focuses on God's love in relation to discipline. Seemingly other areas of the doctrine of God could be used as fruitful lines of inquiry.

88. This could potentially include specifying the role of elders and the role of the congregation in the process of church discipline, or how discipline functions within megachurch and multi-site church contexts.

of their need to repent, and, by implication, to exhort church members to persevere in their faith. Building on the introductory material from chapter 1, chapter 2 has shown that Scripture describes discipline in this manner. This can be seen both in OT trajectories, such as exile from Eden, expulsion from the camp, and ejection from the land, as well as NT teaching on discipline, specifically in Matthew 18:15–20, 1 Corinthians 5:1–13, Galatians 6:1, and 2 Thessalonians 3:6–15. Chapter 3 has demonstrated that, while not using the exact same terminology, leading theologians such as Martin Luther, Balthasar Hubmaier, and Jonathan Edwards conceived of church discipline in a very similar fashion. Chapter 4 delved into greater theological detail regarding eschatological judgment and the perseverance of the saints, and their relationship to church discipline. Further attention was also given to the missional nature of church discipline, and several potential objections to the thesis of the work were answered. Finally, this chapter has named several practical implications for the local church as well as some possible areas for further study.

As such, one can observe that there is exegetical, historical, theological, and practical warrant for understanding church discipline in this manner. Scholars, pastors, and church members should understand the gravity of the realities depicted in this work and take appropriate measures in their churches. Thompson rightly maintains, "The task of ministry is to create the climate in which congregations can be shaped by the cross and pursue the eschatological goal of transformation into the image of the Son."[89] This conviction regarding church ministry entails a robust application of church discipline, wherein one understands that discipline is warning of potential eschatological judgment, and as such is a means by which the saints are called to persevere in their faith and pursue Spirit-wrought transformation.

---

89. Thompson, *Pastoral Ministry*, 162.

Bibliography

Adams, Jay Edward. *Handbook of Church Discipline*. Grand Rapids: Ministry Resources Library, 1986.

Akin, Daniel L. "The Meaning of Baptism." In *Restoring Integrity in Baptist Churches*, edited by Thomas White et al., 63–80. Grand Rapids: Kregel, 2008.

Akin, Daniel L., et al., editors. *A Theology for the Church*. Nashville: B & H Academic, 2007.

Alexander, T. Desmond. *From Paradise to the Promised Land: An Introduction to the Pentateuch*. 2nd ed. Grand Rapids: Baker Academic, 2002.

Alexander, T. Desmond, and Brian S. Rosner, editors. *New Dictionary of Biblical Theology*. Downers Grove, IL: InterVarsity, 2000.

Allen, David. *Hebrews*. New American Commentary. Nashville: B & H, 2010.

Allison, Gregg R. *Historical Theology: An Introduction to Christian Doctrine*. Grand Rapids: Zondervan, 2011.

———. *Sojourners and Strangers: The Doctrine of the Church*. Wheaton, IL: Crossway, 2012.

Alter, Robert. *Genesis: Translation and Commentary*. New York: Norton, 1996.

Anderson, Gary A. *The Genesis of Perfection: Adam and Eve in Jewish and Christian Imagination*. Louisville: Westminster John Knox, 2001.

Armstrong, John H., editor. *Understanding Four Views on the Lord's Supper*. Grand Rapids: Zondervan, 2007.

Arnold, Clinton E. "Early Church Catechesis and New Christians' Classes in Contemporary Evangelicalism." *Journal of the Evangelical Theological Society* 47 (2004) 39–54.

Ashby, Stephen M. "A Reformed Arminian View." In *Four Views on Eternal Security*, edited by J. Matthew Pinson, 135–87. Counterpoints. Grand Rapids: Zondervan, 2002.

Ashford, Bruce Riley, editor. *Theology and Practice of Mission: God, the Church, and the Nations*. Nashville: B & H Academic, 2011.

Ashford, Bruce Riley, and Daniel L. Akin. "The Missional Implications of Church Membership and Church Discipline." In *Those Who Must Give an Account: A Study of Church Membership and Church Discipline*, edited by John S. Hammett and Benjamin L. Merkle, 189–204. Nashville: B & H Academic, 2012.

Augustine. *The Works of Saint Augustine: A Translation for the 21st Century*. Edited by John E. Rotelle. Translated by Edmund Hill. Brooklyn: New City, 1990.

Banks, Robert J. *Paul's Idea of Community*. Peabody, MA: Hendrickson, 1994.

Bargerhuff, Eric J. *Love That Rescues: God's Fatherly Love in the Practice of Church Discipline*. Eugene, OR: Wipf & Stock, 2010.

Basden, Paul, et al., editors. *The People of God: Essays on the Believers' Church*. Nashville: Broadman, 1991.

Bateman, Herbert W., editor. *Four Views on the Warning Passages in Hebrews*. Grand Rapids: Kregel, 2007.

Bauer, Walter, et al., editors. *A Greek-English Lexicon of the New Testament and Other Early Christian Literature*. 3rd ed. Chicago: University of Chicago Press, 2000.

Baxter, Richard. *The Reformed Pastor*. Edinburgh: Banner of Truth, 1974.

Beale, G. K. *1–2 Thessalonians*. IVP New Testament Commentary 13. Downers Grove, IL: InterVarsity, 2003.

———. *A New Testament Biblical Theology: The Unfolding of the Old Testament in the New*. Grand Rapids: Baker Academic, 2011.

———. *The Temple and the Church's Mission: A Biblical Theology of the Dwelling Place of God*. Downers Grove, IL: InterVarsity, 2004.

Beale, G. K., and D. A. Carson, editors. *Commentary on the New Testament Use of the Old Testament*. Grand Rapids: Baker Academic, 2007.

Bell, Rob. *Love Wins: A Book about Heaven, Hell, and the Fate of Every Person Who Ever Lived*. New York: HarperOne, 2011.

Best, Thomas F., and Martin Robra, editors. *Ecclesiology and Ethics: Ecumenical Ethical Engagement, Moral Formation and the Nature of the Church*. Geneva: WCC, 1997.

Bezzant, Rhys Steward. "Orderly but Not Ordinary: Jonathan Edward's Evangelical Ecclesiology." PhD Diss., Australian College of Theology Melbourne, 2010.

Blaising, Craig A. "Premillennialism." In *Three Views on the Millennium and Beyond*, edited by Darrell L. Bock, 157–227. Grand Rapids: Zondervan, 1999.

Blaising, Craig A., and Darrell L. Bock. *Progressive Dispensationalism*. Wheaton, IL: BridgePoint, 1993.

Blomberg, Craig L. *Contagious Holiness: Jesus' Meals with Sinners*. Downers Grove, IL: InterVarsity, 2005.

———. "Matthew." In *Commentary on the New Testament Use of the Old Testament*, edited by G. K. Beale, and D. A. Carson, 1–109. Grand Rapids: Baker Academic, 2007.

———. *Matthew*. New American Commentary 22. Nashville: Broadman, 1992.

Blue, Ken, and John White. *Church Discipline That Heals*. Downers Grove, IL: InterVarsity, 1985.

———. *Healing the Wounded: The Costly Love of Church Discipline*. Downers Grove, IL: InerVarsity, 1985.

Bock, Darrell L. *Acts*. Baker Exegetical Commentary on the New Testament. Grand Rapids: Baker Academic, 2007.

Bonhoeffer, Dietrich. *Life Together*. Translated by John W. Doberstein. New York: Harper & Row, 1954.

Bozeman, Theodore Dwight. *The Precisianist Strain: Disciplinary Religion and Antinomian Backlash in Puritanism to 1638*. Chapel Hill: University of North Carolina Press, 2004.

Brett, Murray G. *Growing Up in Grace: The Use of Means for Communion with God*. Grand Rapids: Reformation Heritage, 2009.

Bridges, Jerry. *The Discipline of Grace: God's Role and Our Role in the Pursuit of Holiness*. Colorado Springs: NavPress, 1994.

Brower, Kent E., and Andy Johnson, editors. *Holiness and Ecclesiology in the New Testament*. Grand Rapids: Eerdmans, 2007.

Brown, Colin, editor. *The New International Dictionary of New Testament Theology.* Grand Rapids: Zondervan, 1975.

Brown, Harold O. J. "The Role of Discipline in the Church." *Covenant Quarterly* 41 (1983) 51–52.

Bruce, F. F. *Commentary on the Book of the Acts: The English Text, with Introduction, Exposition, and Notes.* Grand Rapids: Eerdmans, 1954.

———. *The Epistle to the Galatians: A Commentary on the Greek Text.* New International Greek Testament Commentary. Grand Rapids: Eerdmans, 1982.

Bucer, Martin. *Concerning the True Care of Souls.* Translated by Peter Beale. Carlisle, PA: Banner of Truth, 2009.

Burnett, Amy Nelson. *The Yoke of Christ: Martin Bucer and Christian Discipline.* Sixteenth Century Essays and Studies 26. Kirksville, MO: Northeast Missouri State University, 1994.

Calvin, John. *Commentaries on the First Book of Moses, Called Genesis.* Translated by John King. Vol. 1. Grand Rapids: Eerdmans, 1948.

———. *A Harmony of the Gospels: Matthew, Mark and Luke.* Translated by T. H. L. Parker. Grand Rapids: Eerdmans, 1972.

———. *Institutes of the Christian Religion.* Edited by John T. McNeill. 2 vols. Library of Christian Classics 20–21. Philadelphia: Westminster John Knox, 1960.

Cambier, Jules. "La Chair et L'Esprit en 1 Cor 5:5." *New Testament Studies* 15 (1969) 221–32.

Canham, Michael. "'Not Home Yet': The Role of Over-Realized Eschatology in Pauline Church Discipline Cases." PhD diss., Westminster Theological Seminary, 2005.

Caragounis, Chrys C. *Peter and the Rock.* Beihefte zur Zeitschrift für die Neutestamentliche Wissenschaft 58. Berlin: de Gruyter, 1990.

Carson, D. A., editor. *The Church in the Bible and the World: An International Study.* Grand Rapids: Baker, 1987.

Chan, Francis, and Preston M. Sprinkle. *Erasing Hell: What God Said about Eternity and the Things We Made Up.* Colorado Springs: David C. Cook, 2011.

Chapell, Bryan. *Christ-Centered Preaching: Redeeming the Expository Sermon.* 2nd ed. Grand Rapids: Baker Academic, 2005.

Chester, Tim, and Steve Timmis. *Total Church: A Radical Reshaping around Gospel and Community.* Wheaton, IL: Crossway, 2008.

Church, Keith D. "Self-Examination as Preparation for the Lord's Supper in Light of the New Covenant." PhD Diss., Southeastern Baptist Theological Seminary, 2007.

Ciampa, Roy E. "The History of Redemption." In *Central Themes in Biblical Theology: Mapping Unity in Diversity*, edited by Scott J. Hafemann and Paul R. House, 254–308. Downers Grove, IL: InterVarsity, 2007.

Ciampa, Roy E., and Brian S. Rosner. "1 Corinthians." In *The Commentary on the New Testament Use of the Old Testament*, edited by G. K. Beale and D. A. Carson, 695–752. Grand Rapids: Baker Academic, 2007.

Clowney, Edmund P. *The Church.* Contours of Christian Theology. Downers Grove, IL: InterVarsity, 1995.

Coenen, L. "Church." In *New International Dictionary of New Testament Theology*, edited by Colin Brown, 1:292–96. Grand Rapids: Zondervan, 1975.

Conzelmann, Hans. *1 Corinthians: A Commentary on the First Epistle to the Corinthians.* Translated by James W. Leitch. Hermeneia. Philadelphia: Fortress, 1975.

Cooper, James F. *Tenacious of Their Liberties: The Congregationalists in Colonial Massachusetts*. Religion in America. New York: Oxford University Press, 1999.

Cowan, Steven B., editor. *Who Runs the Church? 4 Views on Church Government*. Grand Rapids: Zondervan, 2004.

Cox, Don. "The Forgotten Side of Church Discipline." *Southern Baptist Journal of Theology* 4 (2000) 44–58.

Craigie, Peter C. *The Book of Deuteronomy*. New International Commentary on the Old Testament 5. Grand Rapids: Eerdmans, 1976.

Currid, John. *A Study Commentary on Deuteronomy*. Webster, NY: Evangelical Press, 2006.

Dagg, J. L. *Manual of Church Order*. Harrisonburg, VA: Gano, 1990.

Davies, William David, and Dale C. Allison. *Commentary on Matthew VIII–XVIII*. Vol. 2 of *A Critical and Exegetical Commentary on the Gospel according to Saint Matthew*. International Critical Commentary on the Holy Scriptures of the Old and New Testaments. Edinburgh: T. & T. Clark, 1998.

Davies, William David, and David Daube, editors. *The Background of the New Testament and Its Eschatology*. Cambridge: Cambridge University Press, 1956.

Davis, Andrew M. "The Practical Issues of Church Discipline." In *Those Who Must Give an Account: A Study of Church Membership and Church Discipline*, edited by John S. Hammett and Benjamin L. Merkle, 205–22. Nashville: B & H Academic, 2012.

———. "Those Who Must Give an Account: A Pastoral Reflection." In *Those Who Must Give an Account: A Study of Church Membership and Church Discipline*, edited by John S. Hammett and Benjamin L. Merkle, 205–22. Nashville: B & H Academic, 2012.

Davis, George B. "Whatever Happened to Church Discipline?" *Criswell Theological Review* 1 (1987) 345–61.

Davis, Kenneth R. "No Discipline, No Church: An Anabaptist Contribution to the Reformed Tradition." *Sixteenth Century Journal* 13 (1982) 43–58.

Demarest, Bruce A. *The Cross and Salvation: The Doctrine of Salvation*. Foundations of Evangelical Theology. Wheaton, IL: Crossway, 1997.

Dempster, Stephen G. *Dominion and Dynasty: A Biblical Theology of the Hebrew Bible*. Leicester, England: Apollos, 2003.

Dever, Mark E. "Baptism in the Context of the Local Church." In *Believer's Baptism: Sign of the New Covenant in Christ*, edited by Thomas R. Schreiner and Shawn D. Wright, 329–52. Nashville: B & H Academic, 2006.

———. "Biblical Church Discipline." *Southern Baptist Journal of Theology* 4 (2000) 28–43.

———. "The Church." In *A Theology for the Church*, edited by Daniel L. Akin et al., 766–857. Nashville: B & H Academic, 2007.

———. "The Doctrine of the Church." In *A Theology for the Church*, edited by Daniel L. Akin et al., 766–857. Nashville: B & H Academic, 2007.

———. *Nine Marks of a Healthy Church*. Wheaton, IL: Crossway, 2004.

———, editor. *Polity: Biblical Arguments on How to Conduct Church Life*. Washington, DC: Center for Church Reform, 2000.

Dever, Mark E., and Paul Alexander. *The Deliberate Church: Building Your Ministry on the Gospel*. Wheaton, IL: Crossway, 2005.

Deweese, Charles W. *Baptist Church Covenants*. Nashville: Broadman, 1990.

———. *A Community of Believers*. Valley Forge, PA: Judson, 1978.

Driscoll, Mark, and Gerry Breshears. *Vintage Church: Timeless Truths and Timely Methods*. Wheaton, IL: Crossway, 2009.

Driver, Samuel R. *A Critical and Exegetical Commentary on Deuteronomy*. 3rd ed. Edinburgh: T. & T. Clark, 1973.

Duguid, I. M. "Exile." In *New Dictionary of Biblical Theology*, edited by T. Desmond Alexander and Brian S. Rosner, 475–78. Downers Grove, IL: InterVarsity, 2000.

Dunn, James D. G. *A Commentary on the Epistle to the Galatians*. Black's New Testament Commentaries. London: Black, 1993.

Eaton, Michael A. *No Condemnation: A New Theology of Assurance*. Downers Grove, IL: InterVarsity, 1997.

Edwards, Jonathan. *Works of Jonathan Edwards*. 26 vols. Edited by Paul Ramsay et al. New Haven: Yale University Press, 1957–2008

Elwell, Walter A., editor. *Baker Commentary on the Bible*. Grand Rapids: Baker, 2000.

———. *Evangelical Dictionary of Theology*. 2nd ed. Grand Rapids: Baker Academic, 2001.

Erikson, Kai. *Wayward Puritans: A Study in the Sociology of Deviance*. Rev. ed. Allyn & Bacon Classics. Boston: Allyn & Bacon, 2005.

Farmer, William Reuben, et al., editors. *Christian History and Interpretation: Studies Presented to John Knox*. Cambridge: Cambridge University Press, 1967.

Fee, Gordon D. *The First Epistle to the Corinthians*. New International Commentary on the New Testament 7. Grand Rapids: Eerdmans, 1987.

———. *Galatians: Pentecostal Commentary*. Dorset, UK: Deo, 2011.

Feinberg, John S., editor. *Continuity and Discontinuity: Perspectives on the Relationship between the Old and New Testaments; Essays in Honor of S. Lewis Johnson, Jr.* Wheaton, IL: Crossway, 1988.

Feinberg, Paul D. "The Case for the Pretribulation Rapture Position." In *Three Views on the Rapture: Pre-, Mid-, or Post-Tribulation*, edited by Gleason L. Archer Jr., 47–86. Grand Rapids: Zondervan, 1996.

Ferguon, Everett. *Christian Life: Ethics, Morality, and Discipline in the Early Church*. Studies in Early Christianity 16. New York: Garland, 1993.

———. *The Church of Christ: A Biblical Ecclesiology for Today*. Grand Rapids: Eerdmans, 1996.

Finger, Thomas N. *A Contemporary Anabaptist Theology: Biblical, Historical, Constructive*. Downers Grove, IL: InterVarsity, 2004.

Firey, Abigail, editor. *A New History of Penance*. Brill's Companions to the Christian Tradition 14. Boston: Brill, 2008.

Fitzgerald, Monica D. "Drunkards, Fornicators, and a Great Hen Squabble: Censure Practices and the Gendering of Puritanism." *Church History* 80 (2011) 40–75.

France, R. T. *The Gospel of Matthew*. New International Commentary on the New Testament. Grand Rapids: Eerdmans, 2007.

Friesen, Jacob T., et al., editors. *Studies in Church Discipline*. Newton, KA: Mennonite Publication Office, 1958.

Frye, Brian Nathaniel. "The Multi-Site Church Phenomenon in North America: 1950–2010." PhD Diss., Southern Baptist Theological Seminary, 2011.

Furnish, Victor Paul. *II Corinthians*. New Haven: Yale University Press, 2005.

Gaffin, Richard B. *Resurrection and Redemption: A Study in Paul's Soteriology*. Phillipsburg, NJ: Presbyterian & Reformed, 1987.

Galli, Mark. *God Wins: Heaven, Hell, and Why the Good News Is Better Than Love Wins.* Carol Stream, IL: Tyndale, 2011.

Garland, David E. *1 Corinthians.* Baker Exegetical Commentary on the New Testament. Grand Rapids: Baker Academic, 2003.

Garrett, James Leo. *Baptist Church Discipline.* Nashville: Broadman & Holman, 1962.

Gentry, Peter John, and Stephen J. Wellum. *Kingdom through Covenant: A Biblical-Theological Understanding of the Covenants.* Wheaton, IL: Crossway, 2012.

Girolimon, Michael T. "John Calvin and Menno Simons on Religious Discipline: A Difference in Degree and Kind." *Fides et Historia* 27 (1995) 1–21.

Goheen, Michael W. *A Light to the Nations: The Missional Church and the Biblical Story.* Grand Rapids: Baker Academic, 2011.

Goldsworthy, Graeme. *Preaching the Whole Bible as Christian Scripture: The Application of Biblical Theology to Expository Preaching.* Grand Rapids: Eerdmans, 2000.

Goncharenko, Simon. "The Importance of Church Discipline within Balthasar Hubmaier's Theology." PhD Diss., Southwestern Baptist Theological Seminary, 2011.

Goulder, Michael. "Already?" In *To Tell the Mystery: Essays on New Testament Eschatology in Honor of Robert H. Gundry,* edited by Thomas E. Schmidt and Moisés Silva, 21–33. Journal for the Study of the New Testament: Supplement Series 100. Sheffield, UK: Sheffield Academic, 1994.

Green, Gene L. *The Letters to the Thessalonians.* Pillar New Testament Commentary. Grand Rapids: Eerdmans, 2002.

Griffith, Benjamin. "A Short Treatise Concerning a True and Orderly Church." In *Polity: Biblical Arguments on How to Conduct Church Life,* edited by Mark E. Dever, 95–114. Washington, DC: Center for Church Reform, 2000.

Grudem, Wayne A. *Systematic Theology: An Introduction to Biblical Doctrine.* Leicester, UK: InterVarsity, 1994.

Guder, Darrell L., and Lois Barrett. *Missional Church: A Vision for the Sending of the Church in North America.* Gospel and Our Culture Series. Grand Rapids: Eerdmans, 1998.

Gundry, Stanley N., editor. *Three Views on the Millennium and Beyond.* Grand Rapids: Zondervan, 1999.

———. *Three Views on the Rapture: Pre-, Mid-, or Post-Tribulation?* Grand Rapids: Zondervan, 1996.

Gundry Volf, Judith M. *Paul and Perseverance: Staying In and Falling Away.* Louisville: Westminster John Knox, 1990.

Guthrie, Donald. *The Letter to the Hebrews: An Introduction and Commentary.* Grand Rapids: Eerdmans, 1983.

Guthrie, George H. "Hebrews." In *Commentary on the New Testament Use of the Old Testament,* edited by G. K. Beale and D. A. Carson, 919–96. Grand Rapids: Baker Academic, 2007.

———. *Hebrews.* NIV Application Commentary. Grand Rapids: Zondervan, 1998.

Hafemann, Scott J., and Paul R. House, editors. *Central Themes in Biblical Theology: Mapping Unity in Diversity.* Grand Rapids: Baker Academic, 2007.

Haines, Stephen M. "Southern Baptist Church Discipline, 1880–1939." *Baptist History and Heritage* 20 (1985) 14–27.

Hall, David D. *The Faithful Shepherd: A History of the New England Ministry in the Seventeenth Century*. Harvard Theological Studies 54. Cambridge: Harvard University Press, 2006.

Hamilton, James M. "The Church Militant and Her Warfare: We Are Not Another Interest Group." *Southern Baptist Journal of Theology* 11 (2007) 70–80.

———. *God's Glory in Salvation Through Judgment: A Biblical Theology*. Wheaton, IL: Crossway, 2010.

———. *God's Indwelling Presence: The Holy Spirit in the Old & New Testaments*. NAC Studies in Bible & Theology. Nashville: B & H, 2006.

———. "The Lord's Supper in Paul: An Identity-Forming Proclamation of the Gospel." In *The Lord's Supper: Remembering and Proclaiming Christ until He Comes*, edited by Thomas R. Schreiner and Matthew R. Crawford, 68–102. Nashville: B & H Academic, 2010.

Hamilton, Sarah. *The Practice of Penance, 900–1050*. Rochester, NY: Boydell, 2001.

Hamilton, Victor P. *The Book of Genesis: Chapters 1–17*. New International Commentary on the Old Testament 1. Grand Rapids: Eerdmans, 1990.

Hammett, John S. *Biblical Foundations for Baptist Churches: A Contemporary Ecclesiology*. Grand Rapids: Kregel, 2005.

———. "Regenerate Church Membership." In *Restoring Integrity in Baptist Churches*, edited by Thomas White et al., 21–44. Grand Rapids: Kregel, 2008.

Hammett, John S., and Benjamin L. Merkle, editors. *Those Who Must Give an Account: A Study of Church Membership and Church Discipline*. Nashville: B & H Academic, 2012.

Harder, Leland, editor. *The Sources of Swiss Anabaptism: The Grebel Letters and Related Documents*. Classics of the Radical Reformation 4. Scottdale, PA: Herald, 1985.

Harper, Brad, and Paul Louis Metzger. *Exploring Ecclesiology: An Evangelical and Ecumenical Introduction*. Grand Rapids: Brazos, 2009.

Harris, Gerald. "The Beginnings of Church Discipline: 1 Corinthians 5." In *Understanding Paul's Ethics: Twentieth-Century Approaches*, edited by Brian S. Rosner, 129–54. Grand Rapids: Eerdmans, 1995.

Harris, Murray J. "Prepositions and Theology in the Greek New Testament." In *New International Dictionary on New Testament Theology*, edited by Colin Brown, 3:1171–215. Grand Rapids: Zondervan, 1978.

Hartley, John E. *Leviticus*. Word Biblical Commentary 4. Waco, TX: Word, 1992.

Haslehurst, Richard. *Some Account of the Penitential Discipline of the Early Church in the First Four Centuries*. New York: Macmillan, 1921.

Hays, Richard B. *First Corinthians*. Interpretation. Louisville: Westminster John Knox, 1997.

———. *The Moral Vision of the New Testament: A Contemporary Introduction to New Testament Ethics*. San Francisco: HarperCollins, 1996.

Hein, Kenneth. *Eucharist and Excommunication: A Study in Early Christian Doctrine and Discipline*. Bern: Lang, 1973.

Hiers, Richard H. "'Binding' and 'Loosing': The Matthean Authorizations." *Journal of Biblical Literature* 104 (1985) 233–50.

Hodges, Zane Clark. *The Gospel Under Siege: Faith and Works in Tension*. Dallas: Redención Viva, 1992.

Holifield, E. Brooks. "Peace, Conflict, and Ritual in Puritan Congregations." *Journal of Interdisciplinary History* 23 (1993) 551–70.

Horbury, William. "Extirpation and Excommunication." *Vetus Testamentum* 35 (1985) 13–38.
Horton, Michael Scott. *The Christian Faith: A Systematic Theology for Pilgrims on the Way*. Grand Rapids: Zondervan, 2011.
———. *Covenant and Eschatology: The Divine Drama*. Louisville: Westminster John Knox, 2002.
———. *God of Promise: Introducing Covenant Theology*. Grand Rapids: Baker, 2006.
———. *People and Place: A Covenant Ecclesiology*. Louisville: Westminster John Knox, 2008.
House, Paul R. *Old Testament Theology*. Downers Grove, IL: InterVarsity, 1998.
Hubmaier, Balthasar. *Balthasar Hubmaier: Theologian of Anabaptism*. Edited by H. Wayne Pipkin and John Howard Yoder. Classics of the Radical Reformation 5. Scottdale, PA: Herald, 1989.
Jeschke, Marlin. *Discipling in the Church: Recovering a Ministry of the Gospel*. 3rd ed. Scottdale, PA: Herald, 1988.
———. *Discipling the Brother*. Scottsdale, PA: Herald, 1979.
Johnson, Dennis E. *Him We Proclaim: Preaching Christ from All the Scriptures*. Phillipsburg, NJ: P & R, 2007.
Johnson, S. Lewis. "Paul and 'The Israel of God': An Exegetical and Eschatological Case-Study." *Master's Seminary Journal* 20 (2009) 41–55.
Keach, Benjamin. "The Glory of a True Church and its Discipline Displayed." In *Polity: Biblical Arguments on How to Conduct Church Life*, edited by Mark E. Dever, 63–94. Washington, DC: Center for Church Reform, 2000.
Keathley, Kenneth. "The Work of God: Salvation." In *A Theology for the Church*, edited by Daniel L. Akin et al., 686–765. Nashville: B & H Academic, 2007.
Kendall, R. T. *Once Saved, Always Saved*. Chicago: Moody, 1985.
Kent, Homer Austin. *The Epistle to the Hebrews: A Commentary*. Grand Rapids: Baker, 1972.
Kingdon, David P. "Discipline." In *New Dictionary of Biblical Theology*, edited by T. Desmond Alexander and Brian S. Rosner, 448–50. Downers Grove, IL: InterVarsity Press, 2000.
Kingdon, Robert M., et al., editors. *Registers of the Consistory of Geneva in the Time of Calvin*. Translated by M. Wallace McDonald. Grand Rapids: Eerdmans, 2000.
Kitchens, Ted G. "Church Discipline: An Exegetical and Theological Inquiry." ThD Diss., Dallas Theological Seminary, 1989.
———. "Perimeters of Corrective Church Discipline." *Bibliotheca Sacra* 148 (1991) 201–13.
Kling, David William, and Douglas A. Sweeney, editors. *Jonathan Edwards at Home and Abroad: Historical Memories, Cultural Movements, Global Horizons*. Columbia: University of South Carolina Press, 2003.
Knight, George W. *The Pastoral Epistles: A Commentary on the Greek Text*. Grand Rapids: Eerdmans, 1992.
Knuteson, Roy E. *Calling the Church to Discipline: A Scriptural Guide for the Church That Dares to Discipline*. Nashville: Action, 1977.
Koop, Karl, and Mary H. Schertz, editors. *Without Spot or Wrinkle: Reflecting Theologically on the Nature of the Church*. Occasional Papers: Institute of Mennonite Studies 21. Elkhart, IN: Institute of Mennonite Studies, 2000.

Köstenberger, Andreas J. "The Identity of the Ἰσραὴλ τοῦ θεοῦ (Israel of God) in Galatians 6:16." *Faith and Mission* 19 (2001) 3–24.

Köstenberger, Andreas J., L. Scott Kellum, and Charles L. Quarles. *The Cradle, the Cross, and the Crown: An Introduction to the New Testament*. Nashville: B & H Academic, 2009.

Köstenberger, Andreas J., and Terry L. Wilder, editors. *Entrusted with the Gospel: Paul's Theology in the Pastoral Epistles*. Nashville: B & H Academic, 2010.

Kuck, David W. *Judgment and Community Conflict: Paul's Use of Apocalyptic Judgment Language in 1 Corinthians 3:5–4:5*. New York: Brill, 1992.

Ladd, George Eldon. *The Gospel of the Kingdom; Scriptural Studies in the Kingdom of God*. Grand Rapids: Eerdmans, 1959.

———. *A Theology of the New Testament*. Rev. ed. Grand Rapids: Eerdmans, 1993.

Lampe, G. W. H. "Church Discipline and the Interpretation of the Epistles to the Corinthians." In *Christian History and Interpretation*, edited by W. R. Farmer et al., 337–61. London: Cambridge University Press, 1967.

Lane, William L. "Covenant: The Key to Paul's Conflict with Corinth." *Tyndale Bulletin* 33 (1982) 3–29.

———. *Hebrews 9–13*. Word Biblical Commentary. Dallas: Word, 1991.

Laney, J. Carl. "The Biblical Practice of Church Discipline." *Bibliotheca Sacra* 143 (1986) 353–64.

———. *A Guide to Church Discipline*. Minneapolis: Bethany, 1985.

Laniak, Timothy S. *Shepherds After My Own Heart: Pastoral Traditions and Leadership in the Bible*. Leicester, UK: Apollos, 2006.

LaSor, William Sanford, et al. *Old Testament Survey: The Message, Form, and Background of the Old Testament*. 2nd ed. Grand Rapids: Eerdmans, 1996.

Lauterbach, Mark. *The Transforming Community: The Practise of the Gospel in Church Discipline*. Ross-shire, Scotland: Christian Focus, 2003.

Lea, Henry Charles. *Studies in Church History: The Rise of the Temporal Power; Benefit of Clergy; Excommunication*. London, 1869.

Lee, Sang Hyun, editor. *The Princeton Companion to Jonathan Edwards*. Princeton: Princeton University Press, 2005.

Leeman, Jonathan. *The Church and the Surprising Offense of God's Love: Reintroducing the Doctrines of Church Membership and Discipline*. Wheaton, IL: Crossway, 2010.

———. *Church Discipline: How the Church Protects the Name of Jesus*. 9Marks: Building Healthy Churches. Wheaton, IL: Crossway, 2012.

———. *Church Membership: How the World Knows Who Represents Jesus*. 9Marks: Building Healthy Churches. Wheaton, IL: Crossway, 2012.

Lenski, R. C. H. *The Interpretation of St. Matthew's Gospel*. Minneapolis: Augsburg, 1961.

Longenecker, Richard N., editor. *Community Formation in the Early Church and the Church Today*. Peabody, MA: Hendrickson, 2002.

———. *Galatians*. Word Biblical Commentary 41. Dallas: Word, 1990.

Longman, Tremper, and Raymond B. Dillard. *An Introduction to the Old Testament*. 2nd ed. Grand Rapids: Zondervan, 2006.

Longman, Tremper, and David E. Garland, editors. *The Expositor's Bible Commentary*. Rev. ed. Grand Rapids: Zondervan, 2006.

Ludwig, Josef. "The Relationship between Sanctification and Church Discipline in Early Anabaptism." *Evangelical Journal* 14 (1996) 77–85.

Lumpkin, William Latane. *Baptist Confessions of Faith.* Chicago: Judson, 1959.
Luther, Martin. *Luther's Works.* 55 vols. Edited by Jaroslav Pelikan et al. Minneapolis: Fortress, 1958–1986.
———. *Martin Luther's Basic Theological Writings.* Edited by Timothy F. Lull. Minneapolis: Fortress, 1989.
MacArthur, John. *The Gospel According to Jesus: What Is Authentic Faith?* Rev. ed. Grand Rapids: Zondervan, 2008.
MacArthur, S. D. "'Spirit' in Pauline Usage : 1 Corinthians 5:5." *Studia Biblica* 3 (1980) 249–56.
Malherbe, Abraham J. "'Pastoral Care' in the Thessalonian Church." *New Testament Studies* 36 (1990) 375–91.
Mantey, Julius Robert. "Distorted Translations in John 20:23; Matthew 16:18–19 and 18:18." *Review and Expositor* 78 (1981) 409–16.
Marcus, Joel. "The Gates of Hades and the Keys of the Kingdom (Matt 16:18–19)." *Catholic Biblical Quarterly* 50 (1988) 443–55.
Marsden, George M. *Jonathan Edwards: A Life.* New Haven: Yale University Press, 2003.
Marshall, I. Howard. *Kept by the Power of God: A Study of Perseverance and Falling Away.* Eugene, OR: Wipf & Stock, 2008.
Marshall, Nathaniel. *The Penitential Discipline of the Primitive Church.* Oxford: Parker, 1844.
Martens, Elmer A. "The People of God." In *Central Themes in Biblical Theology: Mapping Unity in Diversity*, edited by Scott J. Hafemann and Paul R. House, 225–53. Downers Grove, IL: InterVarsity, 2007.
Martin, D. Michael. *1, 2 Thessalonians.* New American Commentary 33. Nashville: Broadman & Holman, 1995.
McClister, David. "'Where Two or Three Are Gathered Together': Literary Structure as a Key to Meaning in Matt 17:22–20:19." *Journal of the Evangelical Theological Society* 39 (1996) 549–58.
McClymond, Michael James, and Gerald R. McDermott. *The Theology of Jonathan Edwards.* New York: Oxford University Press, 2011.
McKnight, Scot. "Apostasy." In *New Dictionary of Biblical Theology*, edited by T. Desmond Alexander and Brian S. Rosner, 383–86. Downers Grove, IL: InterVarsity, 2000.
———. "The Warning Passages of Hebrews: A Formal Analysis and Theological Conclusions." *Trinity Journal* 13 (1992) 21–59.
McMullan, William E. "Church Discipline as a Necessary Function of the Visible Church in the Theology of Balthasar Hubmaier." ThM thesis, Southeastern Baptist Theological Seminary, 2003.
McNeill, John T., and Helena M. Gamer. *Medieval Handbooks of Penance.* New York: Columbia University Press, 1938.
Menken, Maarten J., and Steve Moyise, editors. *Deuteronomy in the New Testament.* Library of New Testament Studies 358. London: T. & T. Clark, 2007.
Menken, Martinus J. J. "Paradise Regained or Still Lost? Eschatology and Disorderly Behaviour in 2 Thessalonians." *New Testament Studies* 38 (1992) 271–89.
Merkle, Benjamin L. "The Biblical Basis for Church Membership." In *Those Who Must Give an Account: A Study of Church Membership and Church Discipline*, edited by John S. Hammett and Benjamin L. Merkle, 31–52. Nashville: B & H Academic, 2012.

———. *The Elder and Overseer: One Office in the Early Church*. Studies in Biblical Literature 57. New York: Peter Lang, 2003.

———. *40 Questions about Elders and Deacons*. Grand Rapids: Kregel, 2008.

———. "The Meaning of Ekklēsia in Matthew 16:18 and 18:17." *Bibliotheca Sacra* 167 (2010) 281–91.

Millar, J. G. "People of God." In *New Dictionary of Biblical Theology*, edited by T. Desmond Alexander and Brian S. Rosner, 684–87. Downers Grove, IL: InterVarsity, 2000.

Minear, Paul Sevier. "Christ and the Congregation: 1 Corinthians 5–6." *Review & Expositor* 80 (1983) 341–50.

Mohler R. Albert. "Church Discipline: The Missing Mark." *Southern Baptist Journal of Theology* 4 (2000) 16–27.

———. "Discipline: The Missing Mark." In *Polity: Biblical Arguments on How to Conduct Church Life*, edited by Mark Dever, 43–62. Washington, DC: Center for Church Reform, 2000.

Moore, Russell D. "Baptist View: Christ's Presence as Memorial." In *Understanding Four Views on the Lord's Supper*, edited by John H. Armstrong, 29–44. Grand Rapids: Zondervan, 2007.

———. "Personal and Cosmic Eschatology." In *A Theology for the Church*, edited by Daniel L. Akin et al., 858–926. Nashville: B & H Academic, 2007.

Moore, Russell D., and Robert E. Sagers. "The Kingdom of God and the Church: A Baptist Reassessment." *Southern Baptist Journal of Theology* 12 (2008) 68–86.

Morris, Leon. *The Epistles of Paul to the Thessalonians: An Introduction and Commentary*. Rev. ed. Tyndale New Testament Commentaries 13. Grand Rapids: Eerdmans, 1984.

Motyer, J. A. *Isaiah: An Introduction and Commentary*. Tyndale Old Testament Commentaries 18. Downers Grove, IL: InterVarsity, 1999.

———. "Judgment." In *New Dictionary of Biblical Theology*, edited by T. Desmond Alexander and Brian S. Rosner, 612–15. Downers Grove, IL: InterVarsity, 2000.

Newton, Michael. *The Concept of Purity at Qumran and in the Letters of Paul*. Cambridge: Cambridge University Press, 1985.

Newton, Phil A. *Elders in Congregational Life: Rediscovering the Biblical Model for Church Leadership*. Grand Rapids: Kregel, 2005.

Obenhaus, Stacy R. "Sanctified Entirely: The Theological Focus of Paul's Instructions for Church Discipline." *Restoration Quarterly* 43 (2001) 1–12.

Oberholzer, Emil. *Delinquent Saints; Disciplinary Action in the Early Congregational Churches of Massachusetts*. Columbia Studies in the Social Sciences 590. New York: AMS, 1968.

O'Brien, Peter T. *The Letter to the Hebrews*. Pillar New Testament Commentary. Grand Rapids: Eerdmans, 2010.

Oden, Thomas C. *Corrective Love: The Power of Communion Discipline*. Concordia Scholarship Today. St. Louis: Concordia, 1995.

———. *Pastoral Theology: Essentials of Ministry*. San Francisco: Harper & Row, 1982.

Oropeza, B. J. *Paul and Apostasy: Eschatology, Perseverance, and Falling Away in the Corinthian Congregation*. Wissenschaftliche Untersuchungen zum Neuen Testament 115. Tübingen: Mohr Siebeck, 2000.

Ortlund, Dane. "Justified by Faith, Judged according to Works: Another Look at a Pauline Paradox." *Journal of the Evangelical Theological Society* 52 (2009) 323–39.

Ortlund, Raymond C. *God's Unfaithful Wife: A Biblical Theology of Spiritual Adultery.* Downers Grove, IL: InterVarsity, 2002.

Overman, J. Andrew. *Church and Community in Crisis: The Gospel according to Matthew.* Valley Forge: Trinity Press International, 1996.

Owens, Wil L. "The Doctrine of Sanctification with Respect to Its Role in Eternal Salvation." PhD Diss., Southeastern Baptist Theological Seminary, 2008.

Pascuzzi, Maria. *Ethics, Ecclesiology, and Church Discipline: A Rhetorical Analysis of 1 Corinthians 5.* Tesi Gregoriana 32. Rome: Gregorian University Press, 1997.

Pate, C. Marvin. *The End of the Age Has Come: The Theology of Paul.* Grand Rapids: Zondervan, 1995.

Pate, C. Marvin, et al. *The Story of Israel: A Biblical Theology.* Downers Grove, IL: InterVarsity, 2004.

Pauw, Amy Plantinga. "Jonathan Edwards' Ecclesiology." In *Jonathan Edwards as Contemporary: Essays in Honor of Sang Hyun Lee,* edited by Don Schweitzer, 175–86. New York: Peter Lang, 2010.

Pennington, Jonathan T. *Heaven and Earth in the Gospel of Matthew.* Supplements to Novum Testamentum 126. Leiden: Brill, 2007.

Perona, Edwin G. "The Presence and Function of Deuteronomy in the Paraenesis of Paul in 1 Corinthians 5:1–11:1." PhD Diss., Trinity Evangelical Divinity School, 2005.

Peterson, David. *Possessed by God: A New Testament Theology of Sanctification and Holiness.* New Studies in Biblical Theology. Grand Rapids: Eerdmans, 1995.

Pfitzner, Victor C. "Purified Community—Purified Sinner: Expulsion from the Community according to Matt 18:15–18 and 1 Cor 5:1–5." *Australian Biblical Review* 30 (1982) 34–55.

Piggin, F. S. "Excommunication." In *The Evangelical Dictionary of Theology,* edited by Walter A. Elwell, 422–23. Grand Rapids: Baker Academic, 2001.

Pinson, J. Matthew, editor. *Four Views on Eternal Security.* Counterpoints. Grand Rapids: Zondervan, 2002.

Piper, John, and Justin Taylor, editors. *A God Entranced Vision of All Things: The Legacy of Jonathan Edwards.* Wheaton, IL: Crossway, 2004.

Polhill, John B. *Acts.* New American Commentary 26. Nashville: Broadman, 1992.

Pope, Robert G. *The Half-Way Covenant: Church Membership in Puritan New England.* Eugene, OR: Wipf & Stock, 2002.

Reymond, Robert L. *A New Systematic Theology of the Christian Faith.* Nashville: Thomas Nelson, 1998.

Ridderbos, Herman N. *The Epistle of Paul to the Churches of Galatia.* Grand Rapids: Eerdmans, 1953.

Rittgers, Ronald K. *The Reformation of the Keys: Confession, Conscience, and Authority in Sixteenth-Century Germany.* Cambridge: Harvard University Press, 2004.

Rivera, Ted. *Jonathan Edwards on Worship: Public and Private Devotion to God.* Eugene, OR: Pickwick, 2010.

Roberts, Alexander, and James Donaldson, editors. *The Ante-Nicene Fathers.* Grand Rapids: Eerdmans, 1950.

Robertson, O. Palmer. *The Israel of God: Yesterday, Today, and Tomorrow.* Phillipsburg, NJ: P & R, 2000.

Roetzel, Calvin J. *Judgement in the Community: A Study of the Relationship between Eschatology and Ecclesiology in Paul.* Leiden: Brill, 1972.

Rosner, Brian S. "'Drive Out the Wicked Person': A Biblical Theology of Exclusion." *Evangelical Quarterly* 71 (1999) 25-36.
———. "Exclusion." In *New Dictionary of Biblical Theology*, edited by T. Desmond Alexander and Brian S. Rosner, 471-75. Downers Grove, IL: InterVarsity, 2000.
———. "*Ouchi mallon epenthēsate*': Corporate Responsibility in 1 Corinthians 5." *New Testament Studies* 38 (1992) 470-73.
———. *Paul, Scripture and Ethics: A Study of 1 Corinthians 5-7*. Leiden: Brill, 1994.
———, editor. *Understanding Paul's Ethics: Twentieth Century Approaches*. Grand Rapids: Eerdmans, 1995.
Roth, John D., and James M. Stayer, editors. *A Companion to Anabaptism and Spiritualism, 1521-1700*. Brill's Companions to the Christian Tradition 6. Boston: Brill, 2007.
Russell, Ronald. "The Idle in 2 Thess 3:6-12: An Eschatological or a Social Problem?" *New Testament Studies* 34 (1988) 105-19.
Ryrie, Charles Caldwell. *Dispensationalism*. Rev. ed. Chicago: Moody, 1995.
Sailhamer, John. *The Pentateuch as Narrative: A Biblical-Theological Commentary*. Library of Biblical Interpretation. Grand Rapids: Zondervan, 1992.
Sairsingh, Krister. "Jonathan Edwards and the Idea of Divine Glory: His Foundational Trinitarianism and Its Ecclesial Import." PhD diss., Harvard University, 1986.
Sampley, J. Paul. *Walking Between the Times: Paul's Moral Reasoning*. Minneapolis: Fortress, 1991.
Saucy, Robert L. *The Case for Progressive Dispensationalism: The Interface between Dispensational & Non-Dispensational Theology*. Grand Rapids: Zondervan, 1993.
———. "Israel and the Church: A Case for Discontinuity." In *Continuity and Discontinuity: Perspectives on the Relationship between the Old and New Testaments*, edited by John S. Feinberg, 239-62. Wheaton, IL: Crossway, 1988.
Schafer, Thomas A. "Jonathan Edwards' Conception of the Church." *Church History* 24 (1955) 51-66.
Schmidt, Thomas E., and Moisés Silva, editors. *To Tell the Mystery: Essays on New Testament Eschatology in Honor of Robert H. Gundry*. Journal for the Study of the New Testament Supplement Series 100. Sheffield, UK: Sheffield Academic, 1994.
Schnabel, Eckhard J. *40 Questions about the End Times*. Grand Rapids: Kregel, 2011.
Schreiner, Thomas R. "Assurance." In *The Dictionary for Theological Interpretation of the Bible*, edited by Kevin J. Vanhoozer et al., 71-72. London: SPCK, 2005.
———. "The Biblical Basis of Church Discipline." In *Those Who Must Give an Account: A Study of Church Membership and Church Discipline*, edited by John S. Hammett and Benjamin L. Merkle, 105-30. Nashville: B & H Academic, 2012.
———. "The Commands of God." In *Central Themes in Biblical Theology: Mapping Unity in Diversity*, edited by Scott J. Hafemann and Paul R. House, 66-101. Grand Rapids: Baker Academic, 2007.
———. *1, 2 Peter, Jude*. New American Commentary 37. Nashville: Broadman & Holman, 2003.
———. *Galatians*. Zondervan Exegetical Commentary on the New Testament 9. Grand Rapids: Zondervan, 2010.
———. *New Testament Theology: Magnifying God in Christ*. Grand Rapids: Baker Academic, 2008.
———. "Perseverance and Assurance: A Survey and a Proposal." *Southern Baptist Journal of Theology* 2 (1998) 32-62.

———. *Run to Win the Prize: Perseverance in the New Testament*. Wheaton, IL: Crossway, 2010.

Schreiner, Thomas R., and Ardel B. Caneday. *The Race Set Before Us: A Biblical Theology of Perseverance and Assurance*. Downers Grove, IL: InterVarsity, 2001.

Schreiner, Thomas R., and Matthew R. Crawford,, editors. *The Lord's Supper: Remembering and Proclaiming Christ until He Comes*. Nashville: B & H Academic, 2010.

Schreiner, Thomas R., and Bruce A. Ware, editors. *Still Sovereign: Contemporary Perspectives on Election, Foreknowledge and Grace*. Grand Rapids: Baker, 2000.

Schreiner, Thomas R., and Shawn D. Wright, editors. *Believer's Baptism: Sign of the New Covenant in Christ*. Nashville: B & H Academic, 2006.

Schweitzer, Don, editor. *Jonathan Edwards as Contemporary: Essays in Honor of Sang Hyun Lee*. New York: Peter Lang, 2010.

Simons, Menno. *Complete Writings*. Edited by John Wenger. Translated by Leonard Verduin. Scottdale, PA: Herald, 1956.

Smith, David Raymond. *Hand This Man Over to Satan: Curse, Exclusion, and Salvation in 1 Corinthians 5*. Library of New Testament Studies 386. London: T. & T. Clark, 2008.

South, James T. "A Critique of the 'Curse/Death' Interpretation of 1 Corinthians 5.1–8." *New Testament Studies* 39 (1993) 539–61.

———. *Disciplinary Practices in Pauline Texts*. Lewiston, NY: Mellen Biblical, 1992.

Stetzer, Ed, and David Putman. *Breaking the Missional Code: Your Church Can Become a Missionary in Your Community*. Nashville: Broadman & Holman, 2006.

Stoddard, Solomon. *The Doctrine of Instituted Churches Explained and Proved from the Word of God: Solomon Stoddard*. London, 1700.

Storm, Melvin R. "Excommunication in the Life and Theology of the Primitive Christian Communities." PhD diss., Baylor University, 1987.

Strange, Alan D. "Jonathan Edwards on Visible Sainthood: The Communion Controversy in Northampton." *Mid-America Journal of Theology* 14 (2003) 97–138.

Strauch, Alexander. *A Christian Leader's Guide to Leading with Love*. Littleton, CO: Lewis & Roth, 2006.

Surratt, Geoff, et al. *The Multi-Site Church Revolution: Being One Church in Many Locations*. Leadership Network Innovation Series. Grand Rapids: Zondervan, 2006.

———. *A Multi-Site Church Roadtrip: Exploring the New Normal*. Grand Rapids: Zondervan, 2009.

Sweeney, Douglas A. "The Church." In *The Princeton Companion to Jonathan Edwards*, edited by Sang Hyun Lee, 167–89. Princeton: Princeton University Press, 2005.

Sweeney, James P. "The 'Spiritual' Task of Restoration: A Brief Note on Galatians 6:1." *Expository Times* 114 (2003) 259–61.

Tertullian. *Apology: De spectaculis*. Edited by Gerald Henry Rendall and Walter Charles Alan Kerr. Translated by T. R. Glover. Loeb Classical Library 250. Cambridge: Harvard University Press, 1966.

Thielman, Frank. *Theology of the New Testament: A Canonical and Synthetic Approach*. Grand Rapids: Zondervan, 2005.

Thiselton, Anthony C. *The First Epistle to the Corinthians: A Commentary on the Greek Text*. Grand Rapids: Eerdmans, 2000.

———. *Life after Death: A New Approach to the Last Things*. Grand Rapids: Eerdmans, 2012.

———. "Realized Eschatology at Corinth." *New Testament Studies* 24 (1978) 510–26.

Thompson, J. A. *Deuteronomy: An Introduction and Commentary*. Tyndale Old Testament Commentaries. London: InterVarsity, 1974.

Thompson, James. *Moral Formation according to Paul: The Context and Coherence of Pauline Ethics*. Grand Rapids: Baker Academic, 2011.

———. *Pastoral Ministry according to Paul: A Biblical Vision*. Grand Rapids: Baker Academic, 2006.

Tidball, D. J. "Church." In *New Dictionary of Biblical*, edited by T. Desmond Alexander and Brian S. Rosner, 407–11. Downers Grove, IL: InterVarsity, 2000.

———. *Ministry by the Book: New Testament Patterns for Pastoral Leadership*. Downers Grove, IL: IVP Academic, 2008.

———. *Skillful Shepherds: An Introduction to Pastoral Theology*. Grand Rapids: Ministry Resources Library, 1986.

Tomlinson, F. Alan. "The Purpose and Stewardship Theme within the Pastoral Epistles." In *Entrusted with the Gospel: Paul's Theology in the Pastoral Epistles*, edited by Andreas J. Köstenberger and Terry L. Wilder, 52–83. Nashville: B & H Academic, 2010.

Tooley, Wilfred. "Stewards of God: An Examination of the Terms *Oikonomos* and *Oikonomia* in the New Testament." *Scottish Journal of Theology* 19 (1966) 74–86.

Tracy, Patricia J. *Jonathan Edwards, Pastor: Religion and Society in Eighteenth Century Northampton*. American Century Series. New York: Hill & Wang, 1980.

Travis, Stephen. *Christ and the Judgement of God: The Limits of Divine Retribution in New Testament Thought*. Peabody, MA: Paternoster, 2009.

Travis, William G., et al. "Perspectives on Church Discipline." *Southern Baptist Journal of Theology* 4 (2000) 84–91.

Turner, David L. *Matthew*. Baker Exegetical Commentary on the New Testament. Grand Rapids: Baker Academic, 2008.

Van Neste, Ray. "The Lord's Supper in the Context of the Local Church." In *The Lord's Supper: Remembering and Proclaiming Christ until He Comes*, edited by Thomas R. Schreiner and Matthew R. Crawford, 364–90. Nashville: B & H Academic, 2010.

Vander Broek, Lyle D. "Discipline and Community: Another Look at 1 Corinthians 5." *Reformed Review* 48 (1994) 5–13.

Vanhoozer, Kevin J. *The Drama of Doctrine: A Canonical-Linguistic Approach to Christian Theology*. Louisville: Westminster John Knox, 2005.

Vanhoozer, Kevin J., et al., editors. *Dictionary for Theological Interpretation of the Bible*. London: SPCK, 2005.

Vedder, Henry C. *Balthasar Hübmaier: The Leader of the Anabaptists*. Heroes of the Reformation. New York: AMS, 1971.

Verbrugge, Verlyn D. "Delivered Over to Satan." *Reformed Journal* 30 (1980) 17–19.

———. "The Roots of Church Discipline: Israelite and Jewish Practice." *Reformed Journal* 30 (1980) 17–19.

Vickers, Brian J. "Celebrating the Past and Future in the Present." In *The Lord's Supper: Remembering and Proclaiming Christ until He Comes*, edited by Thomas R. Schreiner and Matthew R. Crawford, 313–40. Nashville: B & H Academic, 2010.

Vos, Geerhardus. *The Pauline Eschatology*. Grand Rapids: Eerdmans, 1952.

Waldron, Sam E. "Plural-Elder Congregationalism." In *Who Runs the Church? 4 Views on Church Government*, edited by Steven B. Cowan, 187–221. Grand Rapids: Zondervan, 2004.

Wallace, Daniel B. *Greek Grammar beyond the Basics: An Exegetical Syntax of the New Testament*. Grand Rapids: Zondervan, 1996.

Waltke, Bruce K. *An Old Testament Theology: An Exegetical, Canonical, and Thematic Approach*. Grand Rapids: Zondervan, 2007.

Walton, John H., et al. *The IVP Bible Background Commentary: Old Testament*. Downers Grove, IL: InterVarsity, 2000.

Walvoord, John F. *Matthew: Thy Kingdom Come*. Chicago: Moody, 1974.

Walvoord, John F., and Roy B. Zuck, editors. *The Bible Knowledge Commentary: An Exposition of the Scriptures*. Wheaton, IL: Victor, 1983.

Walzer, Michael. *The Revolution of the Saints: A Study in the Origins of Radical Politics*. London: Weidenfeld & Nicolson, 1966.

Wellum, Stephen J. "Baptism and the Relationship between the Covenants." In *Believer's Baptism: Sign of the New Covenant in Christ*, edited by Thomas R. Schreiner and Shawn D. Wright, 97–161. Nashville: B & H Academic, 2007.

Wenham, Gordon J. *The Book of Leviticus*. New International Commentary on the Old Testament. Grand Rapids: Eerdmans, 1979.

———. *Genesis 1–15*. Word Biblical Commentary 1. Waco, TX: Word, 1987.

Westcott, B. F. *The Epistle to the Hebrews*. Grand Rapids: Eerdmans, 1973.

White, Thomas, et al., editors. *Restoring Integrity in Baptist Churches*. Grand Rapids: Kregel, 2008.

Wilkin, Robert N. *Confident in Christ: Living by Faith Really Works*. Irving: Grace Evangelical Society, 1999.

Williams, George Huntston. *The Radical Reformation*. 3rd ed. Sixteenth Century Essays and Studies 15. Kirksville, MO: Sixteenth Century Journal, 1992.

Wills, Gregory A. *Democratic Religion: Freedom, Authority, and Church Discipline in the Baptist South, 1785–1900*. New York: Oxford University Press, 1997.

———. "A Historical Analysis of Church Discipline." In *Those Who Must Give an Account: A Study of Church Membership and Church Discipline*, edited by John S. Hammett and Benjamin L. Merkle, 131–56. Nashville: B & H Academic, 2012.

———. "Sounds from Baptist History." In *The Lord's Supper: Remembering and Proclaiming Christ until He Comes*, edited by Thomas R. Schreiner and Matthew R. Crawford, 285–312. Nashville: B & H Academic, 2010.

Wray, Daniel E. *Biblical Church Discipline*. Carlisle, PA: Banner of Truth, 1978.

Wright, Christopher J. H. *The Mission of God: Unlocking the Bible's Grand Narrative*. Downers Grove, IL: IVP Academic, 2006.

Wright, N. T. *The New Testament and the People of God: Christian Origins and the Question of God*. 1st North American ed. Minneapolis: Fortress, 1992.

———. *The Resurrection of the Son of God*. Minneapolis: Fortress, 2003.

Yoder, John Howard. *Schleitheim Confession*. Scottdale, PA: Herald, 1977.

Zaas, Peter S. "'Cast Out the Evil Man from Your Midst' (1 Cor 5:13b)." *Journal of Biblical Literature* 103 (1984) 259–61.

www.ingramcontent.com/pod-product-compliance
Lightning Source LLC
Chambersburg PA
CBHW062038220426
43662CB00010B/1557